Reflections from La Herradura

A story-telling journey through an enchanting village

Renate van Nijen

Copyright 2016 © Renate van Nijen

All rights reserved. No part of this book may be used or reproduced in any manner whatsoever without the written permission of Renate van Nijen.

ISBN 978-90-824528-1-5

Published by Palcho Publications
info@renatevannijen.com

Images: Renate van Nijen
Cover art work: Renate van Nijen
Interior and cover layout: Ferry Verhoeve

A big thank you to all the participants in the book and also many thanks to: Mel O'Gorman Davies, Robin Connolly, Sue Mowat, Vanessa Bøgstrup and Olga Ruano for their help and support.

Website Renate: www.renatevannijen.com

Table of contents
- The cover of this book 6
- Preface 7

An itinerary of stories:
- The history of 'the horseshoe bay' 10
- Evolution 'from fisherman's to tourist haven' 14

Colourful people
- The happy street sweeper – Francisco Martín 20
- The narrator telling the tales of the storytellers – Raimundo de Haro García 24
- Passion for poetry – Paulino Álvarez González 28

Famous after life:
- A guitar maestro - Andrés Segovia 32
- 'El Ruso', flamenco legend – Manuel Rodríguez Garciolo 35
- A devoted village artist - Pepe Gámez 39

Voicing a story:
- A singing family – Helena Díaz de Haro 42
- The enchanting village choirmaster – Pablo Ruiz Segura 48
- La Herradura, a village of fusion – Lupe Posada 54

A brotherhood of literature:
- A poetic teacher – Reinaldo Jiménez Morales 62
- A prolific writer – Salvador Compán 67
- Uplifting the spirit – Andrés Cárdenas 73
- A seaside poet – Tomás Hernández Molina 78
- A literary couple – Álvaro Salvador / Pepa Merlo 82

Storytelling images
- Inspired by silence – Juanfran Cabrera — 88
- A great loss changed our lives – Fraser Williamson — 93
- Following my bliss – Lauren Sebastian — 99

Sounds of music:
- When Germany meets Cuba – Charly Endres — 104
- Don't die with regrets – Tony Turner — 110
- Musical carpentry – Graham Emes — 117
- From New York to the bay – James Sobers — 122
- Music in visual images – Lino Díaz — 131

Seen through a lens
- The 'Long' way south – Bob Long — 139
- Sharing reflections – Chloe Pettersson — 147
- A Dutch interpretation of Spanish beauty Jeroen Stultiens — 153
- The village photographers – Jose y Nihal — 161
- Saving the rhinos – Charlie Jackson — 164

Flamenco passion:
- A guitar maker's dream – Stephen Hill — 173
- In mind, body and soul – Pablo Escudero — 180
- My life is flamenco – Olga Rodriguéz Garciolo — 186
- Flamenco, a family passion – Ana Maria Aneas Pintado — 190

Living the dream in colour:
- American politics – Anna DiGesu — 197
- An important address – Renate van Nijen — 202
- A nomadic lifestyle – Kerry Broomhead Brown — 208

The past is shaping the future:
- Discovering Andalusia - Juan Franco Quirós   213
- Storytelling pictures from the past – Paco Alaminos   219
- A passion for history – José Ángel Ruíz Morales   223

Arty objects:
- Artistic adventure in an enchanting garden – Rosario González Torres   228
- The jewellery of crop circles – Paolo Sgura   233
- The smell of leather – Lilian Urquieta   240

A different approach:
- Cult, religion and art – Juan Manuel Calvache (Tito)   245
- A colourful castle – Manuel Lecrín   251
- Life is theatre, theatre is life – Josune Sáinz Santana   257
- An artistic chameleon – Antonio Cochera   263

Attraction and inspiration
- Dreaming big, La Herradura a major cultural space – Mario Aguilar   268
- Creating an interest – Marjolein Lu Jong   273

A village of festivals   279

Note from the author   285

Cover Artwork by Renate van Nijen

'Seaside Reflections' is an oil painting representing a horseshoe ('herradura' in Spanish) shaped bay, a typical white-washed Andalusian village, the sea and a flamenco dancer.

Renate's art can be viewed on www.renatevannijen.com

Preface

Someone - a person who was clearly as entranced by the magic of La Herradura as I am - once said: 'La Herradura will either lure you in or spit you out.' Over the years I've been living here, I've seen how true this is, and I can certainly say with delight that my own experience was one of being 'lured in' rather than the alternative.

I'd been thinking about writing this book for a while, but when the idea first came to me, I knew I didn't want to simply write a history book or a guide book for tourists. I had a deep urge to share the story of La Herradura from the individual perspectives of the fascinating array of interesting people here – both those who had been drawn to the lovely village of La Herradura from afar like me and those who had been born and raised here. I wanted to see if they also felt the magic of this almost Feng Shui-perfect 'jewel in the bay', where the sea kisses the mountains and the mountains embrace the sea. Once I started to speak to these people, I knew I wasn't alone in my love for this place and I knew I needed to share their unique stories with the world.

In Spanish La Herradura means 'horseshoe' and the village gets its name thanks to the shape of this shimmering Mediterranean bay. Stroll La Herradura's streets - seemingly deserted out of season - and you might think this is a sleepy, perhaps even nondescript place. But appearances can be deceptive. This mystical village calls out like a Siren to sensitive souls from far and wide - sometimes literally from the other side of the world. Painters, writers, sculptors, musicians, and others with a spiritual approach to life such as healers, teachers of yoga, Tai Chi, Pilates and meditation, have all found their way here, each one attracted by the energy that seems to lift you up - that is, if you are open to it, of course.

La Herradura's beauty can be found everywhere - on the

ground, in the daily life of the Herradureños in the whitewashed little back streets; in the sky, where you often see the many paraglider enthusiasts creating a colourful display throughout the year circling one of the headlands before landing on the beach; and not forgetting on, in and under the water, in this crystal clear haven for swimmers, divers and snorkelers alike.

La Herradura Reflections is not a guide book, but as you read the stories of La Herradura's artists and other 'colourful' people, you will not only find out what drives them, but also learn about La Herradura's history, its evolution and hopes for the future as well as discover its secrets and hidden places.

And who knows? Maybe La Herradura will quietly work its magic on you, too, and inspire you one day to tell your own stories of this enigmatic horseshoe bay...

A Journey of stories

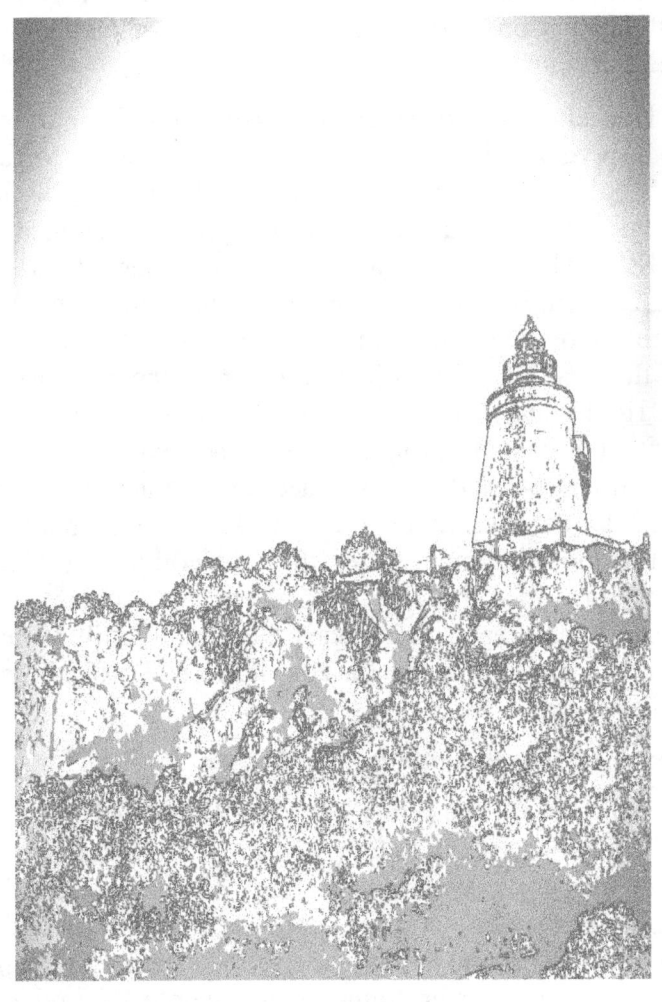

The history of 'the Horseshoe Bay'

The two former watch towers stand proudly on their mountains overlooking the bay and the sea. Each of these monuments has been witness to centuries of change. The tower on the Cerro Gordo dates back to the 16th century and the Punta de la Mona tower is even older - built in the 12th century and converted into a lighthouse at the end of the 20th century.

La Herradura may be steeped in history but this enigmatic bay reveals its past slowly. In fact, 'official' archaeological surveys were not carried out until fairly recently. The first archaeological evidence was unearthed in 1888 when the coastal road from Almeria to Malaga was created. Reports from that time state numerous tombs were discovered in the Baranco de las Tejas (a sandy track off the Paseo Maritimo just along from the pharmacy on the right-hand side. Subsequently, when the motorway was constructed around 1990, a group from the department of Medieval Archaeology at the University of Granada carried out a survey and found the remains of a prehistoric settlement from the Chalcolithic or Copper Age. Since then, no other formal excavations have taken place in the area which means there could still be many ancient treasures in the La Herradura soil which remain undiscovered.

'Unofficial' archaeological finds

In spite of no formal digs since the 1990s, artefacts have still been unearthed before and since - found over the years by people working the land. In most cases, these discoveries were simply kept by the finder and so remained in private hands - one of these being the biggest 'Argaric' sword ever found in the whole of Andalusia. Still, it's from objects like these, found and kept by people working the land, that the region's history can be traced like an evolutionary line from the Copper Age, to an Early Bronze Age and then to the Phoenicians, followed by the Romans.

Arabs in La Herradura

After the Romans, we know that the Moors settled in the area mainly from various Arab texts which refer to a place called 'Jate'. During the Middle Ages La Herradura was known as *Ŝāt*, in Spanish *Jate* which is also the name of the river you can still see today, and which reaches the sea via the shores of the village. Over the years there has been some confusion over these texts which has, in turn, led to some historical inaccuracy. When they were translated at the end of 1900, information sought from a map, on which Almuñécar appeared, showed the village of Jete nearby, not Jate. Historical documents about La Herradura started to refer to Jete instead of Jate. However, because these original Arab texts speak of a marine harbour and a fortified castle, it's clear now that they always referred to Jate and not Jete. Unlike La Herradura, Jete has neither a harbour (it lies seven kilometres from the coast) nor a fortified castle.

It's also interesting to note that when the Arabs came to this area in Spain they arrived at La Herradura, not Almuñécar. At the beginning of 500AD an economic crisis across the entire Mediterranean area led to the disappearance of the salted fish industry - the main commodity of Roman settlements locally. The inhabitants of Jate and the neighbouring towns and villages moved up into the mountains to much safer fortified areas, the so called Castillejos.

When the Christians came

In the 11th century Almuñécar was granted town rights and grew in importance but the Jate area, or La Herradura as we know it today, was not given its own separate administration and so remained an Arab village till the Christians came in the year 1489. With the arrival of the

Christians, the situation along this coast (and beyond) drastically changed. The Christians set about conquering fortified cities like Almuñécar and Salobreña and eventually expelled the Moors. The war which broke out lasted many years and around 1526, Jate, which back then was located more or less where you can now find the motorway bridge, was completely abandoned, its people driven by piracy and war away from the coast.

A 'secret' national disaster

Whilst much of La Herradura's history has been lost, misinterpreted or 'lost in translation', some of the bay's past has been intentionally kept secret. In October 1562, La Herradura became the scene of an historic event which was kept quiet for many years and to this day has remained relatively unknown to the world, even to many people in Spain. This natural disaster, one of the greatest catastrophes in Spanish naval history, happened on the 19th of October and cost the lives of around 5,000 people. The day before, a fleet of twenty-eight galleys, with a mission to defend the Spanish coasts from pirate attacks, set sail from Malaga harbour for Orán and Mozalquivir in Northern Africa. However, when strong winds picked up they were forced to seek shelter beside the Punta de la Mona in the La Herradura bay.

Although these Mediterranean warships were huge, holding more than 500 crew members each, they were clearly no match for the weather. When the wind turned, twenty-five of them crashed into each other and were destroyed. Many of the people in the galleys jumped into the sea, but most were dragged down by the undercurrent or killed by floating debris. Two thousand people survived, mostly galley slaves, whose chains had been broken before the disaster. These slaves were later recaptured. The disaster was kept quiet as Spain didn't want its enemies to know that a large part of its Armada had been lost. The dead were buried on the beach, only to resurface during another heavy storm. People from the area came to help dig the bodies out and to rebury them closer to the mountains but to this day nobody knows exactly where.

This tragic event, for so long kept a secret, now forms part of La Herradura's history and several inhabitants of the village have written about it. It is also mentioned by Miguel de Cervantes in his novel *Don Quixote of La Mancha (Chapter 31)*.

The Italian connection

Back then, like much of the coast of southern Spain, La Herradura was sparsely populated. In fact, apart from a military fortress from the 18th century (now referred to as 'the castle'); there wasn't really a village near the coast until around the beginning of the 19th century when people arrived from Italy. Problems arising after the Napoleonic War left many Italians searching for a new life elsewhere and those who ended up in La Herradura came from Noli, opposite Genova in the province of Savona. The story goes that they came to La Herradura because it reminded them of Noli. Many made their living from fishing and diving for red coral that could be found in deep sea areas near the Punta de la Mona. These days, around 50 of La Herradura's 'original' families have Italian origins and can trace their ancestral roots back to those first Italian settlers.

Although you could say that a big part of La Herradura's history has been uncovered, undoubtedly there are still mysteries buried in the 'hinterland' but the village evolves nevertheless and La Herradura's history will always be in the making.

Evolution, from fisherman's to tourist haven

"Before tourism came to La Herradura people mainly lived by fishing and agriculture," says Juan Manuel de la Cuesta, who is originally from Granada, but has been coming to la Herradura for holidays with his parents since 1957. "There were no apartment blocks on the sea front and there was no promenade, just a sandy track along the beach. During heavy rainfall the river swelled to such an extent that you could not get to the Peña Parda part of the village. When reaching the seafront there were a few fishermen's houses and in the direction of the Punta de la Mona there were little *chozas*, small structures with cane roofs, which although tiny, were nonetheless inhabited. There was only one beach bar. Calle Real was the main street but did not have any houses at the top. There were only a few streets in the village and no supermarkets. For their shopping people went to so-called *ultramarinos* (village shops), a term that referred to products that came from America. There were two village shops in La Herradura. They did not sell American products but rather everything you could possibly need in a household from lightbulbs to paint, locks, tinned food, bottles of wine as well as bread, fruit and vegetables. In those days many villagers only had work for three or four months during the summer time, usually fishing or agricultural work. The rest of the year they didn't have any money so it was fairly normal practice in Spain in those days for the village shops to keep lists of what people bought during the year and villagers would settle their debts when they were paid for their work during the summer.

Life was simple and tough. Many houses in the Fifties didn't even have bathrooms and people just did their business where they kept the animals. But then things slowly started changing. There was still very little tourism, in fact, you could probably only expect to find a few people on the beach on Sundays or in the month of

August. Then some houses were constructed and the first French tourists came to spend their holidays here. They were mostly people from Algeria as France had a colony in Algeria. In 1955 and 1956 the first houses were built on the Punta de La Mona. The land was bought by Prieto Moreno who initially wanted to build houses for a very select group of friends including Andres Segovia. Prieto Moreno was a very well-known and influential figure living in Madrid. He was the conservation architect of the famous Alhambra in Granada and he was specialised in architecture, urbanism and the protection of historical and artistic heritage, but he also designed gardens and published a gardening book. He travelled a lot to Arab countries and was heavily influenced by Arab architecture. At the end of the Fifties the first English people started building houses on the Punta de la Mona in La Herradura. There were about three or four houses and even a street was called after them, Camino de los Ingleses (English Street). Prieto needed money to create the infrastructure on the Punta and started selling off the land but he chose his clients carefully and imposed his vision. The houses were built under his strict guidelines. His idea was that each house had a plot of 1000 square metres and that it would integrate into its surroundings, covered by trees, so that you could not even see the building from the road.

This was still in the time when Franco ruled Spain. Although there was no freedom of press or politics, there was liberty of commerce. Tourists were welcomed. And it's partially thanks to tourism and Spanish emigrants, who left to work in countries like Germany, but also to Barcelona in Cataluña, that the economy started growing. These workers sent their earnings back to their families, which helped boost the local economy and little by little La Herradura started changing. Houses were done up, bathrooms installed and people started buying cars, washing machines and televisions. Men found work as gardeners and women as cleaners. Towards the end of the Sixties tourism started flourishing. More people came to live in the village and construction started on the Cerro Gordo side of La Herradura, also owned by Prieto Moreno. The Moreno family constructed the first chalets in the Los Romeros area, but also came to an agreement with a group of Dutch people who started developing various urbanisations, like Las Palomas and Las Girasoles. These Dutch people did not come here to buy houses, like the English, but to make money through commerce. They were young, in their twenties, spoke various languages and could connect easily with other countries in Europe. They had their office in a street that is still, to this day, referred to as the *Calle de los Holandeses* (Dutch Street). This was at the end of the Sixties and the beginning of the Seventies. At this time there were about four or five beach bars often playing the popular music of the time and creating a free-spirited atmosphere so loved by tourists both from Spain and abroad. During the Seventies the development of the sea front started. Increasing numbers of Spanish people from the interior came down to the South to spend time on the beaches and so more construction was needed to cater for their needs. This was encouraged by people from the village but things were done with little care for quality. There was the attraction of quick money which resulted in poorly constructed buildings that are not very attractive. In 1975 there were only four or five blocks on the sea front but that soon changed. People from northern European countries started buying property, among them English and Belgians but investors also came from countries such as Denmark. At this time apartments started to be built on the Punta de la Mona as well.

The construction boom really took off and at the beginning of 2000, the Carmenes del Mar was created in the Cerro Gordo. This was a disastrous development as the land was not suitable for building. Some of those houses have since had to be taken down and many suffer from serious construction problems due to ground movement. Locals often refer to this area as *los crimenes del mar* (crimes of the sea) and sadly, it wasn't the only development to suffer. The Marina del Este, the leisure harbour of La Herradura, has also suffered from some significant structural problems, but not as badly as the Carmenes del Mar.

In the early days the Marina and its harbour area was very well organised with plenty of gardens, tennis courts and even horse riding. However, planners were forced to make changes, in order to cater for mass tourism, in particular for Spanish tourists who only came during the month of August. It was the downside of the boom and perhaps not well thought through. The Marina del Este is a lovely buzzing place during the summer but in wintertime it can feel rather deserted which is a real shame. The crisis has also had its toll on La Herradura. Nonetheless, now, in 2015, there is still a strong foreign community here, mainly English and German, and the local school usually registers around 25 nationalities, which is rather exceptional for a village of around 4000 inhabitants. The property market also seems to have picked-up a little. People from countries such as Norway, Sweden and Denmark have found their way here again. It remains an attractive place for those who like nature, going on excursions and simply enjoying a typically Spanish atmosphere with beach bars, beaches and not forgetting the typical Granada province custom of serving a tapa with each drink. To many it will remain a tourist haven."

Juan Manuel told me how he loved those holidays with his parents in the Fifties and the Sixties, full of excursions, fishing and time spent on the beach. In 1974 he had the opportunity to open a real-estate agency in La Herradura and has lived here since then with his family, witnessing the evolution first-hand. His love for the village shines through when he passionately explains his hopes for La Herradura's future. "I would like to see an improvement in what we have and no more or very little new construction" Juan Manuel concludes: "I wish that what will be constructed will be done with respect for the environment. Urban laws are made of rubber and can be interpreted in many different ways but I hope the municipal administration is aware of the importance of conserving this special village in the vision of Prieto Moreno... integrated into its environment."

Colourful people

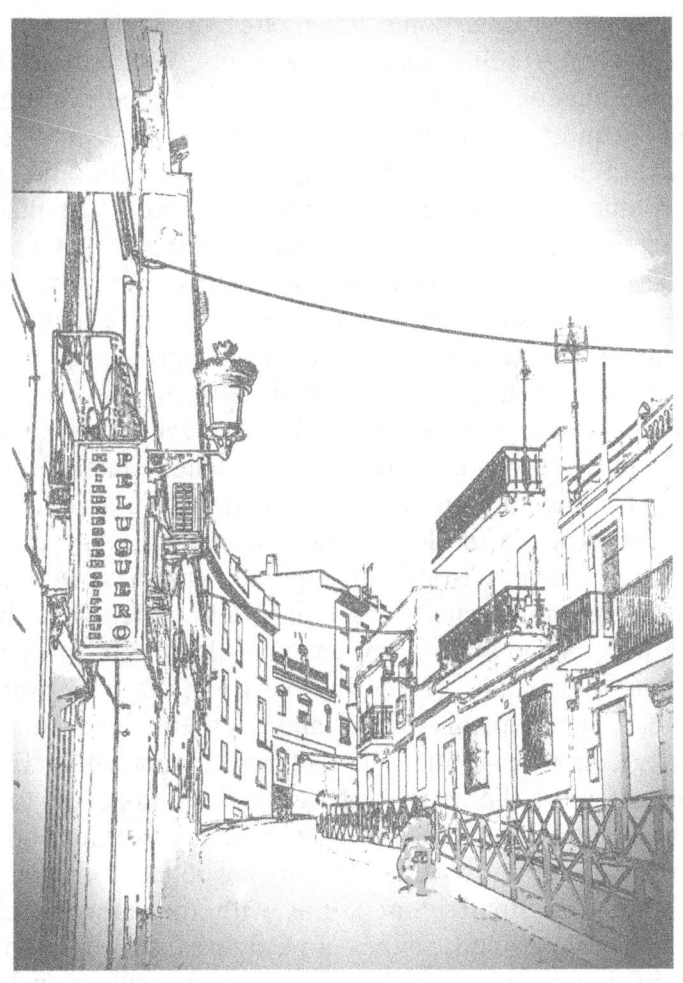

The happy street sweeper

"Madam, about the interview for your book... Just so you know... I always eat my breakfast at 10 o´clock in front of the church." The small Catholic village church feels kind of hidden from the street and doesn´t immediately give you the impression that it is actually a church. The bell tower is only some ten metres up with two fairly small church bells marking the hours, celebrations and funeral masses. A memorial plaque with a medieval figure and a quotation from *The Ingenious Gentleman Don Quixote of La Mancha* (Chapter 31 - mentioning La Herradura), marks the entrance to the church. The plaque is in commemoration of the shipwreck of 19 October 1562 in the bay of La Herradura, where so many lost their lives. A few steps up and you enter the little square in front of the church. The square is protected by an abundance of different types of ficus trees. It turns it into a lovely, lush green space. A few wooden benches offer seats to those visiting the square to contemplate life or to wait for the church doors to open before one of the masses start. To the left of the square there is a covered area supported by Roman type pillars, with a collection of tiles portraying Jesus with a child. Below the image there is a white stand with a tiny image of the Virgin Mary and a memorial plaque on the marble floor. Half the wall is covered with typical Andalusian wall tiles. Their blue, red and green Arab-influenced patterns hypnotically absorb your attention. Four steps up again you gain access to the church, its entrance covered by a veranda-style wooden portico. Entering through the sturdy wooden door you are led into the small church, not with the abundance of golden background statues and figures so common in Spain, but a very sensitive collection of statues on both sides of the altar. The back wall of the church shows an unusual fresco. It is light blue with white in a rather abstract style, painted by the late Pepe Gámez (more about him later). It creates a very calming and tranquil atmosphere.

The day is unusually overcast with clouds, and a few light drops of rain fall down on my cheeks. I hurry to the small church square. One of the large ficus trees gives shelter from the drizzle and I say hello to Francesco Martin the street sweeper, better known as Paco to the locals. I see him practically every morning, six days a week, when I walk my dog along the sea front. Paco always greets me with a kind "Good morning madam." He is clearly passionate about his work, sweeping the streets as if his life depends on it with a never-wavering enthusiasm. His 'Good morning!' greeting is also extended to the local bar owners and early morning walkers, and always accompanied by a smile. Often he rushes towards me after I´ve picked up my dog's excrement with a plastic bag, which he then takes from my hands whilst giving me his blessing with a "Go with God".

Today I am meeting up with him to ask him a few questions. He has just finished his breakfast and clears a bit of space for me on the wooden bench beneath the tree, while carefully folding the plastic bags and putting them back into his rucksack beside him. Lolo, a little dog belonging to one of the bar owners, who always stays close to Paco on his street-sweeping rounds, is sitting in front of him. He is patiently waiting for some more leftovers after he has licked clean the empty tin of tuna fish on the floor. Paco also picks up the empty tin and puts it into a plastic bag with some of his breakfast rubbish. He invites me to sit down. I get the impression that he is excited about the interview. His friendly smile puts me at ease. I am slightly worried that I will not understand everything he will tell me as he has a strong Andaluz dialect and he talks very quickly.

"I love the sea ... I used to be a fisherman," he explains. His passion for the sea is almost tangible. He told me he had been working in Almuñécar for eight years and now works in La Herradura six days a week from seven o'clock in the morning till one o'clock in the afternoon. He is always happy and sweeps with an energy that makes me smile. "I like it when everything is clean", he says. "I want the people who visit La Herradura and the people who live here to think... *it is so nice and clean here.*" He explains that he loves the sea because it is in his soul; he still feels the fisherman's blood running through his veins. But he likes his present job too. The only thing that he doesn't like is that there are people in the village who do not seem to care about having a clean village. He can't comprehend why so many just throw their rubbish in the street instead of in one of the bins that are never far away. Passionately he explains, "It often happens that someone comes out of the tobacco shop where they have just bought some cigarettes, they take off the plastic wrapping and simply chuck it in the street even though I am practically in front of them with my cart and garbage bins." He really doesn't understand that.

We talk about the problem of cigarette butts that lie scattered in the streets and on the beach. They are eaten by animals, even played with by children, he explains, and he can't possibly sweep them all up so on a rainy or windy day they simply end up in the storm drains that lead to the sea, where they are often mistaken for food by fish and birds. Studies have shown that one single cigarette filter contaminates up to eight litres of water and you don't need to be a scientist to understand that this contributes to a serious pollution problem.

Paco also doesn't like it that some people do not respect the designated hours for putting household rubbish out in the streets - that is between eight and eleven in the evening. The rubbish is subsequently picked up by the municipal garbage collection service, but bags that are left outside after these hours often create a problem as stray cats and dogs inevitably try to open the bags looking for something edible. Paco hastens to say that most people do stick to these rules but there always are those who don't seem to care. His dream for La Herradura is that it is a really clean village that everybody can enjoy.

All too soon it is time for Paco to go back to work. I ask him if I can take his picture and he happily agrees. He rummages around in his bag and finds a comb that he expertly runs through his hair, like a young James Dean. We walk to his rubbish cart with its broom, rake and shovel sticking out of the bins. Paco poses behind his cart with the sea shimmering in the background and beams proudly!

Francesco Martin

A narrator telling the tales of the storytellers

The sun has come out and I make my way to Calle Real where I see a small white *Peluquero* sign dangling above the entrance to meet up with Raimundo de Haro Garcia who is the village barber. It is like stepping back in time when you walk into the tiny space. The walls are covered with out of date event posters and calendars mixed in with postcards, old photos and street maps. Two blue, slightly worn, two-seater sofas and a few black office-type chairs offer comfort to whoever walks in. There is only one hairdresser's chair in the old fashioned barbershop where Raimundo cuts the hair of his (mostly male) clients, both young and old. Everybody knows him and he knows everybody. He talks fondly about the foreigners who have made La Herradura their home and happily shares that some of them have turned into good friends. He has seen many changes in La Herradura during his lifetime – particularly how the place has grown from a fisherman's village reliant on almond and olive cultivation into a popular seaside resort where tropical fruit is now being grown, such as avocados and loquats. It has become a 'service industry' village, catering for the needs of tourists. In turn tourists help to boost the local economy – the perfect symbiosis. But everywhere there is an overall Spanish feel and atmosphere.

In La Herradura many of the Spanish inhabitants are either closely or distantly related to one of the original fifty families living here. To this day many bear the same surname. Raimundo was born into one of these families. Married and the father of five children, he is a friendly beacon in this village that he loves. He was born in La Herradura, like his parents, his grandparents and his ancestors, who survived working in the cane industry, picking seasonal crops and going fishing. His grandfather on his father's side was one of these seasonal workers, but Raimundo's father stepped out of this tradition and became the village barber, shaving the beards of the local men. His grandfather on his mother's side was a merchant, making his living buying and selling livestock such as goats, horses and mules. His daughter Gracia, Raimundo's mother, was one of eleven children and ran a tiny supermarket in the space now turned into the barbershop. It was one of two small shops in the village and she sold all sorts of products including sardines and herrings and everything else you could possibly need. According to Raimundo his mother was a very special woman and extremely generous. When someone was sick and needed something, including medicines, she would not hesitate to give it to them for free.

If the walls of the tiny barbershop could speak they would tell some interesting stories, but in a way they still do, dressed – as they seem to be - with such a personal recollection of memories and gifts. There are always people in the shop, some waiting for a haircut, others for a chat. If you need to know something, Raimundo is your man. He is extremely likeable and always ready to share a smile and a kind word. A colourful figure with the habit of shaving off his thinning hair once a year and then leaving it to grow at will again till the next year. He likes to talk and is a natural narrator, vividly recounting the sad, quirky and interesting stories of the local storytellers who come to the barbershop on a regular basis for a haircut or a chat. The barbershop is situated in Calle Real. Practically all towns and villages have a Calle Real. The name comes from *camino de realeza* which means that it was the track where people passed with animals, like horses, cows and goats.

Over the years the street has changed a lot. In the Sixties many houses still had a large corral in front of the house where they kept their livestock such as chickens and pigs. There also were various small-scale bars in the street like La Cabaña, Mesón Pedro and Mesón Sombrero to name but a few. They hosted many *fandango* singing parties. The *fandango* is a form of singing typical for people working the land, also called *fandango cortijero*. In this area of Spain they were also called *Los Verdiales*. It is similar to the well-known *flamenco*. You could picture the 'the flamenco' as a 'family tree' where you have the flamenco trunk with many branches representing the different types of flamenco dance and music.

These days there are only two houses left within the space of the formal corral, both now turned into patios which can be entered from the Calle Rambla del Espinar, which runs parallel with Calle Real. In the 50s and 60s, when the Calle Real still only had the original houses, life was pretty tough. Many men got up extremely early in the morning to help the fishermen. They were paid with a so-called *musa*, which was just a little handout. After that they went into the mountains to work the land, in the olive, almond and fig groves. In those times they also made fig bread and there was an olive mill on the outskirts of La Herradura. Some of the villagers worked in the cane industry as well, which meant travelling to places like Motril, Torre del Mar and Velez Malaga where the cane plantations were very large. La Herradura also had some cane cultivation but only small-scale. It was in the Peña Parda area of the village.

Everybody knew everybody but one of the best-loved people in the village was Frasquito who was Raimundo's uncle. He owned a drugstore in Calle Real. He sold paints and other products and was also the first barber in the village. This profession was passed on to his daughter Helena who became the first female hairdresser. To this day you can see the shelves, where he kept his products on the wall, still standing on a derelict stretch of land where his house used to be, between the Calle Ramblas del Espinar and Calle Real. The wall is covered in orange protection material but still tells a story of the past.

tells a story of the past. Frasquito is most remembered as the 'doctor' as he gave injections and helped people with their health even though he had no medical background. Raimundo speaks with great respect for his uncle as many villagers who are now in their eighties owe their lives to Frasquito. Raimundo was still a boy when he started helping out in his father's barbershop, which was also in Calle Real and more or less opposite the current barbershop. He remembers that his father made him sit on a wooden box to read aloud the newspapers to locals who could not read and write. He loves his work - he likes working in general and cannot see himself not doing something. He has had a few jobs outside La Herradura in places like Barcelona and Granada but La Herradura is his home. He speaks fondly of this home when he remembers his love for sports, a big part of his life when he was younger. Cycling, running, diving, you name it. Life was good in the days when you could hear the sounds of great musicians coming from the beach bars on the playas in the late Sixties and Seventies: the music of Ray Charles, Led Zeppelin, Jimi Hendrix, Louis Armstrong, Lou Reed and Frank Zappa - with the smell of hashish never far away.

Times have changed, but his work as a hairdresser has always given and still gives him a sense of freedom. He likes the fact that he has met so many people, foreigners and Spanish alike, and hopes to get to know many more. His way will always be to inspire with his positive view of life, a smile and friendly advice.

Raimundo de Haro Garcia

Passion for poetry

Paulino Álvarez González walks into the tiny barbershop and starts talking about his life. Paulino has lived in La Herradura since August 1998. He tells me he originally came from Vilardevós in Galicia in the north of Spain. He used to work for the postal services before coming down to Andalusia for work reasons, as he was offered a job in Secondary education. He now calls this village his home. He likes the light and the colours, in particular the sea and he explains how this is a total contrast to the area he grew up in. Vilardevós is situated in a mountainous area, very green but quite grey during wintertime. Every summer he travels back to visit his family but throughout the year he is a familiar face in the La Herradura streets. Since his arrival he has changed jobs several times from working as a butcher and creating sports programmes for a local radio station, to now being employed by Hotel Alcazar on the Punta de la Mona. Paulino has a passion. His passion is poetry and he loves reading, whether poetry, short stories or literature in general. This love originates from the cultural interests of his parents and the environment he grew up in, but also from a natural curiosity and passion for learning. Life's small and big events shape a person but Paulino tells me how three mayor events shaped his life. One was an experience that for many is hard to understand. Involved in a severe traffic accident Paulino had a near-death experience. He is adamant that he saw the tunnel with its magical light and says this changed him so profoundly that since then life has become more precious. The second life event was the sad passing of his parents which also, naturally, had a great effect on him. And the third, well, that was coming to La Herradura.

Having spent his younger years in a rural village in the North coming here was like a road leading to different cultures. As he saw it, it opened up many possibilities to get to know friends from all around the world. He feels that this is an open door to knowledge helping him to change his views on life by opening up different perspectives. Paulino acknowledges that his homeland has a magic to it, but says living in La Herradura has given him inner peace, a more open-minded view on life and more inner riches. In one way the two separated regions complement each other.

Years ago he got in touch with *Amigos de la Herradura* (friends of La Herradura) an association that was created over thirty years ago to promote the cultural patrimony of the village and to recover lost, but once popular traditions. Over the years they have successfully reinitiated the Noche de San Juan (The magical night of San Juan or Summer Solstice), the Dia de los Inocentes (Day of the Innocents) and helped with the Dia de las Cruces (Day of the Crosses) and the San Jose Festival*. The annual poetry contest (*Certamen de Poesia*) is also organised by the association and Paulino is its founder and coordinator. When it started the objective was to make La Herradura known as the special place it is and to mark the history of the natural surroundings of the village. These days there is no particular theme so participants are free to write what they like. Paulino says he created the poetry contest in 2007 because he felt something was missing. There was the famous *Andres Segoviá* contest for classical guitars, but he felt that poetry and music go hand in hand. Poetry is the soul of freedom because it is a vehicle to express the free sentiments of people. Paulino himself does not write poetry but he has been writing about cultural themes for a newspaper.

Every year in July the poetry contest is announced via various media, such as radio and newspapers. There are two entry options: one for everybody provided that it is in Castilian and one for people who live in La Herradura and Almuñécar. The objective of the contest is not just to pay tribute to people who work the land and live off the sea, but to also celebrate to the Spanish constitution that allows people to express their liberty. People from all over South America who have their origins in Spain can send in their entries. The work is judged by a panel of judges, each with high literary credentials such as Andrés Cárdenas Muñoz, Reinaldo Jimenez, Tomas Hernando Molina, Alvares Salvador and Marisa Julian. They also organise the poetry readings and the presentation of books in the garden of local ceramic artist Rosario Gonzalez.

For Paulino what is most important is that people are able to develop their creative voices with total liberty, without limits and without being judged by others and his hopes for La Herradura are clear: To showcase its interesting cultural heritage and to create more cultural heritage for the unforeseeable future.

Paulino Álvarez González

* see chapter: 'a village of festivals'

Famous after life

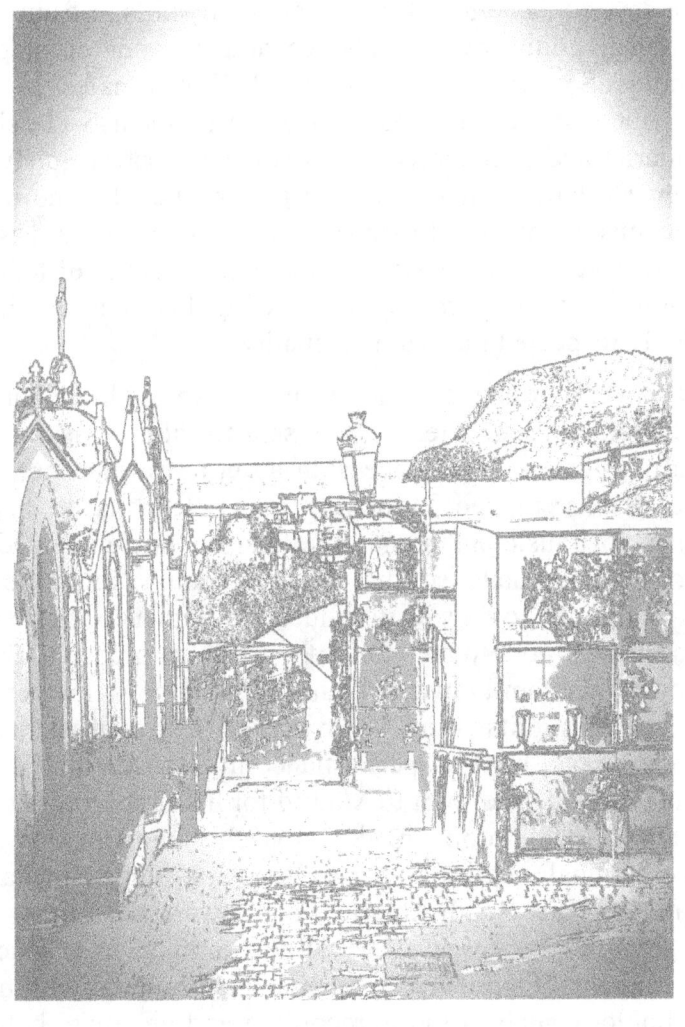

Andrés Segovia, a guitar maestro

La Herradura is known by many musicians as the village of the International Andrés Segovia contest. Every year talented guitarists from all over the world come to the village to show their mastery in an international contest. For several days they demonstrate their skills in front of a classical guitar-loving audience and a panel of judges. Andrés Segovia was born in 1893 in Linares in the province of Jaén in Spain. He was a Spanish classical guitarist and is regarded as one of the greatest guitarists ever. He taught many classical guitar students who have now made a name for themselves. Andrés Segovia was an expressive performer with an incredible palette of tone, a unique way of phrasing and styling his music, and a highly respected musical personality.

At a very young age he went to live with his uncle Eduardo and his wife. He was sent to violin classes, but had a negative experience with a very strict teacher and the lessons stopped. However, it was clear that he had a talent for music and some time later his uncle decided to move to Granada so that Segovia could get a better education. Segovia was introduced to flamenco music but was drawn more to the work of classical composers. Even though his family wanted him to become a lawyer he pursued his guitar studies. He was only sixteen years old when he had his first performance in Granada and just a few years later he went to Madrid for his first professional concert. He soon made himself known on the international stage, playing in, amongst others; in Paris, Barcelona and South America. These were great times for Segovia as there was a revival of the guitar as a concert instrument. His artistry and personality coupled with new technology such as radio, recording and air travel helped make the guitar popular again.

Segovia developed himself as a great flamenco guitar player but his main direction was classical music. He received numerous awards and honours during his musical career but he was especially respected for dignifying the classical guitar as a legitimate concert instrument. In recognition of a lifetime of contributions to music and arts he was given the title of Marqués de Salobreña, by King Juan Carlos I, in 1981.

Segovia felt that teaching was a vital part of his mission to propagate the guitar and he gave master classes throughout his career. He influenced a generation of classical guitarists with his technique and musical sensibility. Being able to say that you had studied under the famous Segovia could gain a guitarist respect, so many claimed to have done so. Segovia used to say that he had not really taught as many students as were claimed and once said: "All over the world I have 'pupils' that I have never met". When Segovia met the architect and politician Francisco Prieto Moreno from Granada, who was much in love with La Herradura, Prieto persuaded the guitar maestro to buy a country house with beautiful views to the sea. Andres Segovia came to La Herradura when he was already in his early seventies. Every summer people could find him at one of the beach bars on the sea front, enjoying his glass of beer. He was a remarkable figure always wearing one of those typical Central American large white shirts hanging loosely over his trousers, a straw summer hat and his walking stick. He continued performing into his old age and during the Seventies and Eighties he spent his semi-retirement in La Herradura. The village soon considered Segovia to be an important neighbour and in 1983 he was named 'Adoptive son of the village of La Herradura and Almuñécar' and the seafront road was named after him, now known as Paseo Maritimo Andrés Segovia.

In collaboration with the Almuñécar Town Hall the international classical guitar contest was created. The great master was still alive and gave his authorisation to the guitar competition. However, he did impose the condition that the competition should be especially demanding as far as the musical ability of the award-winning guitarists went. The first 'Certamen' took place in 1985 and the event continues to attract many guitar music lovers to this day. Andrés Segovia died of a heart attack in Madrid at the age of ninety-four. He was buried at Casa Museo Linares in Andalusia. Although he is no longer amongst us, his name will live on through his legacy; the films made about him, his recordings and the ongoing Certamen Internacional Andrés Segovia in La Herradura.

Andres Segovia - (1893 - 1997)

'El Ruso', a flamenco legend

I clamber up the spread out cobbled steps, using a side-railing to hang-on to, onto Calle Cuesta de Fray Leopoldo off Calle Real, and then take the third street to the right which is Calle Morenas. Along the way I am treated to various pretty views of the old village. Some of these whitewashed houses on both sides of these vertiginous cliff-like streets, too narrow for modern cars to use, are dressed with hanging baskets filled with colourful geraniums. I continue walking along Calle Morenas 'til it opens up into a small square, Calle Las Maravillas, just past a small Discor supermarket. On the left is a community centre where people can go for yoga classes and other activities. It is the neighbourhood where Manuel Rodrígez Garciolo, better known as 'El Ruso', used to live. I am on my way to interview his widow Elena about his fascinating life and musical heritage. I am invited into the tiny living space absolutely filled to the brim with memorabilia and photos. It feels like a shrine. There are two round dining tables each filled with vases, goblets, photos and statues. Every inch of wall space is covered with memorial plaques, plates, prizes, awards and photos, many photos, mostly of 'El Ruso', the children and the grandchildren. Elena is a lively, smiley lady who immediately makes me feel welcome. Now seventy-eight years old and still helping out with every mass in the village church she looks remarkably fit. She was born in Almuñécar but her husband, Manuel, was born in La Herradura. His grandparents' surnames were Garciolo and Ruiz. They were merchants, buying all sorts of things in Almuñécar to sell in La Herradura. Because of the name Ruiz, people would say "the 'Ruises' are coming!" Over the years this became the 'Rusos' (The Russians) hence the nickname 'El Ruso'.

Elena and Manuel came to live in the house in La Herradura in 1958 and the 'Guardia Civil' even knocked on their door a few times as they thought they came from

Russia. She speaks with affection about her late husband, 'El Ruso'. His mother's family came from Genova in Italy, the first to land in La Herradura. Hence his second name Garciolo, which is an Italian name. His father, a goat herder, was a very good singer and loved singing – a love he passed on to his son. Manuel was always singing, on his own, with his friends, or at charity events (to collect money for the church) and at local festivals and *peñas,* places where flamenco singers perform.

At some point Juanito Valderrama, a famous Spanish flamenco and folk singer heard him singing and wanted to take him to Granada to start a singing career. This meant learning from this great master for three or four months without an income, but Elena was pregnant with their first child and he did not want to risk being with no income for such a long period, so he refused. Instead, to make a living, he worked in construction and did a lot of work for Prieto Moreno when he developed the Punta de la Mona. Prieto and Manuel became good friends.

Later, following a motor accident, he could no longer work in construction and so became the caretaker at the local college. It didn't stop him from singing. Manuel could not read or write but he did 'write' his own music. He used a little cassette recorder to record his songs. He was a magnificent flamenco lyrics writer.

Elena recalls: "One day he created a beautiful *fandango a la madre* (fandango is a type of Spanish folk music) which was an ode to his mother". Life was not easy for Elena and Manuel. They lost their first child when he was only one year old, then their second child when it was only six months old. Their third child, a son, survived but then they had another child who died, only six months old. Their youngest child, a girl, survived. Losing three of their five children was a heartbreak that would undoubtedly have been part of the sentiment that went into Manuel's songs and his performances. He was a good man and was always helping others. He did a lot of free construction work for the church. He was not the only one. Many of the other men from the village did too. But Manuel was always generous to everybody. If someone was to say *oh how lovely* about something he owned, he would just give it to them. Elena remembers that one day, when her son was still very young, she went to the bank and discovered 30,000 pesetas missing. This was a significant amount of money at the time. Her husband had not told her anything about this. He had given the money to a man who needed it to visit his son in prison in Granada. He had also given this man, who wore the same size clothes, his wedding suit for the occasion. Elena was only told years later when the man knocked on the door to pay back the money. Her husband never really received money for his singing, and did not want to become a professional flamenco singer, but he became famous nevertheless. He won numerous awards and prizes that now proudly fill the walls of the living room of his house. Other well-known singers, like Camaron, El Chiquetete, Enrique Morente and many more became his friends. He was also very much respected by the *gitano* flamenco scene in Granada. When he was working at the college as a caretaker a friend from Salobreña suggested he make a record. At first he did not want to but they told him it was for the benefit of the local council and school. With the help of the Town-Hall this record was created. To this day the record (now available on CD) is still sold in many shops, and can be bought in places like Granada and El Corte Ingles (a well-known Spanish department store) in Malaga. Sadly, 'El Ruso' died too young of lung cancer in 1997, but he will be remembered. His funeral was a tribute to a great and humble artist and people from far and wide came along to pay their last respects. Elena shows me a copy of her beloved husband's record. On the back it reads: "The antique flamenco of 'El Ruso'"

"With this album we have created an audio recollection of the voice, the artistic sensibility and the knowledge that

Manuel 'El Ruso' has of the flamenco from another era, so that enthusiasts of this type of music can appreciate and enjoy this core folk music, away from commercial productions of the music industry. The salvaging of genuine Andalusian music: El Flamenco."

Manuel Rodríguez Garciolo - (1932 - 1998)

Pepe Gámez, a devoted village artist

Just off the main square in La Herradura, la Plaza de la Independencia, and to the left of the stage, you can walk up a few steps and then turn left into one of the old village streets. This then opens up into a lovely little square with some trees, plenty of plants in pots and also a ceramic portrait of Pepe Gámez, made by local ceramicist Rosario González Torres. A glass cover protects the statue and at its feet there are five white ceramic flowers, also by Rosario, paying tribute to this much loved local painter. This is the area where Pepe lived for most of his life. Pepe was born in La Herradura during the Civil war and died in February of 2013. Just past the statue a tiny street takes you into another square, the Plaza of San Jose where a statue of the Immaculate, made by Pepe Gámez, still stands proudly in the middle of the square. The old church in this square is long gone, as it became too small to cater for the growing village, and now the area provides space for shops and houses.

Pepe put his stamp on La Herradura in many ways. Most of the old families will have one of his paintings adorning their walls. He was a generous man and often gave his artwork to newlyweds. He also was a very good-looking man, like a movie star, and potentially he would have been able to break many hearts, but Pepe had no time for that. He had a different kind of passion, and he was religious in his passion. He did not want to take on the responsibility of a family as that would have meant having to stop doing what he loved most...art.

In the year of 1958 he went to live with his father's brother in Madrid to participate in sculpture workshops. He learned a lot there but felt like a burden to his uncle and aunt who had to feed four children in times when money was scarce, so Pepe returned to the village. Back here, his unstoppable desire to be a painter and sculptor meant instead of a formal education, he would go on to teach himself. His perseverance and undoubted talent paid off and during his lifetime he was to receive many commissions amongst which were the restorations of a church in Vittoria in Pais Vasco in the north of Spain and the Church of Carmen in Motril. In the Seventies and Eighties Pepe sold many of his paintings to foreigners who came to La Herradura on holiday or to live permanently here and, of course, many locals bought his well-loved art. Devoted to art he dedicated his life to painting, sculpting and the church. The church was important to him as although he wasn't your typical religious person, he had great faith. The fairly modern church in La Herradura was 'touched' by this local artist in many ways. Statues of Jesus and the apostles there are by his hand and the lovely altar backdrop depicts a modern and rather abstract representation of a white light above a vague image of a city or town. He was a true artist, living with art all his life.

When he was a young man he used to have a studio near the new church and also one in the house where he lived. In the last years of his life he could be found every morning and afternoon in the studio of Rosario González, always behind a painting, with classical music coming from an old radio in the corner of the studio. He was a very sensitive person and could fill up and get really emotional just listening to Mozart's Requiem. He also was a very generous man and during harsh times, people from the village preferred to come to Pepe than to the priest. Pepe would take them to the local supermarket and buy them some bread or milk. He was much loved and always made people laugh with his fantastic sense of humour and story-telling ability. He was an elegant man and although greatly missed, his presence is still very much felt as he lives on in his statues and paintings generously spread throughout the village.

Pepe Gámez - (1934-2013)

Voicing a story

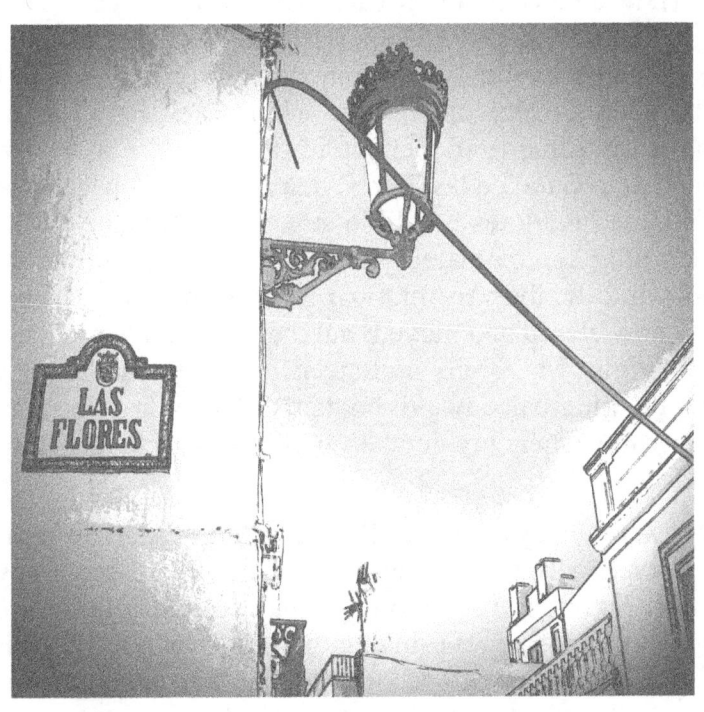

A Singing Family

"Singing is in our blood, in our genes. My entire family sings. In the village everybody knows my family and we are referred to as the tobacconist family. I am the daughter of Helena de Haro and Ricardo Díaz Valero. People in the village know me as Heleni. Practically my entire family, grandparents and great-grandparents come from La Herradura. Like many La Herradura families, my ancestors came from Genova in Italy. I grew up with my parents in Calle de las Flores, above the old tobacco shop. Calle de las Flores is a little street just off Calle Real, to the right approximately twenty metres after El Salon, known to be the very first bar in La Herradura. The shop has now closed and moved, but the place is used for social gatherings. My family no longer lives in the house above, but the little balcony still holds many memories of a long ago time when my mother used to sing to the Virgin Mary.

We were always singing. People could hear us from afar and especially my mother when they were passing down the street or coming in to buy a pack of cigarettes. Often, when my mother was singing, my father played the guitar and sang harmony to accompany her. I remember when I was still a young girl, how friends of my parents passed through the shop and came upstairs to make music, almost every night. There was no television. There was instead plenty of music with violins, guitars, bandurras and singing, lots of singing. Even some foreigners participated. These evenings were, so to speak, the first jam sessions in La Herradura. 'El Ruso', the well-known flamenco singer and part of our family, also came to these events. My great grandmother had five children. She was known in the village as 'Maria the ironer' because she was very good at ironing clothes. It was a very humble family. Many people in the village are closely or distantly related. For example, my grandfather from my mother's side is the uncle of Raimundo who is the local barber. My grandfather was called 'Frasquito' and was very important to the village. He was very artistic, but in those times people had to work the land or become fishermen.

During the war my grandfather had to join the military and he ended up working in the infirmary. That is where his passion to help others grew and when he came back to the village he practically became the doctor in La Herradura. Everybody went to see him when they fell ill. Even the official doctor from Motril who came to the village once a month said: 'Frasquito, you can do this, with all the experience that you have you are very capable.' My granddad never had a chance to study medicine but he had a passion and was an avid reader. He had two children. A boy, who was a very good singer as well but who sadly died when he was nine years old, and my mother. My mother was the oldest and was always singing. A close friend of my mother's mother, known as La Marquesica, who was also from La Herradura, went to live in Seville when her daughter Ana was still a young girl. Ana loved dancing and went to a dance academy in Seville. She ended up being a famous dancer and actress who played in various well-known movies. She was called Ana Esmeralda and had many friends in the flamenco world. Ana heard my mother sing when she was only twelve years old and wanted to take her with her to make her famous, but my grandfather did not allow it, as in the old days, dedicating yourself to the world of arts was not considered respectable for women. Instead he brought a woman over from Malaga to teach my mother how to become a hairdresser. My mother was only twelve years old and was running the first hairdresser shop in the village. There was a wooden floor and she was always dancing and singing.

Many people in La Herradura played the violin or sang and with the help of the local music teacher some sort of theatre group was created, which my mother was part of. My parents were very much in love but my father's grandfather wanted my father married to someone with land, with money. My parents were also related. My great-grandmothers were sisters; my mother's mother and my father's mother were cousins, so my parents knew each other very well from a very young age. At that time my father was living in Galicia because my granddad was a military man, a captain in the marines. My father did have some girlfriends before my mother, but love is a mysterious thing and one day, when my mother was performing in the theatre he was in the audience and she dedicated a song to him. The rest is history. Music really united them. My mum was very good at singing the *copla*, which is not flamenco but a typical Spanish style of popular songs, mostly sung in Andalusia, but also sung in Madrid. Apart from the *copla* my parents also sang a lot of Spanish *boleros*, however, never professionally. If they performed during local events they didn't ask any money for it.

My mother was a very religious woman and she sang many *saetas* dedicated to moments of suffering. The *saeta* is a typical Spanish Catholic song dating back many centuries. The old *saetas* probably originate from the recitation of psalms under the influence of liturgical music. They vary greatly in form and style, but are perhaps best known for their mournful power during Holy Week in Spain. The song is performed during the religious processions that slowly move through the streets in towns and villages in southern Spain carrying statues of holy figures. It is often sung from a balcony and may be addressed to the statue of Jesus, depicting his agony in the Via Dolorosa, or to a statue of mother Mary suffering from his death. My mother was well known for this type of song and people came especially to our house to listen to her singing on the balcony. The *saeta* sounds like flamenco singing and is very difficult to sing. She was rather shy and did not show herself whilst singing a *saeta;* it was not about her but was out of respect for the suffering. People loved her singing and the men from the village who carried the statues during the procession always stopped beneath the balcony to listen.

My mother was a true artist. She also painted, in oils, but never for money. She helped create the statues of Christ and the Virgin Mary for the village church. She made their eyelashes from my hair and that of my sister. So our hair was dressing the eyes of her beloved statues. She always sang to them. My mother died on the 28th of March, on a Good Friday, the day that Christ died. She died at exactly three o'clock, and some people believe that Christ also died at three o'clock. When my mother was laid out, the procession with the Virgin Mary passed below the balcony. It was as if the Virgin came out to see her. We were looking down from the balcony. It was so touching, everybody was crying. It was emotional and special, because of the day, because of the hour, because of the Virgin. My mother had dedicated so much of her life to the Virgin; her songs, the hair of her children and now it felt as if the Virgin was paying her respects to her. The funeral was amazing; there was a huge crowd paying respect. Both my parents were much loved in the village. Everybody still stops me in the streets to talk about them. Both my parents fell ill with cancer in the same year, but my mother died two years after my father. My life was wrecked. I was only twenty years old and the youngest in the family. I have an older brother and sister.

The legacy our parents left us was a great love for music. We all sing but we weren't encouraged to be professionals. Our studies came first as they thought a musical career was too difficult to survive on, but it didn't stop us from making music. My brother studied in the evenings to pursue a singing career. He became a tenor and has worked in some musicals and has even performed in Germany. He is a great composer too, but in the end he chose a different career and became the religious education teacher in the village school. My sister has never sung professionally, only during some village events. We all play instruments. I play the 'bandurria', my brother plays the piano and guitar, my sister plays guitar and so does my nephew. My niece is the only one who doesn't play an instrument but she sings. I went to study in Granada, but I was always singing. One day, when my mother was still alive, she gave a recording that I had made of me singing, to a friend of hers who organised weddings. This friend of my mother contacted me after my mother had died and offered me a job as a singer for weddings and other events. It was a life-saver for me as singing was the only thing I really wanted to do. I sang professionally for seven or eight years, but then life got in the way and I started travelling, something I love doing, exploring new horizons. However, music is never far away, it is in my family. My nephew sings professionally. He lives in Valencia where he is part of a group called Wonder. I currently work in the family's tobacco shop, but I have plans to get back into singing. I miss it. I always listen to music, singing along during music programmes on the television or radio, but I want more. I know that I have potential but I need to improve my singing so I am working on that through technical vocal classes in Granada. My favourite music is jazz and I love to sing in the style of Halie Loren. I think she is fantastic and inspirational, but I also love singing the bolero and soul. For soul you need a group to accompany you but for jazz and bolero that is not necessary. At the moment I am working with Carlo Martin, a jazz guitarist for future performances. For me music needs to move me and communicate something. I am always listening to it and I like it when it awakens emotions within. Now that I am getting older I realise that it is important to appreciate art of all kinds. Music, dance, but also painting, sculptures and so forth. There is always a story behind a picture or a piece of music. There is time and effort, years of practice, studying. You can appreciate that when you truly observe or truly listen. I like to convey that as well when I sing. I like people to truly listen when I perform my songs, to let the music become part of them, allow it to touch them because when you get touched by music, when you sense an emotion, you will have a beautiful experience. It certainly works like that for me. Music is, has always been and will always be my nutrition. I need to sing. It is in my blood…it is in my genes."

Helena Díaz de Haro

The enchanting village choirmaster

Just beneath the Carmines del Mar there is a small cove, which is only accessible by a path in the National Park of Cerro Gordo. Both the cove and its surroundings are called Calaiza. Pablo lives just above it and often goes out for an inspirational meander to the tiny beach. We meet at his house and together we walk down the pathway through the enchanting area with stunning sea views. We find a nice shady space on the beach and express our shared appreciation for the sea and the village of La Herradura.

Pablo is one of the younger interviewees to take part in this storytelling itinerary. His thick black hair is held together in a ponytail and I cannot help but take a look at his hands. They look totally right and artistically suited to do his job. I am also impressed by his straight back and confident and calm appearance, but not surprised. I ask him whether he was born in the village and he starts talking.

"I am from Almuñécar but have been living in La Herradura for three years now. I was interested in finding a tranquil setting where I can play my grand piano without disturbing the neighbours and I found it in the Carmines del Mar. It is a big house and I was fortunate to be able to afford to rent it. It is perfect for me. I like the village but it is hard to explain its attraction. There is, of course, the natural beauty but the same goes for neighbouring towns and villages such as Almuñécar, so that is not really the reason. There is something else here. The easiest way to describe it is that it has an energy of its own with really good vibes. It is something that you feel inside and I believe that this is why it is such a special place for artists. To me it gives me peace of mind. The fact that it is rather small and therefore easy to connect with other people does help. This is a village with a strong sense of family, where people know each other and keep an eye out for each other. It makes it feel safer, with less aggression than in bigger towns."

Could you then say that the village has changed your life?

"Yes, absolutely. I was able to realise my dream here".

You are still very young if I may say so, and you have already realised your dream? That is impressive!

"OK, perhaps I should say that I've realised my first dream so far! I wanted to find the right place and the time to develop myself more through study and practicing and I have managed to create that. I can live doing what I love doing most, my passion for music, with my teaching, giving concerts and now also being the director of the village choir, I can do all this and still be close to my family in Almuñécar. Most musicians have to go to a big city, somewhere in the world, away from family. My family is very important to me.

I had a strong intuition about coming to La Herradura. Finding this house, where I can study combined with fantastic views to inspire me, was like an omen. I work every day but it feels as if I'm always on holiday. You could say that I am an example of becoming what you dream of. If you have that strong feeling, fuelled by a passion that is calling you so loudly that you feel that you just have to do it, then you have to follow your intuition."

Wise words. So how did you get involved in the choir?

"The choir was one of those coincidences, although I have to say I don't believe in coincidences, I believe everything happens for a reason. When I came to la Herradura I was immediately contacted by Roberto Ruggiero who was the former choirmaster, who sadly passed away in 2012. He told me that, as a pianist, I would be perfect to become the new choirmaster. I felt somewhat uncertain as I had never done anything like that, but he told me that he was sure I was capable of it. I have now directed the choir for quite some time and it has been a process of learning and growing. Apart from it being an enjoyable and interesting experience it is also very complementary to my personal and musical training. A pleasing side-effect of all this work is that it has helped me to meet people from the village who have taken me in as if I am part of one big family. I am treated very well and that is really wonderful.

Musically it is also interesting. I use music that I like and I then try to adapt it to this choir. It is a choir where people come and go so it is a challenge to get the right combination of what I like and what they love and can work with. Personally I have never sung professionally and it is not specifically what I studied, but throughout my years of musical education I have been singing in choirs. In the La Herradura choir I have to sing everything, from soprano, alto, and tenor to bass. So currently I am actually singing quite a lot so that is very enjoyable. With the choir we also give concerts and we always attend at the San Jose church mass. When the choir was founded it had about 40 members and was able to put on more concerts. Nowadays there are around 20 people but I hope this number will grow. However, no matter how you look at it, it is an achievement that a village of this size has a choir at all. It is curious. In the south of Spain there is no long tradition of choirs as there is in the North. In the South, the most normal type of choir is a *rociero* choir. These are choirs that sing during a special Spanish celebration called Las Cruces where crosses are created in the streets by the locals that are then visited by these choirs. With their popular hymns, traditional folk percussion and guitar music they animate the audience. There is also a *rociero* choir in La Herradura and some people sing in both choirs. The choir I direct is a classical choir."

Where have you studied?

"I studied piano, first in Granada and then at the

Conservatory of Madrid."

Have you always had an interest in music?

"Just recently I was thinking about that, and wonderful childhood memories popped into my head. I remember the feelings I had watching the light reflected on the sea in a residential area of Miramar in Almuñécar where I was born. That light was so beautiful and somehow it was connected to classical music. My family did not have any musical training, but they ended up with a collection of classical records and my father used to play these. I was very young, not even six years old, but I have very clear memories and sensations of these moments. I would even go so far as to say that it was a most sublime feeling; that music in combination with the magical light reflection on the sea and the intense colours of the bougainvillea everywhere you looked. When you listen to music by Mozart when you're a baby or a small child you think that it is normal. I was also lucky to have a neighbour, Eduardo, who used to play classical music records when I visited him. When I was six years we moved to the centre of Almuñécar and my life became more like that of other children. But the seed had been planted and all this has led to where I am now. At school there were the normal music classes that every child participated in, but I happened to be one out of every thousand or so that then continued to pursue a music career."

Did your family support you in your decision?

"Oh yes, I have great parents and they have always supported me."

How do you describe yourself as an artist?

"I am a pianist. Apart from being the director of the local choir, I give concerts and am now also embarking on a new journey, composing. Apart from that, I give private piano lessons, to adults as well as children. I have a very gratifying job. So I am lucky to be able to be a full-time musician. I used to give quite a few concerts when I was younger, also abroad, for example in Poland, Belgium, Germany, and even in the United States when I was still a student, but I have chosen to slow down, because I want to find myself as an artist and concentrate on my musical development for the time being. When I do give a performance it is usually a recital but I also work in ensembles."

Do you have to put yourself in a particular mood in order to play?

"When I need to capture a certain emotion like sadness or happiness in a music piece I sometimes think of sad moments or a happy moment in my life. To make myself sad I can, for example, think that one day my family might not be there anymore. It is not totally necessary to do this every time. You can play beautiful music without tapping into these emotions, but when you do, it can be explosive and more magical.

It never gets boring. Even if you played a piece, for example Beethoven's Piano Sonata No.21 in C, Op.53, 'Waldstein', a thousand times it will sound different each time. It all depends on your state of mind and perhaps your physical state and there is of course the interpretation. It is beautiful to put feelings into a work. As a pianist you are not always in the same mood and you have to work on finding that special state of mind and that special place to convey the right emotions! Playing the piano at a high level is like a mix between flying and an energetic massage. You are playing with energy, with the intense perception of climbing and descending, which takes you from here to there and back. Sometimes, it is a transcendental sensation and feels like the best experience I can have in life. It is hard to explain this to people who have not experienced it. In fact people might see me play and think that I am very sad but that is not necessarily the case."

What is your dream for the future as an artist?

"My dream for the future is that my interpretation of the classics of Mozart, Bach, and all these great composers that I love so much will emerge in such a way that people can distinguish my personal touch. I try to make the most of the beauty of the music that I am sharing with others. When someone can truly resonate with music it can move them into harmony, peace or love, but most important for me is that I am actually living my dream right now. I play the piano every day, I am surrounded by nice people and I can play the music that I like to play."

Do you have a wish for La Herradura?

"I like the energy here but it would be great if there were more young people on this wavelength. I do miss that somewhat. I realise it is perhaps more difficult to find younger people who already have found this sensitivity. I would like, both Almuñécar and La Herradura to be places that attract even more interesting personalities like athletes and artists alike and to nurture cultural tourism with more people contributing and reflecting the wondrous natural beauty of this area. It is not just about the sun and the beach. This is a very special area that could grow into something even more wonderful."

We walk back together to Pablo's house. I thank him and tell him that I really enjoyed the interview. We say goodbye and I head home with Mozart's Piano Sonata No. 11 keeping me company in my head.

Pablo Ruiz Segura

La Herradura, a village of fusion

"Lino, my husband, and I share the same point of view both musically and professionally and we agree on where we want to get to," says Lupe, a Cuban born musician and singer. She was only six years old when she started studying classical piano at the music school. "I entered to study the piano but I also loved singing. I come from a very artistic family, some of whom are successful both in Cuba and abroad. My uncle is an artistic photographer, my mother is a professional singer and has won national awards, my sister is a painter and my brother is a musician too. When I was eleven years old I also started painting. However, I was more or less forced to study piano and this required many hours of study. It was hard for me as I was a free spirit and wanted to express my creativity freely.

At some point I was able to convince some teachers to let me sit for art exams and ended up graduating in both art and music. Although I was educated in art and classical piano, I was always singing. When I was seventeen years old my mother fell ill and I had to replace her in a performance during a political event in Cuba. From there on I knew...*this is what I want to do.* I told my mother that I wanted to sing professionally and that was the start of my singing career."

Her full name is Adaleydis Amador Posada but professionally everybody knows her as Lupe Posada. She grew up in Camaguey, a city in central Cuba, but in 2006 she moved to La Herradura with her family.

We agreed to meet for the interview at the La Herradura lighthouse. You can reach the lighthouse via two different routes; either by way of the Camino de la Ermita or via the Camino de la Torre. Today I turn left on the seafront onto Paseo Andres Segovía and drive up the Calle Ctra. de la Playa. I go straight ahead, where the road splits with a sharp curve to the left, and enter the Camino de la Torre. The winding road takes me through a scenic route with unexpectedly pleasant views of houses, partially hidden from curious passers-by behind lots of green trees. I am also treated to an occasional spectacular sea view. I keep following the Camino de la Torre until it bends sharply right at a sign that says La Aldea and soon I find myself at the foot of the lighthouse.

Lupe and I take in the beautiful view over the village and the bay on one side and over Marina del Este and the sea on the other side.

Why La Herradura? I ask her.

"Lino and I were living and working in Italy when my mother came to La Herradura in 2005 for work during the summer season. She loved the village and the area, the beach and the weather. Back in Italy she told us about this. It sounded like the perfect place for us and we decided to move to Spain. Lino came first to find a place to live and make some contacts and I then followed with our first child who was born in Italy.

I first went to Italy when I was nineteen years old with a contract as a pianist to the Trento area in the North. After having worked for this company for a year I decided to start my own family business with my mother, my stepfather and two other musicians. We called it *Salsa Loco*. Other musicians joined the group and we ended up travelling all over Italy and part of Europe, playing mainly Latin American music.

After two years I decided to create a show group called *'Le Cubanissime Son las que Son'*, with dancers and Cuban costumes. My mother was part of the company but wasn't in the show group. She is a traditional Cuban music artist. I dedicated myself to the show and we travelled during the summer months performing at many Latin-American festivals, both in Italy and internationally including throughout Latin America. Through this we achieved a certain fame. We even worked with music publishers like EMI Music. I was very busy but it felt as if I was losing my identity, I wasn't happy. There was satisfaction with what I had achieved but it was not really the music that I personally preferred and that satisfied my soul.

With the encouragement of my brother, who was my musical support at the time, I decided to return to Cuba to find musicians to create a new group. I also needed to find myself again and go back to my roots. I went to my home town of Camaguey and started a fusion music project that included powerful instruments like the *tres cubano* (a guitar-like three double-stringed chordophone) and the trumpet and *batas*, which are Cuban drums that are used for the Rumba and the Guaguancó, and which are an important part of our Afro Cuban culture. During this project I met Lino. He was special because of his music style and also for the fact that he, himself, had invented and created an amazing instrument – a combination of the *requinto ecuatoriano* and the *tres cubano* in one instrument which he called the *treaquinto*. We created an entire show in Cuba with the collaboration of an important studio and then presented it in Italy one and a half years later. We even created a video clip called *Lupe Mátale la Pena* which can be seen on YouTube. We are also in various Le Cubanissime clips on YouTube.

Whilst we were working on this project Lino and I became a couple. Our first child was born and I discovered that one of the most precious jobs in life is being a mother. Being a well-known artist was not something I liked. People stopping you in the streets, always having to play that role, it didn't really suit me. What I wanted was to reconnect musically, I wanted to breathe again. That is when we decided to come to La Herradura.

We came and we stayed and living here in La Herradura not only gave us a sense of serenity, it has also given us peace of mind. The village has become our home. It has something mystical. La Herradura also made it possible for us to experiment musically and to find out what we really wanted. We both love jazz music. I like to sing jazz but we both also like fusion and musically you could say that my Cuban roots always come to the surface. We are both influenced by Cuban music which is logical as in Cuba there aren't many other musical influences and it was Cuba where we both grew up and got our musical formation."

So could you say that La Herradura has changed your life?

"Yes it has. La Herradura has given me tranquillity. Our second child was born in La Herradura and I feel protected here. It is a small village and all the mothers know each other and that creates the sense of protection. One of our children has autism and is musically very talented but he needs some special attention. I feel very safe in La Herradura, all the mothers meet at the school gate and this creates people protection. If your child runs off there will always be one of the mothers nearby who knows your child and will tell you where it is. Our oldest son also loves music and he too is very talented. He learns really quickly. When his father plays the flute, the piano or the ukulele he just picks up the skill. It all comes very easily to him.

Generally speaking, for children it is also fantastic to be able to talk and play with children from other countries. All the children of foreigners that come to the village go to the same class to learn the language but what they get in addition is a wealth of cultural information. This creates a nice, pleasant environment. My son now says that as an adult he wants to travel the world because he has received so much information about other countries, which has created a healthy curiosity in him."

Getting back to the music side of your life, can you tell me a bit more about that?

"The basis of what we do is jazz music but Lino has a rather complicated and fascinating musical concept. He is very exploratory and likes to experiment a lot. I do love jazz but I also feel influenced by Celia Cruz, a Cuban singer. Both our musical influences mix well and we now perform as *Timbalito Street*. We allow ourselves the liberty of creating the same musical theme in different styles and forms. It is difficult to define ourselves musically but people identify with what we do and that is the goal. That is what is important. I play several instruments including the piano, but when I play with Lino my main contribution is to sing and provide some percussion.

I also perform without Lino and still participate in shows given by my mother's group. My mother, Consuelo Posada, has returned to Cuba because she felt the need to sing again. Now in her sixties, but still very fit, she performs a lot, and can be seen on television and mentioned in articles in the Cuban press. She is happy. Sometimes she performs in Spain with her group and then I join in. I also participate in the music group of my brother, Luis de la Cruz, who still lives and performs in Italy. So you could say that I am involved in different types of music, jazz with my husband Lino, Latin with my mother and Latin rock with my brother – and this diversity is something I enjoy very much.

Musically Lino makes me feel safe and he also supports me in my other musical adventures. People say that we have created something amazing and I think that is true. We understand each other, both musically and personally I feel we have created a perfect union."

So where do you get your inspiration from?

"I like listening to the radio and any type of music I hear can inspire me, both the good and the bad. It catches my attention and makes me curious. This can, for example, be on the radio or music screaming from a car window passing by."

Do you perform regularly in La Herradura?

"With *Timbalito Street* we perform every Monday in El Tinao, one of the local bar/restaurants. In fact, you could say that Timbalito Street was 'born' in El Tinao. The audiences can vary, sometimes there is a fantastic ambience with people really appreciating what we do, but sometimes I feel we are seen simply as background music. It's usually a very pleasant situation and the best thing is that we can perform the music we like and experiment. It is like our music laboratory."

Are you a full-time artist?

"I consider myself a full-time artist and I cannot imagine my life without music. But I am also a mum. When I am cooking I am singing and when I'm singing the children are listening, it is part of me. I also compose, but I do not compose for me - only on request, when people ask me. I sing and make music because I like to. There is no deeper message. I know that I did not like the 'reaching fame' side of it. That is not me. You are always performing, wearing the right clothes, high heels, you name it. It makes it hard to be who you really are. It is true that we were making a lot more money than we are making here, but the difference is here I can be myself and do what I love, which is being a mother and a singer/musician. I feel more satisfied, more complete."

So how do you see the future of La Herradura?

"La Herradura is already open to many types of cultural events and music and it would be wonderful if it attracted even more artistic people. Some people are afraid that this might ruin its tranquillity, but I don't think that will happen. Cultural events will not ruin that. The village is protected by the sea and the mountains and that cannot be broken, that is impenetrable. I suggest people should not be afraid, just go with the flow and let it be and teach future generations to keep an open mind in order to experience the wonderful sense of freedom that comes with that.

Culturally La Herradura is very rich, but in my opinion it is important to unite in a musical, artistic and cultural collaboration. It would be brilliant if there was more interaction between the various musicians and artists, writers and other creative people, and coming back to my passion, music ... I would love to see more musical fusion. Sometimes musicians are afraid to merge, afraid that it will change their culture. But I feel it only adds to it. My belief is that you will not lose it but rather you might create something really special. There should be no fear of playing together. Music is a language and it can touch people. Let's speak the same language! Let's turn La Herradura into a village of 'fusion'!"

Lupe Posada -
www.facebook.com/lupeadaleydis.amadorposada

A brotherhood of literature

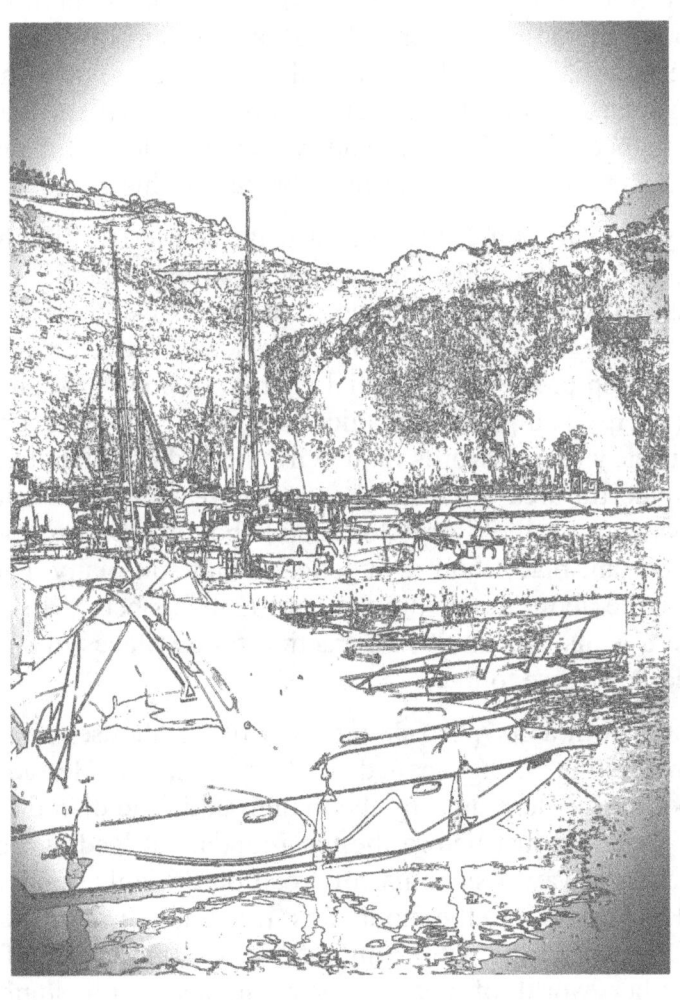

A poetic teacher

"We have named it *Cofradia Literaria de La Herradura*, which is a brotherhood of literature. It isn't an association but a group of writers who have a love for this village in common. We meet in the garden of the studio of a local ceramic artist called Rosario Gonzalez, who happens to be my sister-in-law and decided to form this group. We come together on a regular basis to talk about books, about literature in general and about our love for La Herradura. As a brotherhood of literature we have organised various literary events both in the village and in Almuñécar and Granada and we hope to do so for many years to come. It is inspiring to be part of this group.

My love for La Herradura is a bit like art, difficult to explain, not tangible but a feeling, a strong attraction. It is easy to love the surroundings, the mountains, the sea, but not every village or town is blessed with such a startling backdrop or the same special energy. In poetry the theme of energy is a point of magic, therapeutic even. As a poet it is easy to find words to give tribute and gratitude to this wonderful area in Spain. For many years I have written poems about the Cerro Gordo and about the bay as a very important place, both energetically and spiritually. I love to write about the nature that surrounds us here. I believe there is also an intuitive attraction to the places in which people choose to live.

I was born a *cortijero*, in a cluster of farmhouses that are part of the village called El Cerval de La Herradura. Exiting La Herradura by the main road in the direction of Malaga and just before the big roundabout leading up to the motorway, a steep narrow road on the right hand side takes you up into the mountains. It is a favourite track for many walkers. Within minutes you find yourself in another world of peaceful surroundings with stunning views of the verdant beauty of the river Jate valley.

Walking up the road you can see beautiful examples of small and large houses and the ruins of *cortijos*, local farmhouses on a plot of private land. You might be treated to a smile by one of the locals working their land surrounded by custard apple trees as well as mangos, avocados and loquats. Approximately seven kilometres further into the mountains you reach the small hamlet of El Cerval. My parents still live there. When I was a young man I used to help my parents on the land and I also worked in bars in the village during the summer months to pay for my studies in Granada. I studied language and speech therapy. I lived away from my village for a total of fourteen years for work reasons.

In addition to my love for poetry I also love my day job as a teacher. My wife and I lived a busy working life in Murcia but then our daughter was born and we were consumed by a strong longing to return to La Herradura where we were both born and grew up. We wanted our daughter Lucia to grow up in a small village that sits by the seaside but also in the mountains. We were fortunate that I was able to get a transfer as a teacher to the village of Jete, within reasonable driving distance from our house, and that's where I continue to work, at the primary educational level. I am a teacher by vocation. This is very important to me. Every day I love my work more and more. I feel blessed to be able to always find a reason to learn more about myself and life through the eyes of children. Their young minds are still so pure, and they are so totally in contact with their natural purity and are real fountains of energy.

We live in the village in the midst of my wife Teresa's family. Our home is surrounded by a lush patio, full of trees and plants in pots. It's a tranquil little haven and we also like to go to our plot of land outside the village. We have planted some vegetables and fruit trees and like to simply go there to work the land and take in the enchanting view over the La Herradura bay and the mountains.

Nature is the prime source of my inspiration - it feeds my poems. A poem in my latest book is called *Arte* and it is about searching for my necessity to write. I don't know if there is a clear answer but there are various ingredients. One of these is a primitive part in me, a need to express myself. I write because I feel the need to tell my story, to share it, a sort of validation of my life. I also look for my spiritual essence through my poetry. The cornerstones of this quest are primitive, rational and spiritual, but the truth is that it is not necessary to find an answer. In the poem *Arte* there is a line that states that art and/or poetry is the searching for a place that is hard to get to and only a few reach, but once they are there they realise that they will never fully arrive.

I once asked the late local artist Pepe Gámez why he always made the same painting. He said that he had never completely achieved what he was searching for and for that reason he had to continue. My poems often deal with a moment of existence that leaves some wondering or doubts without always giving clarity. When I write there is a part of me that is in the flow, uncontrollable, that is my voice. I try to write as clearly as possible as I am aware that some people find poetry difficult to access. Every artist has his or her style and his or her voice, I don't believe you choose your mode of expression, it just comes to you. You cannot choose authenticity - that is a gift.

The poetic voice is important as it shows individuality. Nature is hugely important in my poetry. I always talk about nature and I don't feel any need to use something else as my muse at the moment, but should that change in some future then that is fine too, as long as it is a natural process. When I sit down to write I don't really start with a message, but the message comes to me whilst writing. I get in touch with my emotions and a poem transcends emotions such as love, unity and humanity. For me it is important that we all live in harmony with the nature that surrounds us. Those who love their natural surroundings will respect it and help conserve it. I like to write about the sensitivity needed to understand the pain and the joy of the world.

I believe that we should not dwell on the negative when something potentially bad happens, for example, the recent over-construction that has ruined much of the landscape, but I try to look for the good in it. This idea is embodied in my children's books to create awareness and to prevent it from recurring. I write about the landscape, about loving the mountains and the sea, and about the importance of not polluting it but looking after it. The same applies to animals. I like to teach about sensitivity and about loving people, nature, animals and living together in harmony. I write two types of poetry books, one for adults and one for children. The children's books also have illustrations. Usually the various publishers I work with find an illustrator for my work. To date I have had five adult poetry books published and five children's books, of which two are poetry and three are theatre plays. At the moment I am working on two infant literary projects, and on a poetry book for adults, called *La Alberca* (The swimming pool) - the latter incorporating my experience of country life, my relationship with nature and how I experience that spiritually.

Usually special moments inspire me but it depends on the book that I am writing. My first book was about memories from my childhood. I like to include the influence of our past, our parents, our upbringing and the places in which we live. I am concerned not just with description but transforming an observation into an emotion, of dealing with something more profound, more mysterious and spiritual. Poetry is about placing yourself on the boundary of the real world and the incomprehensible and indescribable. It's about looking for that border and looking into that space that is ineffable. Words can only get us close to the territory that we cannot name, the border we find so difficult to cross. The poet in me is a man who reflects the image of that border on the surface of the water. When you look you will find that the reflection is the truth, like a mirror. But words cannot enter the water, the sounds of nature remain on the surface, the brush stroke of a painting cannot enter and neither can the sounds of music. But the idea of God, the idea of the soul, can be mixed with your emotions. La Herradura is part of that inspiration.

When I left my village at the age of twenty-four I looked at the landscape in a different way. Although raised in an agricultural environment with parents who taught me about working the land and love for the land, when I came back after my years in Almeria I had changed. It was as if everything had manifested and I had come full circle. I had learned to view the world from another perspective through reading many books, meeting interesting people and my studies. When I came back I looked at my village with different eyes, with poetic eyes. I valued the landscape more than ever before and poetry helped me to look with the colours of my palette of words to admire the emotions that this environment caused in me. I rediscovered the beauty of this area also through the eyes of my precious daughter. My bond with La Herradura had never been broken but now I recognise its tranquillity and happiness on a daily basis whilst I walk along the beach or work the land. This place is so special that I hope we will all work together on its conservation, so that my daughter, when she is an adult woman, can enjoy this very same poetic landscape."

Reinaldo Jiménez Morales - www.reinaldojiménez.com

A prolific writer

On a grey, drowsy afternoon in early April I follow the signs to the Marina del Este leisure harbour for an interview with Salvador Compán, an award winning Spanish writer. Down from Hotel Alcazar the road passes some modern, yet Spanish style urbanisations, treating you to a spectacular view of the sea and the impressive sight of villas built on the edge of a sheer cliff of orange-coloured rock. At the sea front I find a parking space to the right and walk down some steps towards the beach bar on the Playa de Los Berengueles beach. I pass by some rocks rising from the sea and watch the slightly choppy water revealing the bright red layer of orange coral (asteroid calicularis) which is attached to the rocks just below sea level. A group of divers are taking off their gear looking happy and satisfied. I recognise the owner of one of the many diving schools in La Herradura. It is too chilly to sit outside so I enter the beach bar and sit down at a table in front of the window with a view of the beach. The music is loud enough to enjoy but unobtrusive enough to hold a normal conversation. I am early for my meeting and so I order a cup of coffee and a glass of sparkling water. There is a lovely big gas heater in the centre of the space, giving off a pleasant heat and the atmosphere is comfortable.

There are a number of other visitors that are possibly best described as alternative or artistic, certainly not the typical tourists you see on Spanish coasts, easily recognisable as such by their dress-sense – i.e. bright colours, t-shirts, shorts and flip-flops no matter the weather. I observe a couple a few tables away from me. It looks as if they are discussing a serious subject, their heads close together but not necessarily amorously. He looks concerned and holds her hand. I can see fear in her eyes and she shakes her head, kind of powerless, without any fight left. I get the impression that he is trying to convince her of something important. She looks frail and vulnerable, almost vague, like a sad poem. I'm sure she is Spanish. He on the other hand looks northern European and could be a teacher or a professor with his glasses sliding down the bridge of his nose. I imagine it is Scott Cover, one of the leading characters in *Palabras Insensatas que tu comprenderás* (Silly words that you will understand), a novel by Salvador Compán, who just walks in. It is the first time we have met and I introduce myself.

After ordering a drink he starts talking: "I was born and raised in the land of olives, in Úbeda, in the province of Jaén, which boasts a wealth of Renaissance palaces and churches and is a World Heritage Site but I currently live in Seville. We have an apartment in La Herradura in the Marina del Este. My wife and I bought it in 2001. We like the fact that it is almost a deserted village in winter and spring time but maintains a pleasant atmosphere in summer with mainly Spanish tourists. We like to enjoy an appetizer or a nice meal on the sea front and, weather permitting, take a swim in the sea. We come here whenever we can but we don't have a fixed timetable, because I am a pensioner now. Before my retirement I was a teacher. I worked in various towns and cities including, amongst others Santander, Ibiza and Brussels. The latter was to give pre-university classes to emigrants and children of Spanish diplomats, and from 1983 to 2011 I taught Spanish literature in Seville. I am now a full time novelist, but also still produce other types of written work, like prologues for books and art exhibitions, literary interviews and articles for various newspapers. My literary work mainly consists of novels. What interests me most when I write is the human psyche and in particularly 'desire', a recurring theme in all my books and, in my opinion, one of the most important driving forces in a human being. There is no novel if there is no contradiction. Often doubt and desire serve as the motor which drives the main character. This desire can be sexual, an ambition or any other type of desire that can lift the character out of normality. Take for example, love. A desire for love or indeed a lack of love is always central in my novels. My inspiration is the observation of reality and when something sparks an idea, I turn it into literary material. It almost becomes an obsession. An idea gets into my head and I cannot let go of it. It can be a metaphor or a fragment of reality. What is important is how one handles the metaphor. For example, in one of my novels set in Granada, the spark that I am talking about came to me through a mural that I saw. I became obsessed with it. The mural portrayed Ángel Ganivet, an important writer from the nineteenth century. I wondered *what's behind this painter, what is his story?* Little things inspire me hugely and I can go in any direction. For example, a girl goes to school every morning with a blue jumper with brass buttons. When she is on her way to school she meets another child but they go in different directions. One of my novels called *Tras la mirada* (Beyond the glance) which was set in Córdoba was inspired by this observation. The observation then becomes the core of the novel, the children the motive and it extends into a full blown fictional story.

Another one of my novels was based on something I witnessed in a bar in Seville. A man, dressed in a red jersey, was sitting at the bar, drunk and crying. It was the 6th of January, *Día de Los Reyes* (Three Kings Day), an important national celebration in Spain. He was all on his own. I asked him: 'What is the matter? Can I help?' Approximately one hour later I saw him again in Calle Sierpe, one of the main streets in Seville. It affected me to see how people made an effort to avoid him, walking around him in a large circle. He was extremely drunk and I wondered what his story was. There is always a story behind a story. This moment in time resulted in *Cena de Reyes* (King's Dinner), that tells a fragment of the life of a lonely man.

Often the observation turns into a fixation, a mechanism that then becomes a search. I like to discover and unveil that which lies beyond the surface of reality. That is what makes it literature. Something you might look upon as evident and obvious is not always the reality. I love the searching that leads to creating something that did not exist before. I consider myself very lucky. My life has always been easy. I wanted to become a literature teacher and I achieved that. I wanted to write and communicate and achieved that too. When I was studying for my bachelor exams in mathematics and chemistry I realised that a scientific career was not what I wanted from life. During my pre-university years I discovered a great love for writing poetry and reading in general and I wanted to have a career in this field. I told my parents that I wanted to change my study to literature. Although they tried to persuade me not to, they stood behind me when I took this big step. Changing my study to literature was hugely important to me. It enabled me to make the choices that I have made and to never have to do anything that I didn't want to do. This doesn't mean that I haven't worked hard to get to where I am now, but I have been fortunate enough to do precisely that which fulfils me and I still do that to this day.

I also have another passion. Painting and drawing, something I remember doing from a very young age. Painting is more like a hobby to me, but the drawings are part of my existence. I have created travel journals during my longer travels and my novel *Cuaderno de Viaje* (Travel Journal) was chosen as a finalist entry in the important Spanish 'Finalista Premio Planeta'. I now tend to create mostly pen drawings and I like to combine them with my literature. This combination of writing down what I experience and then depicting it in images is what I am doing in these travel journals, like an old-fashioned romantic traveller. I am not sure whether they will ever be published; I create them because it gives me immense personal satisfaction. However, the book I am working on at the moment is a good example of a combination of literature and my drawings. This novel is about a character who is narrating his life by means of a graphic novel. It will be my seventh novel. There is nothing that helps me more to get in a state of total self-absorption than painting or drawing, a very pleasant sensation.

Writing on the other hand is a process of going within, of reflection, taking inspiration from your surroundings and fusing them with your ideas. Creative writing communicates with reality. The metaphor is the main actor in the creative process combining realities that are separated but eventually merge. I like to draw my surroundings, but also draw on my surroundings for my writing. La Herradura is no exception to this. I have known La Herradura since I was a youngster, enjoying the clean beaches during holiday time. My novel, *Palabras Insensatas que tu comprenderás* is in fact set in Marina del Este. Scott Cover is a fictional figure who has come to the area for its tranquillity, to be in close proximity to the stars, to the sound of the waves, the tops of pine trees near his terrace and bird song. He came here to write. In the story he helps a woman who is suffering from abuse.

My inspiration for this book was a real life story in a time of Spanish modernism at the beginning of the twentieth century. In the nineteen twenties there was a remarkable woman, Maria la O Lejárraga García, sometimes known as María Martínez Sierra. She was a Spanish feminist writer, dramatist, translator and politician and she wrote successful novels as well as theatre plays. A famous theatre play, called *Canción de Cuna* (Lullaby) was even turned into a movie both in Hollywood and in Spain. It was a best-seller at the time. She was a prolific writer but she did not sign her own work. Her husband did. Gregorio Martínez Sierra enjoyed the fame of being a successful theatre producer and dramaturge. The reality was a case of tremendous artistic exploitation as all the theatre plays, novels and stories were in his name, but were in fact written by his wife María. In a way my novel tries to make up for this, through a new María Lejárraga, a woman who resembles her; a modern day woman who is a poet and in this case abused both physically and mentally by her husband. She is the writer, not her husband, but this secret makes it impossible for her to leave him. Exposing this secret could ruin her husband.'

The situation is very complicated but the North American writer Scott Cover is going to intervene. The entire novel takes place in La Herradura with its epilogue taking place in 'Hotel Cartago' which is in reality Hotel Los Fenicios.

The subject is something close to my heart, I am not a different person when I write and I strongly believe that nobody is more than anybody else. This comes through in all my novels – in this case Scott is fighting the abuse of the lead character Luisa Lasarte; fighting for her dignity and to recover her autonomy. You could say that the novel is about equality which is, to me, the elemental principle of justice and solidarity."

Our meeting has all too soon come to close. I press the stop button on my Samsung tablet which has recorded Salvador's story. I thank him for his contribution and watch him leave. Whilst I get ready to go I take one last look at the couple at the other table. There is a little shine in her eyes and a hopeful smile adorns her face. They get up and walk into an unknown future, perhaps laid down in a Spanish novel.

Salvador Compán - www.salvadorcompan.com

Uplifting the spirit

We meet up at the Peñón de las Caballas, a big rock in the sea in Marina del Este. One arm of the leisure harbour has been built on the rock which allows for a pleasant walk around the marina to marvel and wonder at the different leisure boats that calmly rock in the seawater.

Andrés Cárdenas likes to go out for a walk, always taking a little notebook with him to record feelings inspired when overlooking the bay and sitting on a rock like the one in Peñón de las Caballas.

He was born in a village called Bailen in the province of Jaén, but he has been living in the city of Granada for 34 years. Since 1995 he has been coming to La Herradura regularly, often just for the weekend. For 32 years he worked for a popular newspaper called IDEAL and for a long time he was the paper's summer chronicler. He used to come to the area to write reports and stories. This is how he first found La Herradura.

"I like the Granada coast, and in particular the La Herradura Bay. One day when I was still a young journalist, I was in La Herradura and said to myself: *Someday I will have a house here!"* That moment arrived when after he inherited some money from his parents, he bought himself a house in the Carmenes del Mar suburb in the Cerro Gordo part of the village.

"At the moment there is a lot of controversy about that area, people say it should not have been developed at all because its terrain is unstable. Some of the houses have indeed been seriously affected by the natural movement of the mountain range - thankfully not mine - but there still is much concern amongst the owners. In the end I decided I would take the philosophical approach and simply enjoy the time that I spend in La Herradura whilst I can," says Andrés.

He likes the village because of its quietude, which is

somewhat affected during the summer months, but he still loves to stroll along the sea front on the beach. "That is pure medicine to my soul. I live in Granada and whenever I feel a little negative I just say to myself... *I am going to La Herradura.* Here I can find that pace of mind that my soul sometimes needs."

Andres knows many people in the village and likes to come here to talk to friends, visit some bars or just go for a walk. La Herradura is his safe haven. "It is a place where I can always find someone to talk to or enjoy a few beers. I think we are all shipwrecked in some way or form, we are all survivors of life and if we have a place where we can come to after a 'bad storm' then we are very fortunate. For me La Herradura is like a trunk to hold onto that keeps me afloat. The village is also special to me because it is here that I have found a wonderful group of like-minded writers. One day I was talking to Tomás Hernandez, Álvaro Salvador and Salvador Compan and the idea presented itself to us to create a brotherhood of literature in La Herradura. Soon Reinaldo Jimenez, Pepa Merlo and Juanfran Cabrero joined our group. We meet up frequently to have a chat over a glass of wine and to recite poems for example. We usually also meet when the prize for the poetry competition in La Herradura is presented. Most of us are members of the judging panel for this competition. The ethos of the group is to exchange ideas and gain knowledge. We organise literary events and hold poetry readings. We also like to give talks and often help out - when someone is presenting a book for example."

At the moment Andres is Head of Communications at a medical college in Granada. He has been writing journalistic columns for more than 30 years. In these columns he writes about the human nature of ordinary people. He has a colloquial, direct style and tends to use humour as a vehicle to reach his readers. Andres often says journalism feeds his body and literature feeds his soul. "My passion is writing novels and fictional stories but that does not make you much money. You can take three or four years to write a novel, but then, with some luck, it might be read by a thousand people. So writing novels is not something I do for money; it is just the best way I know to spend my spare time"

Why do you write and what do you write? I ask. "I have written several types of books. There are the historical novels, essays, travel books ... besides that there are bundles of my journalism articles. But what I like most is writing fictional novels, taking an idea and transforming it with words into something that readers can enjoy. One of my favourite pastimes is sitting on a rock, watching the La Herradura bay, contemplating and writing down things that occur to me in my little notebook. One day I remembered someone telling me about the 1562 shipwreck. I was looking at the Punta de la Mona and I could not believe that nobody had even heard about this maritime disaster. This is when I decided to write *La Luna de octubre* (October moon) in which I narrate this tragic event.

I tried to imagine what it must have been like as there is little historical account. Only a history teacher, Mari Carmen Galero Valazio has done so. She has written a very complete documentary-style book in which she gives all the facts about the shipwreck. I used these facts as a base for my book, which is a work of fiction. My objective for the book was to remind people, and in particular people from the province of Granada, of this event.

I have since spoken about the La Herradura shipwreck at many forums and I'm always surprised that most people had not even heard of it. I was amazed that such a major story had been kept quiet, but later, after some investigation, I found out that Philip II himself had forbidden people to speak about the disaster to ensure no Berber spies in his court would find out that Spain had been left without a Spanish fleet to defend its coasts. For this reason a blanket of silence was created around the tragedy".

Andrés Cárdenas says that the inspiration to write comes from life itself. "Things people say, or what I experience when I observe my surroundings, inspire me to write" he says. "For a writer it is important to know how to observe. Any detail can serve me as inspiration". He also says that he likes to use humour as he feels it is important to uplift people's spirits with stories that make them laugh. "I use humour as my weapon. An example of this is a novel called *La Vidente Ciega* (The Blind Clairvoyant) about a blind girl who can see into the future. This book takes place in Granada and apparently it will be translated into English, as there are quite a few English speaking visitors coming to Granada, but there are not many books about the city in English."

I ask Andrés whether there have been any special events in his life that have turned him into the person who he is today and he explains: "Lately I have had an experience that has totally changed my life and the way I view life. It was the birth of my grandchild. I never thought that such a small child could fill a gap in my life that I didn't even realise existed, that it would give so much meaning to my life. When you get to a certain age it is easy to become slightly pessimistic about the future, but when I am with my grandson I feel that he has kindled my desire to live. Throughout my life many things have happened but this new-born baby has made me realise that it is not worth living your life in an angry state of mind."

What are your plans for this future that you now see more positively?

"I am currently working on a very personal novel, it is partially invented but it is about things that happened in my life. However it isn't an autobiography. I take parts of my past that I think could make an interesting read, but with an ironic, humorous touch. Life is depressing enough as it is. When people open a newspaper or watch the news on television they can easily feel overwhelmed by stories of corruption, murder, terrorism or other depressing events. I feel that people are given very little opportunity to laugh. That is why I like to introduce some humour into what I write. My life has, so far, not been particularly interesting, but when I lard it with a tone of humour, stories from my childhood in the 1950s and 60s can become an interesting read to others. I like to be able to put a smile on people's faces. Some people are like a closed room and I would like to open a window in that closed room, to make them feel better through my words. In one word, I like to spread a sense of optimism.

I feel that sense of optimism for La Herradura as well as it could become a reference point of cultural importance. It has a strong ecological identity with a nucleus of art, music and literature. It is an ideal place for people to sense the beauty in life!"

Andrés Cárdenas -
https://www.facebook.com/andres.cardenasmunoz.1

A Seaside poet

"It was the summer of 1974, when I came to La Herradura for the first time; a few hours spent between the old campsite and the beach bars. That brief visit inspired me to write a poem that appeared in my book Sphinx, over time the only thing worth mentioning is the affectionate foreword written by my friend and teacher, César Simon. Who could have known that forty years on, in 2004, this is where I would have my home and my friends? Back then I lived in Valencia and the idea of returning to the south of Spain was one of those desires that lived inside me. I spent eighteen years in Valencia, first as a student and then as a professor at the Faculty of Philology. The last six of those years I worked in the Instituto Mariano Benlliure. I still have many loyal friends, old colleagues from the Faculty and the Institute, some already retired like me, and others are students.

I came to Valencia in an unexpected and haphazard manner. One summer morning, a friend from Alcalá la Real, where I was born, asked me if I wanted to accompany him to Valencia where he was going to enrol for university. It was a hitch-hiking trip, filled with incidents, that took us three or four days. Valencia felt like a modern city to me, with some splendid libraries, which no longer exist, and two or three clubs where you could go for a drink and hear live music or go and see the almost clandestine film projections that did not make it to the commercial theatres. I stayed in Valencia until I turned forty, living through its social and cultural fervour of the late 1960s, during its political transition and its claim for freedom, and I attended many interesting lectures. I enjoyed the friendship of Juan Gil Albert, the poet of the Generation of 27 with whom I shared an admiration for Jaime Gil de Biedma. It was Gil Albert who lent me the first book I read by André Gide, *Diarios* (diaries), which I am reading again right now. Gil presented a long poem by me called *La manera en que muerdes tus labios cuando esperas* (The way in which you chew your lips when you are waiting). It was the last time we saw each other. We never knew that the hug next to the portico of the Cathedral was to be the final farewell. During my time in Valencia I tried to visit Granada once or twice a year. I used to do these trips with friends and spend a few hours in the famous Alhambra; I became a non-official guide to them. Now that I am living a lot closer I go there a lot less. The poem *La manera en que muerdes tus labios cuando esperas* originates from one of those trips. In 1986 I started working at the Instituto Antigua Sexi in Almuñécar. I spent the best years of my professional life in those classrooms. I remember, with gratitude, how I was welcomed by my colleagues and the many friends I made there and, above all, my students who were the best I could have hoped for. When I arrived at Almuñécar I came to La Herradura to look for a house. No luck. Almost twenty years later, in 2004, I found a place to live and started writing again after many years. Almudena, my wife, read the poem of the Alhambra one day and told me that I should write again because that poem was so well written and had such a deep tone. During my years in Almuñécar I had become an avid reader. As a result of this and Almudena's suggestion, I wrote my first book, which was also an encounter with poetry, called *El viaje de Elpenor* (The voyage of Elpenor). I discovered the character in Los Cantos (the songs) by Ezra Pound who is amongst the poets that I most admire. The journey of Elpenor is a book of stories and love poetry. I was surprised, when I came to live in La Herradura, what little I knew of its history, considering I had lived so close. I had read one or two books in the past but not with the interest that I felt many years later. I came to know that the sudden sinking of the Armada of Philip II had taken place on these usually serene beaches and that in a few hours more than five thousand people were killed. I found a lot of information about this tragedy in a book by

Carmen Calero, a teacher. Thanks to this I knew of the existence of the soldier Fernando Moyano and the long poem which he wrote, describing the shipwreck. He was one of the few survivors. As a result of my interest in this event I wrote *Un viento inesperado* (An unexpected wind). This book was published with the support of my friend Juan José Ruiz Joya, Javier Sánchez Contreras, director of the Municipal Library and Almudena. Inspired by the light on the beaches; the sea, different each day; the time that passes in this peaceful village manner, I wrote *Peñón de las caballas* (Rock of the mackerel). Incorporated into the passages are the primitive burials studied by Doña Joaquina Eguaras, the beloved Doña Joaquina who taught Arabic on the Cuesta de Chapí in Granada; I also talk about the off-season swimmers of late autumn; about the man who sat in a wheelchair watching the flight of the birds from behind the glass of a window and the old men talking through the incidents of the day, sitting on the benches of the promenade along the beach; about the Peñon de las Caballas that are right opposite where I live; about the date trees and the bars where I go for a drink and to talk with friends. In a house higher up in the village in Las Gaviotas, a house so close to the clouds, I wrote *Última línea* (Last line) whilst I was reading books about soldiers and battles. And so, forty years after my first visit to La Herradura, I came back to stay."
Tomás Hernández Molina

During the interview Tomás explained to me that he lives in Marina del Este. For the greater part of the year this is a rather quiet area in La Herradura where you could even go for a walk and not see a single person. But in summer and weekends the pavement café areas of the restaurants directly by the harbour are filled with tourists and people from La Herradura who are treated to beautiful views of the boats that dock in the port throughout the year. Boats that tell a story without revealing too much, transformed easily into stories, songs and works of art in the minds of artists.

A literary couple

Of all the interesting spots and historical sites that are part of La Herradura Los Castillejos cannot be left out. Los Castillejos is up in the mountains and not that easy to get to. Evidence of human occupation can be found among the rocks. When the Roman Empire fell apart a time of disruption occurred and the unprotected, vulnerable coastal areas in the Mediterranean were susceptible to piracy. There is evidence that in 1520 Jate (the historical name of La Herradura) suffered a piracy attack and people were made slaves. Those who could, fled to the mountains. Settlements were created in the area now known as Los Castillejos. The Castillejos are in fact two, not very high, peaks beside each other. It is a rocky area and there are remains of old cisterns and of antique walls in the gaps between the rocks which can still be seen today. Now it is a place of calm and contemplation where the sweet music of nature is all that you will hear.

Los Castillejos would have been an interesting place for a meeting with two of Spain's respected authors, but alas, the face-to-face interviews never took place. Instead I'm looking at several sheets with answers on a questionnaire sent via email. Unforeseen circumstances dictated appointments had to be cancelled, but both Pepa Merlo and Álvaro Salvador certainly merit being mentioned in this book about artists, writers, musicians and other interesting characters of La Herradura. Both are members of the La Herradura brotherhood of literature.

Álvaro Salvador Jofre, commonly known as Álvaro Salvador, was born and still lives in Granada to this day. He has been coming to La Herradura for more than twenty-five years, attracted by its tranquillity, the quality of life and pleasant climate. He feels that its easy access from towns such as Malaga and Granada is a big plus as well.

Since he has been coming to La Herradura the majority of his work has been written in the village. He mainly writes poetry, but he has also written a few theatre plays and two novels. He feels inspired by many things and is interested in topics such as love, eroticism, the passing of time and social issues. He finds the surroundings of La Herradura very inspirational.

Álvaro is a professional writer and doctorate in Romanic philology and works as a Spanish and Hispano-American literature professor at the University of Granada. In addition to that, throughout his working career he has presented courses, seminars and lectures in various universities around the world.

As a writer, Álvaro Salvador's work has embraced all genres, including essays, and novel writing and writing for the theatre, although he is mostly known for his work as a poet which is summed up in two anthology books *Suena una música*, 1973-2008 (2008) and *PoPoemas* 1969-1975) (2014). He is also a regular contributor to various newspapers and periodicals in literary criticism such as *Cuadernos Hispanoamericanos, Ínsula, Litoral, Hora de poesía* and more.

Several of his poems have been translated into other languages, mainly into English. Álvaro has recently published his latest book, *Fumando con mis muertos (2015)*, which is about the passing of time, losing loved ones and about the recapitulation of events already lived, trying to get away from an elegiac tone whilst searching for the query of the present.

His poetry is in line with a trend which was developing in Spain at the end of the twentieth century, called *poesia de la experiencia* (poetry of the experience). Writing gives him great satisfaction. He can express in a poem what he feels and what his readers feel they can identify with. However, teaching, being in contact with young people is also something that gives him great pleasure and he believes it prevents spiritual ageing.

Álvaro feels enriched by the accumulation of all his life experiences which has shaped him into the person he now is. He is grateful and feels lucky to have met and known such a great variety of people many of whom are now close friends. He refers to people with whom he has shared his life in distinctive periods. Generally speaking he feels that all writing contains some ethics, some more explicit than others. In his personal work his aim is to transmit useful values which can help people live a better life.

He feels that La Herradura will continue to inspire him when he and his wife Pepa Merlo come here for visits. They both feel that La Herradura is a special place, although they agree they have witnessed some regrettable changes over the years during the economic boom. They hope and trust that the village will conserve the specific character it still has. They both feel that what has been an enchanting village for many deserves to keep its own unique personality.

Pepa Merlo has been coming to La Herradura since the nineties yet she still longs for those pre-development days when the village, to her mind, was idyllic and charming and above all, very quiet: an ideal place to come to relax and disconnect. She especially remembers the inviting ambience of the village. She now feels, especially during the summer months, that this tranquillity is hard to find. However, she acknowledges that La Herradura is still an ideal place to escape the interior and to contemplate by the seaside.

Pepa Merlo, who graduated in Spanish Philology, was raised in Granada, but she is originally from a small village called Pinos del Valle in the Valle de Lecrín. Pepa has published various books including: *Todos los cuentos, el cuento, Diputación de Cádiz (2008); El haza de las viudas (2009); Colección Espuela de Plata* (with a prologue by Almudena Grandes and cover page by Juan Vida) and *Peces en la Tierra, an anthology of women poets from the 1927 generation (2010)*, in collaboration with the *Centro Generación del 27* centre in Málaga.

With *Peces en la Tierra* (Fish on earth) Pepa Merlo has recovered the missing voice and poetic production of writers of the Generation of '27. During an interview with Europa Press Pepa indicated that the intention of the publication is to 're-vindicate the poets of 27'. During the time of the Republic and also from the beginning of the 20th century until the year 1936 women were publishing books and moving in artistic circles but during the dictatorship they were excluded. A woman's place was considered to be in the home, looking after the family.

About her life as a writer Pepa explains: "A writer is always a writer, in one way or another. Apart from personal opinions, views and visions regarding how we approach life are more like the vision of a photographer through his lens. Details of landscape, of light, of a passer-by, for example, can spark an idea for a possible story.

However, making a living from writing is difficult in these times with its many economic challenges. Even in cases where a writer can live solely from literature, they have to give conferences, press talks, book presentations and workshops or classes in order to pay for the costs of daily living. What is important, if you have to get a job on the side to survive, is that you find a job that is related to your passion, in my case literature."

Back to her writing career; Pepa has the opinion that the life of a writer is a continuous period of learning. In her work she talks about life itself. She doesn't pretend to send a message through her work, but she likes to invite people to reflect on things.

Writing is not her only creative outlet. She is fascinated

by photography. "I love seeing the world through the lens of my camera, seeing the details that the eye does not discover at first glance. With a zoom you can enter a world full of surprises." She also has a love for cinema and particularly the *Cinema de verano* (summer cinema) during the summer months in La Herradura. She very much hopes those nights will never get lost.

You could say that both Pepa Merlo and her partner Álvaro Salvador share a passion for culture in general, arts, literature, cinema and ….music; including the sounds of the music of nature still to be found, fortunately, in many spots in and around the village of La Herradura.

Álvaro Salvador - www.alvarosalvador.com

Pepa Merlo - www.pepamerlo.com

Storytelling images

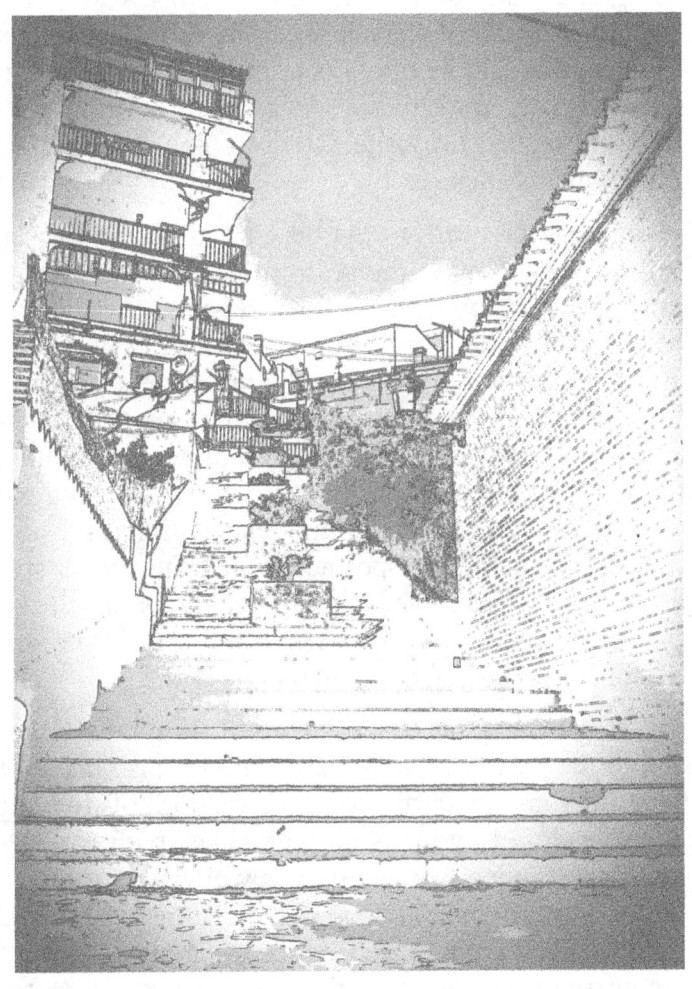

Inspired by silence

"Just outside the entrance to the village of La Herradura" says Juanfran Cabrera, "there is a lush green roundabout planted with grass, tropical plants and trees and it is one of the favourite places for the wild La Herradura parrots to congregate and sing their sunset songs. Close to the small urbanisation of Cañada Real, more or less opposite the fuel station and next to a cute little garden centre, this residential area has buildings painted in a warm yellow colour, the second favourite exterior colour in this area of white washed villages.

It is only a short walk to the beach and during the day I often make my way to the seafront to get some fresh air, take in the sea view and go for a relaxing walk. I could not live without the sea; I grew up with it, by it and in it. It is in my blood as my grandparents were fishermen. Often I take my canoe out for some me-time. I absolutely love being on the sea, feeling its tranquillity, something I actually need. Floating on the sea I can watch the rocks for hours on end, rising with grace and strength from the sea. It's a mesmerising spectacle when the waves splash against these impressive, natural sculptures and it has a hypnotic effect on me, like staring into a fire. The sound this creates is comforting for me.

Something I really like doing is to sail from La Herradura beach to the playa of Cantarijan, which is also part of the village. It's a wonderful spot consisting of two sand beaches enclosed by rocks on both sides, with two beach restaurants, called *chiringuitos*, which cater for its visitors. Cantarijan is known amongst naturalists as a nudist beach, but many also go there simply to enjoy the stunning sea views whilst enjoying a drink or something delicious to eat. This lovely beach can also be accessed by land. There is an exit sign on the old road from La Herradura to Nerja with its spectacular sea and mountain views and you can follow this sign towards the sea. The road winds in graceful curves through the landscape of green trees and wildly growing shrubs from the lower end of the Cerro Gordo down to the Cantarijan playa. The Cerro Gordo is famous for the wild mountain goats or ibex (capra pyrenaica), that live here.

I was born in La Herradura where my parents ran a hostel. As a young guy, like so many lads in the village I used to spend my holidays and spare time working in bars and in my family's hostel. It was a way to earn some pocket money and at a later stage to finance my studies to become a comic writer and illustrator. I was the youngest of four children, which meant I got more freedom than my siblings, including the freedom to choose my own career. Nobody else in my family had any artistic desires or talents so it was not a logical choice for my family. They supported me nonetheless. There are two big loves in my life, the sea and drawing. As far as surviving is concerned, I guess I am a bit of a masochist, opting for the 'harsh' life with little money, as trying to make a living from art is not necessarily the easiest route to create a comfortable life for yourself. There have been moments in my life that I've tried to work in full time jobs to make more money, but I couldn't stick with them. The longest I was able to hold down an ordinary job was one year, but it made me unhappy. It showed me that I had to follow my own path, my passion. It was the only way to make me feel content inside.

I lived away from La Herradura during the years of my study at the faculty of Fine Arts at university in Granada. It is truly one of the most beautiful cities in the area, oozing with history, magic, Arab atmosphere and artistic energy, but when I finished my studies I came back to live here. I just have to live near the sea. During my city life as a student I often imagined that the constant hum of cars passing by in the streets was the sound of sea waves. Generally speaking I don't like big towns or cities and prefer to live in a village and La Herradura is a special village. It is very cosmopolitan. I love the fact that I can meet people of so many different nationalities here and can learn about their cultures. It really helps you see things differently and you don´t have to go to a library to become more informed about what's out there. It has certainly broadened my knowledge and that is just great. I have been self-employed for a long time now and have worked for different editorials and private clients. It is a challenge to make a living as a comic writer and I therefore also work as a graphic designer and illustrator. I guess you could say that there was one important event in my life that has had a major impact on my life as a comic artist. When I was only eighteen years old I got the opportunity to get to know professional authors like Luis Alberto Maldonado who became my teacher. Before the internet he was a comic writer and went to Barcelona to work for a publisher. A Japanese publisher travelled to the United States and Europe looking for comic authors who had something special and Luis was selected. For many years he worked in Japan for important clients and I became his assistant. My work was mainly drawing-in the backgrounds and that taught me a lot. It was an amazing experience and school of learning. Then, for many years, I had the privilege of working from home, for a comic magazine in Barcelona, called *El Vibora*. This magazine ran for twenty-five years in Spain and was very well known.

Now I work for other comic magazines, contributing stories. Apart from all this I work on my own books and have published various pieces. I love my work. I get my inspiration from real life stories and historical facts. The information gathered in my mind comes to fruition in the dark hours of the night when my creativity blooms. When there are no footsteps, no street noise of neighbours telling each other that same old story of long gone days, no mopeds whizzing past or the voices of children having a good time, all carried on the wind. All you can hear during the night is the gentle sound of the sea with the soft soughing of the waves on the pebbled beaches reaching up to the highest-situated houses in the village. In the silence of the night my concentration level is much higher and the images in my head come to life and end up on virgin paper.

A comic is a method of communication. A lot of people think of a super hero when they think of comic books, but that is not my interest. I suppose the correct word for my work is graphic novels. I don't like super heroes very much and instead I like to tell real-life inspired stories. I don't have a specific theme and just use a story that I find interesting and feel that could appeal to people. A comic can be a very accessible medium to talk about history. It's a great way of reaching people who normally would perhaps not pick up a book. I really like it when people who don't read much like to read my comics. That gives me enormous satisfaction. Of course, by reading comics, children can be taught history as well. The lively images in comics can bring historical facts to life. One example is the book I created about the shipwreck that took place in 1562 in La Herradura called *Naufragio en La Herradura*. I created this book in 2012 in collaboration with the local council in remembrance of the 450th anniversary of this incredibly sad event. All the proceeds from this book go to the Red Cross.

My images are words, but I also like to write stories so it is fantastic that I can combine the two. I can always find an interesting real-life account, or something that interests me that I can turn into a visual story. At the moment I am working on a series of five books, *Los Caballeros de la Orden de Toledo*, together with Javierre, a screenwriter who writes the stories. In December of 2015 we were given the Expocómic award, for best national work of 2015, for this series. It was already incredible to have been nominated for this, but to then take away the award felt like madness. I actually met Javierre quite a few years ago when he contacted me to ask me whether I would be willing to draw the images for a story he was writing and I accepted. Whilst he was writing and profiling the script I was creating the characters and looking for a style that was in line with the story. The series is based on the friendship between poet and play writer Federico García Lorca, filmmaker Luis Buñuel and painter Salvador Dalí. The stories take place in the capital city of Madrid. They are not 100% biographical but give an excellent idea of how these inspirational artists were living their lives during the Roaring Twenties.

This is my passion and I feel really grateful that I can do what I love in my lovely village of La Herradura that has kept its charm, its tranquillity, fascination and magic for many years. I sincerely hope it will stay this way and for the silence to continue inspiring me."

Juanfran Cabrera - https://juanfrancabrera.wordpress.com

A great loss changed our lives

"An indescribable loss led us to make the decision to pack up, sell everything and leave. Our dream, the last chance to have a child of our own, fell to pieces when we lost our baby during pregnancy after years of IVF treatment. We were heartbroken and devastated with deep holes left in our souls. Our dream had turned into our nightmare, but somehow we needed to find the strength to move on, taking our baby with us in our hearts.

A friend told us about La Herradura. It sounded appealing and we decided to come over here. It wasn´t a decision taken lightly. We needed to take my wife´s sister's son into account - a child whom we had raised as our own for seven years, and who had to come with us. We also needed to consider our 'parental' responsibilities towards the two young children of a local single mother. I am their father figure.

What made the decision easier was that my primary income comes from being a children´s book illustrator so we are in the fortunate position of being very mobile, as far as where our base is concerned. Over the past thirty years I have been able to build a name for myself, working for several publishers and different people in my home country of New Zealand where most children are familiar with my name. My paintings mainly sell in New Zealand but that doesn't mean I have to live there – these days it is easy to ship my finished works to the gallery that represents me.

So, we took the jump and it didn´t take long at all for us to fall in love with La Herradura. It was a feeling, an instant connection. I had spent my entire life near the sea in my own country and totally love that but this village offers more. We love the people here. Apart from it being such an interesting mix of artists as well as writers, musicians and guitar makers from all sorts of nationalities

– we love the Spanish locals too. For us it is extremely important that the village has still maintained that Spanish feel which we appreciate so much.

I can honestly say that La Herradura has changed my outlook on life. Spending a significant amount of time in a different culture gives you a whole different idea of how you want to spend your life. I now know that it is important to me to live in a civilised community and that is what this village has taught me. La Herradura holds certain values and offers a warm social life. This is very different from my experience of New Zealand, which is a harsher place and still noticeably a settler colony with a predominantly pioneer mentality, a bit rough and tough. I love the cosmopolitan atmosphere in La Herradura and I really fit in here. It is the same for my wife and my son, who has Tongan nationality like my wife. Although still a kid, he now says that he is half Tongan and half Spanish.

The first time we came here we only stayed for three months. It had such a profound impact on us, with La Herradura already feeling like home, that we promised ourselves we would come back for longer periods. We returned in April 2014 and have, so far, enjoyed an amazing summer and winter. Our son chose not to come with us this time and stayed with his birth mother. Even though we miss him greatly, contact via Skype keeps us close.

We were able to rent an interesting, quirky village house, which seems to have shifts in mood. Sometimes it feels a bit cave-like and rather melancholic and then it changes into the most welcoming, warm and open place. It suits my personality perfectly and inspires me to create my artwork. The house is situated in a typical Spanish neighbourhood with a few local shops, accessed up the vertiginous 'killer' steps, beside the village church square – the imperfectly tarmacked steep little streets lead up to our front door. Whichever way you walk from where we are you are treated to that typical Andalusian view of white washed houses set along winding, narrow streets with their colourful pots of hanging geraniums dangling in the wind. The sounds of the village waft on the gentle air, the revving of a motorbike is never too far away, nor the church bells ringing at a pleasant distance or the chatter of locals sharing their adventures. For us it is perfect and we can improve our language skills talking to our lovely Spanish neighbour Elena, the widow of 'El Ruso', the famous flamenco singer.

The sea is also very important to me. I have a deep need to live near the sea. I love swimming both in the summer and during the colder seasons. It is like having an inner connection with oneself and I have come to see the sea as my spiritual home. I often feel like a wave coming out of the ocean to then return to it in a rhythmic cycle. Simply sitting by the sea or walking along the beach, watching its colours, its movement, noticing its smell, listening to the sounds of the pebbles gently rocked by the waves, has a calming and soothing effect on me.

I have spent my whole life by the sea. I was born in New Zealand in Thames on the North Island. My life has been an accumulation of challenges, temptations, and survival. Progressive loss in all manner of ways has been the most determining thing in my life but it also turned me into who I am now. If you always have success you might settle for something comfortable but not necessarily be happy. If your comfort has been stripped away you have to find something interesting in what would seem less than favourable circumstances.

Going to the Kingdom of Tonga and getting married to my wife were very important in my personal transformation. Tonga is as far away from European culture as you can imagine. It's a very cultural island where community is totally integrated into family life. At the end of the day everyone helps and feeds each other.

My father, a European family doctor, was like so many of the people I knew in New Zealand. There was work and then there was family, but others were not included. The door was not open to anybody. Loisi, my wife, who is from Tonga, is awash with humanity. Everybody can stay with us and is welcomed. This is a significant change in outlook but also a significant challenge for me. It has forced me to really reconsider what I took for granted as a person - about being a lot more relaxed with not having so much and what it means to look after other people. I have learned to transform loss and sadness into something creative instead of letting it get on top of me. I have learned about giving up the idea of control and I sail along on my journey, rather than trying to force my will onto everything. I now consider myself as being on a spiritual path. I walk, I paint and I cook. I meditate and I read. I read, virtually exclusively, theology books of various types. I am immersed in this path all the time. I do everything with attention – when I read, when I walk, when I cook. I bless my food before preparing it with a 'Namaste'*. I love cooking and I find it a spiritual exercise to feed my family. I generally like to adapt my cooking to the place where I am, using local ingredients.

Life is a learning path and I am learning to see the sacred in everything and make it part of my spiritual life. I feel spirituality is in everything; when I cook, when I swim or when I paint. You could say that I have a creative approach to spirituality. Creativity comes naturally to me. I have always done creative work. It allows me to have some freedom and be sort of irresponsible. You *can* create the life that you want. My friends have the goods, the houses and the cars but they often say, 'You've got the life!' It is not just what I really enjoy doing, but it has allowed me to be able to create an interesting and different life. Whatever I am doing, thinking, reading or praying, all seems to lead to story-oriented ideas that I then paint. My story-telling paintings came after my children's books and are quite illustrative. Still, I do not like to explain my artwork and prefer to let people read their own story into my images.

I tend to express my ideas in concepts. It starts with a conceptual idea, rather than an expressive idea. The painting grows whilst contemplating the idea. I do have a reason for doing my work but I don't pretend to have a specific message. However, I do find inclusivity important so I guess, if there is any message in what I do, it is that there is a place for everybody. In my children's books especially I like to show the funny and amusing side of things but I try to include many different types of people, for example, gay people into the story. In this way I try to portray the diversity of life, that it is fine to be different. I like children to know that school can often be cruel. I also have a problem with moralistic religion as it has such a narrow view of who fits in and who doesn't.

It is important to me to keep the children in mind. All 'my children' belong to ethnic minorities and I am painfully aware of the subtle ways of discrimination that the three children we are bringing up have to deal with. In New Zealand we look after a girl who is half Tongan and half African, a boy who is half Tongan and half European, and then my boy who is full Tongan but wants to be half Spanish. We miss them and at the moment they are all begging for us to come home. Antonio, whom I call my son, would like to live with us again. This request has made us decide to return to New Zealand three months earlier than planned, but we have every intention of returning to La Herradura, hopefully with all three children.

I do have a wish for La Herradura. I hope it will stay as it is, as Spanish as possible, but for its artistic and creative community to flourish and increase. Not for it to become a swirling English hangout but for the Spanish culture to lead things with its beautiful flamenco dance, singing and music. We are now sad to say goodbye but it won't be a farewell. We will be back soon to this wonderful place ... our home."

Fraser Williamson - www.redshark.co.nz

*'Namaste' is a form of greeting in India and it is a way to honour and show respect or gratitude. Literally it means 'my soul honours your soul'

Following my bliss

"I like to sit here at my desk after a brisk walk home up the hill. Several times a week I walk down that hill from our small apartment in Cotobro, passing the 'Flor de Hierro' by Feliciano Hernandez who was a friend of Prieto Moreno - an iron sculpture in the form of an abstract tropical flower opening up to take in the sunlight. I stroll down into the village via Camino Real, which turns into Calle Real. It is not strikingly beautiful but it has its charm. I observe the bustle of the awakening village. Shutters are pulled up with a wooden clatter, youths on mopeds whizz by on their way to school and mothers take their children to the various schools in the area in their cars. I watch a lady clean the footpath in front of her door, first sweeping the dust onto the street, then mopping it with some strong, flowery smelling soapy water. The street has a mixture of old and new architecture, the new sometimes feels out of place to me. I prefer the older houses, some of them showing off their inevitable decay of 'growing old' in a charming and artistic manner. Here and there I can peek into the narrow streets off the Calle Real with their irregular steps leading to village houses that can only be reached on foot.

Whilst I walk down the hill I contemplate my life. It is a very meditative walk and I like to remind myself of thinking positively and being grateful for the wonderful things by which I am surrounded, things that are happening and that are coming my way. It is always nice to be in the village, meeting up with interesting friends, getting inspired by the waves, the sound of the wind in the palm trees and the sun rising higher in the sky, warming my skin on a rather chilly winter's day. It is bliss. My favourite word.

Yes, it is nice to be back home. I feel physically tired from walking up the hill, but fulfilled and happy. I make myself a cup of English tea in a mug decorated with a heart design. I add a bit of honey and milk and sit down at my desk. I take in the amazing view from our living room window, my desk sits right in front of it. Every day I am treated to the ever-changing spectacle of nature over Marina del Este. Early mornings and early evenings, the mesmerising colours of subtle clouds left by a sunrise or sunset fill my heart with warmth. I feel blessed to be able to work in such a beautiful spot. What lies behind me was an interesting path to get here.

I was born in London and am the eldest of six children. I have four sisters and one brother, all of them special to me. I love them all to bits. We grew up in Westgate-on-Sea, a village in Kent, to where my parents moved when I was a young girl. Graham, my partner, and I go back every year and visit both our families, usually at Christmas time and in the summer and we find that really enjoyable. Before we came to Spain, Graham and I lived in Cornwall, which is fantastic for artists and musicians like us. We absolutely loved it there and should we ever go back to live in the UK then we hope to be able to live there again.

At the time, Graham's thirtieth birthday came up and I wanted to give him something special. He was a full-time musician and wanted to upgrade his student guitar for a concert level guitar. I remembered him once telling me that he would love to build his own guitar. I asked him whether he would like that experience as a birthday present. Tears welled up in his eyes. I thought *Yes, we can do this* and started searching the Internet to find out more. I was working for a children's musical theatre charity that was situated in an old chapel. I remember sitting at my desk, freezing cold, with a hand-knitted hat on and my hands kept warm by colourful woollen gloves. I found several guitar building workshops in England, but then I saw the photo of La Herradura and information about Stephen Hill's one-month-long guitar making courses at the European Institute of Guitar Making. It was comparable at the time with buying a new guitar. Graham loved the idea. We sold everything we had, bought a small van, converted it into a camper van and set off for southern Spain. It was September 2011.

Needless to say, we fell in love with La Herradura. So much so that we've decided to stay for the foreseeable future. We are now renting a tiny, but beautiful, one-bedroom apartment just outside the village. Although Graham still loves being a musician he has now become a guitar builder himself and he is really enjoying that. Life is not always easy and often we have to scrape things together to pay our rent, but we seem to manage. We don't need much. We are happy. We've been together now for over ten years and are very much in love. We are grateful to be alive, to live in such a wonderful place, with amazing friends, being able to do what we love most: following our bliss.

My bliss is painting, illustrating and writing. In the UK I worked in a culture and education company, focusing on creativity in the English education system. The most important thing that I learned there was that everybody is creative and that in order to fully express our innate creativity, our well-being is of paramount importance. An occupational hazard of working in the creative and cultural sector is that you continuously ask yourself the question: *How am I expressing my creativity?* After several years I was inspired to pursue my own creative path fully. In the beginning it was mainly for myself, but over time I realised it has everything to do with well-being and it has gradually evolved into a desire to facilitate others in discovering their innate creativity as well. This is the theme of the book I am currently writing. I now consider myself a full-time artist, illustrator and writer. Apart from mainly creating illustrations and working on commissions for clients, I am developing my own style, finding my true brand or voice. This is how the 'Doodle smudges' emerged. 'Doodle smudges' have become my illustrative style and they appeal to both children and adults. 'Doodle smudging' is a term I came up with to describe a process of accessing creativity when you feel without inspiration. You randomly throw a few colours on a page and try to see images in the paint or ink smudge, which you then 'doodle' over. It is a way of freeing the mind before a creative activity. I am developing a doodle smudge app for iPad so that other people can do it too. I am working on this in collaboration with strategic storyteller and friend Elizabeth Adams. It is an app for the love of creativity and to take the terror out of the blank page. I love painting as well and have had exhibitions in Cornwall, France, Kent and participated in group exhibitions in Spain. However, I am currently more focused on my book and on commissions. I would like to think that over the coming years I can build up a new body of work for exhibition. I like what I do. I like that I can bring beauty, visual beauty, to the world. That has always been important to me. I remember one of my art teachers telling me that I made things more beautiful than they were during life drawing classes. It was an important observation, I still do that - I do actually always see that beauty. I also love colour and like to bring a lot of colour into my work. What I do makes me happy and I can spend many of my days smiling at the characters that come from my imagination. They become my friends.

I take a last sip of my tea and look out of the window, the sun is shining over the harbour in a wonderfully blue sky and I see its reflection on the sea and on some of the masts of the sailing boats in the far distance. I feel happy and blessed. Happy and blessed that we had the courage to just follow our hearts, to follow our bliss. That is my message to everyone. Dare to listen to your heart so you can discover your bliss and follow it too!"
Lauren Sebastian www.laurensebastian.com

Sounds of music

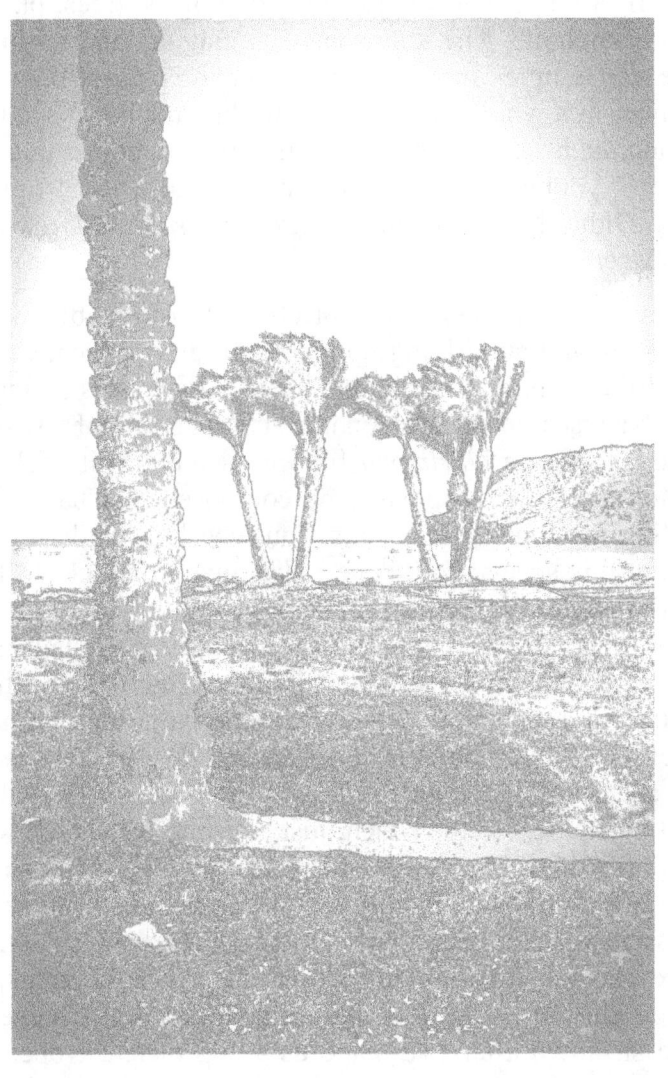

When Germany meets Cuba

I absorb the soothing sound of a saxophone near the seafront. The sun is about to set and I look at the small, raised patch of green grass in the middle of the La Herradura beach with two sets of palm trees on each side. Charly Endres is leaning against one of the trees, playing his saxophone. The atmosphere is magical and idyllic at the same time. In the background a Spanish flamenco dancer in a white dress with light blue touches is walking along the beach, close to the gentle waves, contemplating. She is young, beautiful and mysterious, a lonely gypsy girl. Didier Marechal sings s*iento Suspiro del Moro en mi Corazon.*

Then my eye catches the bright red convertible wood-dressed Morgan driving up the Punta de la Mona. Charly is still playing his saxophone but this time he is sitting on the back seat of the car. A naive style painting of a woman about to kiss a *chirimoya* fills my screen. I sit back and enjoy the 'La Chirimoya' song composed by Charly, now filling my living room via a YouTube link whilst I think about this special fruit. The *chirimoya* is thought to be a fruit native to some parts of Southern America, but it was then transported to many places including Andalusia in Southern Spain. Even Mark Twain mentioned the fruit, calling it 'the most delicious fruit known to men.' It has a creamy texture and is very sweet and is often referred to as a custard apple. In the inland areas of La Herradura, but even close to the beach, just over the Rio Jate bridge, towards the Cerro Gordo side of the village, you can see the efforts of farmers cultivating this popular fruit which has clearly inspired Charly Endres, the talented German saxophonist. I'm thinking about this when he rings my doorbell. I open the door and immediately like his energy. We sit down after I've made us a cup of tea; I open the questionnaire document on my computer and ask him where he comes from and what music means to him.

Charly explains: "I was born in Aachen in Germany close to the southern Dutch border. Music first caught my attention when I heard Dixie music on the radio. I must have been about ten years old and immediately fell in love with the clarinet. Since then music has been a constant and dominant part of my life. I had already been playing the flute for many years but always dreamed of having a clarinet. My parents bought me a clarinet when I was fourteen years old. I was over the moon and rapidly managed to master the various types of music that appealed to me. At the same age I joined a school band. It was my first music group. By the time I was twenty I had become a member of a student band; a good dance band and I was able to finance my study with earnings made from that. We played everything, from dance music, like the cha-cha and the Wiener waltz to disco music. We were able to cover it all and had a great time doing so. I studied music, sports and pedagogy and became a teacher at a high school with classical education, but you could certainly say that it was music in particular that has coloured my entire life in a very positive way. It is impossible for me to imagine my life without it; it would be like part of me was missing. Being a clarinet player it was a logical step to take on playing the saxophone. During my music study I also had to learn classical music which is why I play German flute as well. I just love making music. I have written some pieces as well, but I would not call myself an avid composer. Although I am open to all kinds of music, including classical, my greatest passion is jazz music. Musically I was very much influenced by John Coltrane and after seeing him at a live concert in Belgium, jazz became my favourite music. From that moment on I started playing Bebop Jazz and I was part of a jazz quartet called *Cremer-Endres-Quartett*, a German-American band. We were still students and participated in various festivals. We even won the Bilzen Jazz festival in Belgium which allowed us to go on tour in

Belgium, France and Luxembourg.

Our home country has been Belgium for a long time now and I am still very much involved in music. In Belgium I met a young professional band that allows me to join in every now and then during their concerts. They perform under two different names, depending on the lead singer, as there are two. One band is called the Didier Marechal Band and the other one Aquis Combo Aachen. They have gigs in Belgium, Holland and Germany. However, I must say that I feel like I am now laying down some musical roots in Spain too."

So I ask him how he ended up in La Herradura and listen to his story. One of his daughters studied Spanish in Granada and Charly and his wife came out to visit her. After having spent some time with her they decided to explore the surroundings and embarked on a motorcycling trip through Andalusia. From Granada they came down to the coast over the mountains via the old mountain pass, called the *Suspiro del Moro, and landed in Almuñécar. They very much liked the atmosphere but continued their trip and ended up in Otivar in the Alpujarras region where they bought a little house which they renovated ten years ago. One day, remembering Almuñécar they came down to visit the area and stumbled on La Herradura. This was five years ago. It was the day Charly met Lino Díaz, a talented Cuban pianist and composer who lives in La Herradura. They became friends and Lino introduced him to the local music scene which is significant, considering the size of the village. Every Monday Lino plays his music in a bar-restaurant called El Tinao. It is one of the places in La Herradura where musicians gather and perform. These musicians come from Granada and other Spanish places, but there are also many musicians of other nationalities, including Dutch, English and French. Charly regularly joins in with Lino and his wife Lupe, who is a singer, during their performances. Apart from his love for jazz, Charly has since also learned to appreciate and love Spanish flamenco music. He met Pablo Escudero, a local flamenco singer and guitarist and this led to Charly being invited to participate in some flamenco music concerts. The biggest concert was in the Majuelo Park in Almuñécar in 2013 - a concert with ten great Andalusian musicians from Córdoba, Malaga and Jaen and, on this occasion, Charly. "A fantastic experience," he says and continues: "You could also say that music is a social glue. It brings people together, both musicians and audience, and the Spanish love music. I have met so many nice people in La Herradura. To share music, and especially to improvise, is something I very much love. Creating something new with like-minded good musicians when nothing is laid down is something magical and with Lino this comes so naturally. He only needs a theme for us to create musical euphony. "In jazz improvisation, each musician does his or her own thing around the contours of a basic theme or set of chords. There are many variations of these themes and each has a certain harmony. We introduce the musical theme to the audience and then the improvisation starts. Each musician does his own thing - one might concentrate on rhythm, for instance - but I only focus on harmony. At the end of the piece we go back to the basic theme again to finish."

Now a pensioner of four years and the proud father of two daughters and granddad to three grandchildren Charly travels back and forth to Belgium and Germany, to play in his band and to look after a 97 year old aunt, he then returns to La Herradura where he and his wife have rented a house for the past three years. He loves the area, it allows him to immerse himself in his two great passions; music and sport - skiing and paragliding. He also loves the Spanish people in La Herradura whom he finds very welcoming and friendly and he mentions the many likeable foreign people he has met here. He feels fortunate and appreciative that he has been living a very good life without major traumas or horrible events and always sees things from the positive side. He no longer feels a need for fame and enjoys the relaxed atmosphere in Spain. His years of being recognised in the streets lie behind him and he says he prefers it that way. He is happy in this little village on the Costa Tropical. Out of love for La Herradura and the region Charly wrote the song *Chirimoya* and made a video of it with his *Didier Marechal Band*. He explains that it was just a bit of fun and doesn't have much in common with his usual type of music.

Currently Charly has to go back to Germany every three weeks or so to look after his elderly aunt. He does this with love as he feels that it is nice to give back to the world, but Charly also has a dream. He and his wife are hoping to live here permanently in the future and then he would like to do something with his teaching, pedagogy and musical life experience. One day he hopes to give free music classes to unprivileged children in La Herradura as he feels there are so many children whose parents cannot afford music lessons. "It would be great if the municipality could perhaps invest in instruments and a space so these kids can play and, who knows, even create a small orchestra."

The interview has come to an end and I feel that we have become friends when we walk down Calle Acera del Pilar after the interview. We reach the sea front and say goodbye just as the sun is setting between two sets of palm trees on the raised patch of green grass in the middle of the beach. I hear a pleasant melody in my head…*siento Suspiro del Moro en mi Corazon.*

Charly Endres

*Suspiro del Moro (Moor's sigh) is referring to a mountain pass in the Spanish Sierra Nevada. According to legend the last Moorish sultan of Granada, Boabdil (Mohamed Abu Abdalahyah), after being ejected from Granada by the Catholic Monarchs in 1492, looked back as he was crossing this pass, and with a loud sigh expressed his longing for his Granada palaces, in particular the famous Alhambra and he started crying. His own mother, Ayesha, full of fire, condemned his tears and said: "You cry like a woman for what you were unable to defend like a man".

Don't die with regrets

I watch people enjoying a drink or a bite at one of the beach bars on the beach, a choppy sea dressed with sunshine in the background. A strong wind pleasantly massages my face as I stroll along the sea front on my way to an interview with Tony Turner. He lives near the La Herradura castle, close to the beach and is a remarkable figure in the village. He is a big guy but transmits a nice calm energy. Happy blue eyes glisten in his friendly face. A grey ponytail and hands and wrists full of silver bracelets and rings distinguish him from the crowd.

We take a seat in one of the sea front pavement cafes sheltered from the wind but warmed by the sun, and order a coffee. I explain the thinking behind my book on La Herradura; how I want to focus on the 'arty' people who live or have a second home in the village and how I hope this book will bring greater awareness of the special quality of this little village. I explain that it's part of a vision to get La Herradura on the map as an artistic village and encourage visits by people who would respect its culture, its integration, the sea and natural environment and its inhabitants. Tony agrees. It feels nice to talk to him, easy. I ask him where he was born as I know it wasn't in La Herradura.

"I was born in Hull in Yorkshire in the United Kingdom. I was married with two grown up sons who had flown the nest, one living in Scarborough and the other one in Dubai. My wife and I had somewhat grown apart, leading separate lives. She went on holidays on her own and I did what I loved most, getting together with other musicians to play music. I was a pensioner and before I came to Spain I lived for many years in Scarborough. The music scene there was fantastic. I built some really close friendships. I used to organise open mic events for young people and those kids often came with their parents. All of them are very grateful to me to this day and whenever I return to the UK, I am warmly welcomed by them. This musical side of my life was very interesting and fulfilling - together with other musicians I organised a lot of charity concerts. The musicians played for free and the money went to good causes. I've since done a similar event called Starfish in La Herradura with Stephen Hill. I like doing those kinds of things."

So how did you end up in La Herradura?

"Something happened that had a major impact on me. A very good friend of mine became sick. I feel tears welling up when I think of it. He always said he wanted to become a writer and had taken early retirement, but soon after he fell sick with leukaemia and died within six months. I was devastated to have lost a good friend and cried so much that day. He was a big guy like me, but this cruel illness had reduced him to next to nothing. The moment I saw the relatively small coffin coming down the aisle during the burial service, I realised that I had to follow my life-long dream to go and live in the sun. I felt an overwhelming feeling that I did not want to die with regrets and knew I had to follow that strong inner urge to simply pack up and go. My wife was different from me and had never shared that dream. Sadly it was the end of our marriage, which was very hard for everyone involved, but it was something that I simply could not ignore.

I decided to take my van that I had turned into a campervan and drive to Fuerteventura to visit my brother, who was living there. I had been there a few times and loved it. I had already booked the ferry from Spain to Fuerteventura, but when I road-tested the van I found it had some electrical problems. I was worried that this could happen again, so, whilst traveling through France, I decided to look for another place to head to in southern Spain. I googled language schools and windsurfing near the sea and La Herradura came up. It was total faith, my coming here.

I parked my van next to the windsurfing place on the beach run by Rob Kolenbrander and his wife Katti. I became good friends with them and helped out at their school just because I enjoyed it and was an experienced windsurf instructor having worked at my brother's windsurfing school back in the UK. I slept in the van on the beach, but when it got too hot in summer to sleep in the van, I rented a house. I am very fortunate because I have two pensions so I can afford to pay rent and have a nice standard of living here and I appreciate that very much.

I have now been living here for over six years and really love my life. I do feel a little guilty for not speaking Spanish very well; ideally I would like to be able to hold a good conversation with the Spanish people. I don't feel that they should adapt to us and learn our language."

Could you tell me why La Herradura is special to you?

"I must say that I like the fact that there are many different nationalities mixing here, but admit I would like to see more integration, especially from the British. I cannot complain about the Spanish - they are amazing, extremely welcoming and they seem very positive about all these different nationalities coming to their village to build a new life. I had brought some instruments with me and met another musician called Charlie Jackson. We started playing in the Oasis bar every Friday and Saturday. We played for free, I was playing guitar and singing and anyone could join in, a so-called jam session setup. The main thing was music: people who would normally only play at home started playing in public. It was pure pleasure just being together with lovely people playing music. It felt like being in paradise, on the water during the day and playing music at night time."

What does your daily life look like?

"I guess the main reason for me coming here was that I wanted to live in the sun and I have accomplished my dream of living a hundred metres from the sea. I always liked woodcarving so here I am, getting a tan and creating wooden sculptures in the sun on my terrace. When I am tired I can just go out to the sea windsurfing or in my kayak, taking my two dogs that love the water with me. It is just an incredible lifestyle and freedom. It's a stress-free life and I only mix with people that I like. I don't like to be part of an English clique. People tend to gossip too much about each other and the real story gets tarnished as people like to make the story more interesting. In the beginning I'm sure I was one of their subjects, living in a van on the beach like a hippy, probably thinking I was dirty with my long hair. Foolish really, as I was probably cleaner than most of them, swimming in the sea every day, having a shower on the beach, but they never bothered me. Curiously I have more close friends here now than I had in the UK, which is rather remarkable when you think I've only been here six years. These are really close friends that I feel I can call when I need to talk to someone or when I need help. Both female and male friends, kindred spirits."

Why do you do what you do, can you explain that?

"I used to be a schoolteacher in the past. I ran a residential school in Surrey with a small farm at the school. Kids would come out from London every week, accompanied by two teachers, learning about woods, animals and farm life. My wife, an artist, illustrator and art teacher, got pregnant and we moved to Yorkshire. I used to be a cricket player and wanted my son to play for the Yorkshire cricket team. However, you can only join the Yorkshire cricket team if you are actually born there. My wife went to live with my sister in Yorkshire to give birth to our child and we bought a smallholding in Lincolnshire.

When we left Surrey I was in charge of teaching at the social services' Scawby Grove Observation and Reception Centre with residential observation for kids in care. This centre provided an assessment service to see whether there had been any kind of abuse and whether the children could go back home or had to be taken into care. It was a multidisciplinary assessment of one month. I was trained as an art teacher, having studied pottery and sculpture, and as a PE teacher. So it was my job to assess these kids as a teacher. A very big influence on my life was the birth of our daughter when I was forty years old. She was born with both Down's and Turner's syndrome and she died when she was only nine months old. This changed my life in many ways as I decided that I wanted to work with children with special needs. I felt that this was what I was meant to do with my life."

Where did the music come in?

"Music has always played a very important part in my life and that was certainly also the case working with kids with special needs, moderate or severe learning difficulties and specifically children with all sorts of handicaps, physically and/or mentally. Music will always get you a response - it was an essential part of my work. By the time I took early retirement I was a supply teacher and working at schools for kids with severe learning difficulties or disruptive kids and delinquent kids. I used music as a behavioural instrument."

What do you like about your life now?

"I used to make love spoons for family and friends. Carving a spoon is a selfish pleasure because I know people who get them will love them. It is the kind of pleasure that you get when you buy something for someone and you know they are going to love it. The pleasure of giving is fantastic. I also like to take people out on the sea in my kayak, especially people who have never been on the water. I know that they will love it, as a mere hundred metres from the shore it is peaceful and you can talk, it is so serene. I love introducing people to the sea. The sea has always been important to my family. One of my sons is a double British windsurfing champion and my other son runs a surfing school and shop. When I visited my son, who has two very young boys in Scarborough last year I could witness that he is passing on his passion for the sea to his children. I saw him paddling out into the waves with his then two-and-a-half year old son sitting on his back and coming back he put him in front of him on the board. It was magic. My other son is expecting twins and I am looking forward to be a grandfather to these kids. It is one of my drives to remain fit so I can do water sports with them. There is an interesting similarity between water sports and music. Both can be enjoyed by people with handicaps or elderly people with physical complaints. I like that."

Has La Herradura changed your life?

"It has given me the freedom to do what I want to do. That is so wonderful. I live my life from day to day, I don't plan ahead. My life is dependent on the weather. I go with the flow. I have also been writing more since I have been living here. I write rhyming poetry and then put it to music. When I perform in public I do both covers of other artists and my own music. I used to have an Irish band in England, so I played a lot of harmonica, guitar, banjo and mandolin music. That influence still shines through in my gigs. I play a musical cocktail, a mixture of blues, pop, Irish and self-penned original music. I like other people joining in as performing with other musicians is giving me so much joy.

I love La Herradura for having given me the opportunity to live my life the way I do. The recession has affected the village and that is sad. It would be nice if cultural tourism could be the norm here but I hope it will not attract the package tour industry. I think it simply is not that kind of place and I hope it stays like that."

I agree, and tell him I have to go. Tony tells me he has enjoyed the conversation and the feeling is mutual. It was really nice: lifting the veil of an intriguing man that until now had only caught my eye from a distance with his extravagant, beautiful presence when making his way through the village. We pay for our coffees and say goodbye, the Spanish way, a kiss on both cheeks and a warm smile. My step even happier than before...the wind blowing away my thoughts.
Tony Turner

Musical carpentry

"We sit on the beach and I put my arm around my lovely Lauren, she lays her head on my shoulder. We look at the sea, so calm today. Like a mirror, reflecting a flock of seagulls gliding through the sky in search of fish. Once spotted they dive down with immaculate precision. There seems to be a shoal of fish and the birds are having a feast. Lauren and I talk about how we ended up in La Herradura. I look at her and express my gratitude. In a way it is thanks to her that we are in this village, because she was the one who first suggested the idea of going to the Costa Tropical to build a guitar, when she said, 'Darling, I have found Stephen Hill's European Institute of Guitar Making! You could go there to build a guitar for a month and I could make art in the meantime.'

There was no persuasion needed. We sold up whatever we could and drove down in our renovated camper van, Bruno, through France, and arrived in Tarifa in August 2011. Our plan was to go travelling for six months and to spend one of those months in La Herradura so I could build my guitar. We came here that September and in La Herradura the travelling stopped because I fell in love with guitar making and Stephen offered to let me continue working in his workshop. Lauren was also happy to stay and pursue her artistic career here, something she could do from anywhere. One month turned into years.

People often mistake me for a Spanish person as I have olive skin and jet black hair, but I was actually born in Margate, a seaside resort in Kent in the UK. It is interesting how life sometimes allows you a sneak preview of your future without you realising it. Or perhaps I could say that various seeds were planted unknowingly. For example, when my dad was a young guy he worked for some time in a guitar-building factory in Erith for Vox. He was working on the production line, but in a way he was involved in the process of making guitars. At a later stage, my father and brother worked as carpenters and had their own construction company. I worked for them sometimes, but mostly on groundwork and the decoration side of things. Interestingly though I probably enjoyed working with wood more. Opposite my father's building yard in Ramsgate there was an electrical guitar maker. I used to visit him and was fascinated by the concept of building guitars and I asked him a lot of questions. However, it never occurred to me then that I would one day be making guitars too, especially not Spanish guitars. At that time I was into heavy metal, rock and blues music.

In addition, my mother moved to Spain, to Barcelona and then Cadiz, and Lauren and I visited her there. She introduced me to flamenco music and I realised that this was very impressive guitar playing and I wanted to learn it. I took lessons for three months in Cadiz which gave me some grounding. I didn't so much want to become a flamenco guitarist, but I wanted it to be part of my technique. I am passionate about all music and also love classical guitar, but with flamenco, the way the right hand is used really helps a guitar player to express him or herself and become one with the guitar. For me this is a perfect playing style and I guess you could say it has heavily influenced my approach to guitar playing and song writing. There is an addictive side to my nature, in a sense. When I find something that I really love doing, I feel a need to express myself and for that to happen. In my head I believe I have to become really good at it, not to prove anything but to simply become as good as I can be at it. Then, I don't have to consciously think about the technical aspects anymore and can just enjoy doing it. As far as playing the guitar is concerned, this allows me to have a perfect balance with my song writing, which is driven by expression.

I love expressive song writing. I don't know why exactly

but the guitar building took over. It was just something I had to do. It came along and I felt a need to pursue it to the end, even though there is no end to it, just as there is no end in music. Before leaving the UK I was a full-time musician, now I am a guitar builder in my own right, although I do not want to lose touch with the musician in me. I do believe, however, that I should give all I have and all my love to pursuing something that feels right. Also, to be OK with change and doing something else when inspired; that freedom to be able to change when something comes along and to simply follow my heart. That is how it works for me.

In a way you could say that La Herradura has changed my life. I never planned to be a guitar maker and we never planned to live in Spain, just to come here, build one guitar and then move on. I now see being a guitar maker as my career path, so that is definitely a massive change. I have noticed that this happens to other people as well. They come here for a week and stay for a lifetime. La Herradura also made us change our thoughts on life, it helped us look at ourselves in a deeper way and made us think about what we really want from life. It is hard to explain, it's been like a healing process, thinking about what really matters and what is really important in life. There is a special energy here, a feeling, which cannot be explained in words. Apart from that it is a very relaxed and welcoming place, people are friendly and there doesn't seem to be a lot of stress here.

Music is still very important to me. When I was a full-time musician I practised six hours a day. Now, I try to practise playing the guitar at least half an hour each day. It is important to me to find a balance. In the beginning that was very hard, I had to work long hours to create a guitar as each one required seventy percent more of my time than it does now, as I was still learning. There was little time left for music. At the moment, however, the balance is coming back and I am finding some time to play my guitar again. I still write songs and Lauren has also taken up singing. We love singing together and we like to do some recording in our spare time. There are bars in La Herradura that offer live music on a weekly basis and often there's a sort of open mic set up where we can join in and perform a few of our songs. This is part of the magic of this place. There are many musicians and artists here and plenty of people who enjoy listening to music too. There is true support for those singing in front of others, genuinely influenced through passion and love. However, with the smallness of this place and with the community being so friendly there is a risk of becoming distracted and spending a lot of time just meeting people and having a coffee or a drink. It is really nice, but if you are not careful you could just do that all day, every day.

I try to be disciplined about my working life and go to Stephen Hill's workshop every morning. Stephen is a really special man and has become a very good friend. I still learn from him and he is extremely generous with his knowledge. We get on really well, it is a blessing to be able to learn from someone so experienced and skilled and who carries no fear or resentment that he might be nurturing the 'competition'. He has become an important part of my life here.

It is time to go back to the workshop. We shake the sand off our clothes and walk in the direction of the statue - a sculpture by Miguel Moreno, dedicated to those who died during the shipwreck in 1562. The statue is situated right opposite Calle Acera del Pilar, the main street out of La Herradura. There is a remembrance plaque and the statue is placed in the midst of some large stones. Behind the statue you find a small round space with a few benches for people to sit and relax. To me, the statue portrays eloquently the pain and desperation that must have been felt throughout this area when the awful event took place.

Lauren and I say goodbye to each other. She sets off to meet a friend and I walk up Calle Acera del Pilar. When I reach the oldest cafe of the village, El Salon, I turn right and immediately left again. I enter the workshop, where Stephen has just come back from his break and says hello. I soak up the smell of wood and varnish and walk to my workbench. It is always a bit daunting when I start building a new guitar to see the many pieces of wood involved. It is a massive job. I can write a song in ten minutes or maybe in a day, but with a guitar it takes a good one hundred to one hundred and fifty hours for the initial dream to become the final object. It is a beautiful feeling though when you finally put the strings on and play the instrument, especially as it has been such a long journey from start to finish. The sense of reward is immense, all those hours working with the wood, the smells, the taste and the joy of doing something really well and knowing that you've done the best you can, knowing that it is really high quality. Because of the expense of building a guitar, it has to be perfect...as close to perfect as can be. All this is highly fulfilling.

Someone asked me once whether there is a message in what I do. Yes there is, the message is love. Just try and love what you do. Also, try and love what others do. Express yourself and keep the passion for what you are doing. Have love for your creations, it doesn't matter whether that is a guitar, a painting, a song or even a plate of food, anything really, as love will come out in the flavour of what you are doing, thus passing on the passion. I realise this is exactly what I am doing now... it feels great. I clear the work surface and pick up a bridge that I finished earlier this morning, ready to put on the guitar. I just love what I do. I am happy."

Graham Emes - www.emesguitars.com

From New York to the bay

Wikipedia says: 'James Sobers (born May 13, 1974), a.k.a. BluRum13 is an American rapper (MC/emcee) and producer under the pseudonym Killa Platypus. Originally from New York City, he spent most of his formative years in Washington D.C.'

An impressive list of career highlights, contributions and collaborations follows, amongst others, and I quote: 'BluRum13 began a live show collaboration with acclaimed Spanish jazz drummer Mark Ayza, and also founded the dub-hop/electro step group Indigenous Invaders with DJ Toner (Granada). Indigenous Invaders appeared live at the world's first YouTube music festival "YouFest" in Madrid on September 28, 2012.'

I am intrigued and look forward to meet the man behind the information. We sit down at a table at El Realengo, one of the beach bars and an apparent favourite spot for the many paragliders that descend on the stretch of beach alongside the beach bar after their mesmerising display in the air.

We watch a group of young men and women squeezing themselves into their wetsuits. La Herradura is well known for providing some of the best reef dives in Europe. There is an abundance of choice - from the quiet sheltered coves of Marina del Este to the white sand nudist beach of Cantarriján. The Costa Tropical has a number of protected bays that allow for year-round diving. Lying at the foot of the Sierra Nevada mountain range, this rocky shoreline offers a rich heritage of natural wonder and hosts a profusion of multi coloured marine species.

Diving schools from the entire region come to the village with groups but La Herradura has fine diving schools to cater for the diving enthusiasts, taking both beginners and advanced divers on an unforgettable dive. The divers are putting weight-belts, air tanks, fins and other equipment into the rubber boat. Off they go. We order a drink and James tells his story.

"My name is James R. Sobers II, but I am artistically known as Blurum13. I was born in Long Island New York and I am the proud father of my two wonderful boys. We live in La Herradura more or less permanently but we regularly go to Canada which was the last place we lived before coming to Spain as a family. My wife, Elisabeth is from Montreal. In a period in my career, when I was already relatively successful I was touring extensively with a group called One Self and this touring experience introduced me to the whole southern coast of Europe. Back home I talked about it with my wife and I vowed I had to come back. We first ended up in London and at a party we met a woman who was buying real estate in the Almuñécar and La Herradura area. My wife and I had lived for eight years in Canada and had both spent much of our youth in small towns and we were looking for a similar setting. We took this woman's telephone number and gave her a ring a couple of years later when we had our first child and had the opportunity to spend four months in the area. This was one of the few places we discovered where we could take our kid with us into a bar. We felt that was a step up from the 'control society' and the fact that we could see the sea and visit the beach every day was something we found difficult to beat. Now, having lived here for quite a few years we love the fact that people really know each other in the neighbourhood, which is, apart from anything else, a real bonus when you want to learn the language.

The village is definitely special to us, one of the reasons being that we can just be ourselves here. In the hip-hop music scene everything is a performance and when living in any city, when you leave the house, you become a performer. No matter how small or large a celebrity you are there is an expectation that you have to perform like a rapper all the time. The rapper scene has also changed with expectations that can be rather self-destructive, whereas before, hip-hop was a voice to the voiceless and the opportunity to create a community for the voiceless.

This expectation of performance is rather funny. If I want to go to a nightclub I cannot go by myself, I have to go with a minimum of three friends to create the impression that I attract people. Then, at some point during the night, more people are phoned to enhance the illusion. The club manager will continue that illusion by giving us free drinks ... I never get to dance or sing. It is always a performance. There was a time when it had very little to do with how you looked. It was about getting your perspective across in a poetic way that created emotions and explained the thoughts of the moment. It was a real skill, but then people started to show up with less skill and more flash and wardrobe than was needed. If I only wear a black jumpsuit as a rapper there is no merchandise. Rappers are now supposed to wear three golden chains and a few gold teeth, it has become hilarious. If I don´t go outside with a lot of bling on my hands and my hat with a sticker, which I hate by the way, my value is less in the eyes of the public. Here, in La Herradura, people don't care, no matter how popular I am and I like that.

The journey I've made to get where I am now is perhaps not what you expect of a rapper. My mother was working for the city hall and my father was a member of the Green Berets. My father taught me that 'it is better to be paranoid than it is to be afraid but to learn the difference between the two.' He added: 'Everything in your body, including your emotions, is there for a reason. If you listen to what an emotion is telling you, you will always make the right decision and then I don't need to teach you anything else.' He also told me that I needed to find out about my responsibility to myself.

I grew up in Maryland about twenty miles from Washington DC, in what was quite a rural area at that time, surrounded by a lot of farmland. While I was growing up there was still quite an active Ku Klux Klan movement. I vividly remember us being called 'niggers' and even being shot at when I was only seven years old. There were a lot of racial threats. I intuitively sensed that very same atmosphere when I was offered a job that seemed so good that it felt like it was a trap many years later. At the time I worked as a youth counsellor and in a relatively short time I had worked my way up to Youth Counsellor Director. At the same time I was going back and forward to Canada for music gigs. Then I got offered the job of Regional Director. I was twenty three-years old and I would have had responsibility for looking after twelve camps with seven-hundred staff, even though I had no real management skills. However, some older authority figures involved let me know that they were suspicious of the fact that I had dreadlocks. To me it felt like old times had returned, so I listened to my instinct and turned down the role. I left my job and went to Canada to work with a band, which that year played at the Samuel Jackson golf tour tournament. For me that was a huge success, personally and financially. Afterwards I decided to go back to the US and become a professional musician.

In my younger years I was inspired by jazz music. My father had a large record collection and he had also been a radio DJ at some point. I also remember there was always a lot of music in our house. My dad would play music by great musicians like the legendary Grammy Award–winning jazz saxophonist Charlie Parker who, with Dizzy Gillespie, invented the musical style called bop or bebop.

I used to go with my father when he went around the city, as he had a job that allowed him to drive his own vehicle. I recall sitting in the back of the car with its red interior, with the music blasting out of the radio, and from my car seat, which was facing forward, I remember being able to look up and out of the window. As a small child I remember seeing lots of colours. My imagination was very vivid and I recall seeing a guy being a purple colour and he blended into the blue sky whilst the trees reflected their magic on the interior of the car. This experience probably triggered something in my DNA and I now realise that my vision of colours and memories from when I was a kid are very similar to the ones I had on a mushroom trip later in life.

My father also played the clarinet. In those days music was imperative for African Americans. You just knew how to sing and how to move. It was intertwined in our churches with gospel music. There was a point in the ceremony that we would celebrate by singing hymns. As a child that was all God needed to be, the rest wasn't important. You just wanted to dance and get a cracker which they used to hand out. There is an interesting comparison with what I do these days as well. When I hold the microphone the people in the audience bow their heads. This is typical for classic hip-hop fans; they put their hands up and bow their heads. It is like praying.

Hip-hop became more and more present in the music scene in the mid-eighties and I got involved. Initially by doing some writing here and there, then in the early nineties I was creating demos and got involved in local collaborations. I have a brother who is ten years older than me and he would bring that early hip-hop music home. I have now made a name in the business and am referred to as an artist who likes diversity. This diversity and my voice are my strength.

I try to get myself into a space where I can compose and feel inspiration. I can be inspired by almost anything, by life itself. I remember being in a studio for a session with some other musicians. It was a very blank studio, no pictures, just a black sofa and a little green light in the corner. There were four of us writing a song. My friend asked, 'Does anybody have a topic?' and I suggested the dark studio. I simply wrote a song about the studio. The words and the music become like a ballet. It involves balance and control, but it really is about taking an experience and turning it into 'art'.

From a writer's perspective I try to write differently with every song. I have been called a singer but I would not classify myself as a singer. However, the rap is a song. You will not understand my music if you are not inspired to listen to it and if you are not comfortable with yourself at the time you listen … you won't feel it.

I compose both alone and with other people but mostly give my attention to the lyrical side. As a rapper I have a preference for lyrics that are based on empowerment. I also work for other people. When people hire me it usually concerns a rap, when I am doing my own work I am a bit more involved in the musical creation. My current band is called The Blurum13 Experience. We are working as a trio - a DJ, a drummer and a bassist and we perform in a very hip-hop format. We interweave hip-hop with the songs that I and other people have written.

On paper my main audience is New York, California and England but I have also performed in France, Germany, Spain, Russia and other Eastern bloc countries and I was, actually, the first rapper to perform in Serbia. Performing for a crowd is magical. To me music is something that fills you with energy - it is the language of pure energy. You start playing and someone next to you hears a melody and starts singing, and another person comes along and starts to dance. It is instantly a congregational experience that can fill me up with tears.

There is nothing like a crowd becoming one entity. Looking at 10,000 people is different from anything else. Their attention is supposed to be yours but they are people until you remind them that they are an organism that is called a crowd. There truly is a crowd mind. There is always an improvisation aspect to my show and I used to do so-called heavy free style. Some friends would write down a word that I gave them. Nobody else would see this word. There then comes a point during the show where I start doing freestyle and I just make things up. For example, I can describe the crowd during a rap and then I will ask them for words. If it is a 'quick' crowd I can ask them for a word during the rap, in the case of a 'slow' crowd I stop the rap and ask them for a word. Inevitably, in over fifty percent of the time, the word that comes out of the audience is the very word that I planted into the crowd. The reason for this, in my opinion is that when you have their total attention they are so involved that they become interactive ... when someone says 'yeah' the entire crowd says 'yeah'. It's fascinating; it becomes one voice, one crowd. I am also grateful that I can reach such a large audience. That is part of why I am doing this.

For a period of about five years I stopped the intensive touring because my first son was born. I did not want to miss anything of those first few years of his life, so I worked from home and I concentrated on making more music. Apart from creating music I am also a 'rap broker'. I get people together to create things. I have over thirty printed releases and I have been involved in many projects. However, one of my next projects is a pop venture. It is a group that has been in the making for over nine years. I wanted to take a group that is undeniably talented to the point where they are good at whatever music they make. This is very difficult to do. I had to catch the musicians while they were young and groom them. We still have the same core of people as we did when we started.

The entire music industry is rather particular. There are circles of success and the people in those circles have more influence than other people and it is a challenge to get in. Being a good artist is not necessarily straightforward and Amy Winehouse is a perfect example. When she was popular nobody knew she had a drug addiction, but when she was not popular that was the way she was portrayed. I am by no means that famous but these are challenges that we come across and have to face. Our group is called True Ingredients and it is an amazing group of minds. There are two environmental engineers, a musical prodigy and a young lady who has been singing with Gladys Knight as a back-up singer ... the talent is phenomenal and most importantly, we all recognise the traps in the industry.

Through science, with the help of some talented lab rats, we discovered a way to sonically help people listen to themselves. We did not invent this but we found some theories and helped put it into practice. What we think of as musical skill has been altered! You can do this through harmonic resonance. If you find a pure A you will see the seismographic symbol. We have gone back to those original sounds but this has taken a long time because we had to wait for technology to catch up with when we first had the idea, which was when there were no iPads and no tablets. The human mind works on repetition. If you repeat something six times, whether the person wants to remember it or not, it is more likely to stick. Pushing pop music feels like something light and fluffy but it is not.

The exact opposite of the above is my Indigenous Invaders group. The same technology is employed to make the music, but what is different is that it is organic music meeting electro music. The tone is aggressive, not the music itself but the sound, thanks to huge harmonic reverberations. Indigenous Invaders is Spanish based. We have a Spanish webmaster, a Spanish producer and blogger. We have a person who monitors all activities online and directs these.

Do I have any other passions? Well I like to draw, I love pen and ink. Within the hip-hop scene there is a lot of graffiti - 'Spray can realism and cubism' is what it should be called. At an early age you learn about perspective and colour pallets through the hip-hop scene. However, I also have another passion. I am very much interested in what makes people laugh. I like to set up funny situations and test people out. So you could say that "funny things" is my hobby."

Two hours have passed. We see a group of divers returning to the shore, unpacking the rubber boat, looking satisfied. I ask James whether La Herradura has changed his life and he explains that it hasn´t changed his life as his life was already changing and La Herradura was part of that change. 'And you know what … I speak a lot more Spanish, which has definitely changed my life' he adds. I have one more question for James '*Do you have a specific wish for the village?*' and he has: "I wish for it to grow, because I don't want anything to stay the same, but I hope it will grow without losing itself. It doesn´t need to be anything but La Herradura."

James Sobers - blurum13.com trueingredients.com indigenousinvaders.com

Music in visual images

There is something for everyone in La Herradura. Like many seaside villages there are plenty of bars and restaurants to cater for the villagers and the expats escaping the cold, wet winters in northern Europe as well as the mainly Spanish tourists during the summer months. One of its nicest customs, as in most of Granada province, is the serving of a free *tapa* (a small snack) with every drink, but, nice as this is, it's not what makes La Herradura so special. It's the unashamed abundance of cultural events happening twelve months of the year in the many bars and restaurants, the Civic Centre, the Castillo and the Plaza Nueva, also known as Plaza de la Independencia – all offering space for artwork or the organisation of musical events, artisan markets, dance classes, yoga, theatre or cinema. There is something for everyone.

For a relatively small village it is also about the mixture of very talented people of different nationalities who have made La Herradura their home. Treating yourself to a coffee, a meal or a tapa in one of the many bars and restaurants is a pleasure in itself but keep an eye out for small or large posters on the announcement boards or blackboards outside these establishments and you will be surprised by the choice of offerings in a welcoming environment whilst enjoying a bite or a drink.

Today, Monday, I am meeting up with Lino Diáz, a Cuban classical and jazz pianist in El Tinao, a bar-restaurant in Calle del Koala 5, a side road off the sea front. This is where Lino plays his music live, as he does every Monday, together with his wife Lupe. We sit down in the outdoor restaurant area, opposite the entrance of El Tinao and I listen to his story.

"I am from the province of Camaguey and I live in La Herradura with my wife Lupe and our two boys. What I like here is that it is a Mecca for artists. We sort of came here by accident. My wife's mother and stepfather came to La Herradura for seasonal work and they fell in love with the place, with its kind people and because the climate was so comparable to the climate that we are all used to in Cuba.

We were at a stage in our lives where we longed for tranquillity. When you are in a creative process you need to be in a place where you can find tranquillity both physically and mentally. The wonderful views, the sea and the pleasant ambience cause this creativity to multiply. Although we lived in a nice area in Italy by Lake Garda, we liked what we heard about La Herradura and we have never looked back.

La Herradura has given me so much. In a sense I have become an adult here. Our first child was only one year old when we arrived and our second child was born in the village and it is fantastic to be a parent to my wonderful sons. I always have had a positive view on life but it has not always been easy and I have had to take on other jobs to survive. I have worked as a waiter in La Herradura to be able to care for my young family, like so many artists and actors who have to take on jobs on the side. There were many challenges on our path, but these challenges make you grow. I have changed a lot since we came here, not so much as an artist but as a person, and in a very positive way. Now I am in the situation that I can dedicate myself to music full time and that makes me very happy, I am grateful for that.

If I have to describe my music it is mostly jazz, but I also work on producing what I would describe as New Jazz. I sing as well, but I am not a singer. My wife Lupe is a professional singer. I compose music and write lyrics for genre songs. I am a singer/songwriter. As a composer I compose mainly jazz music and I am producing my own jazz album, which is where my heart lies. Jazz is my passion and the most important music to me.

I remember while still a very young child liking jazz musicians. I loved to listen to Oscar Peterson, Louis Armstrong, Miles Davies and John Coltrane and have certainly been inspired by these great masters of jazz. Strangely enough playing jazz is a fairly recent phenomenon in my musical career - I only started to dedicate my time seriously to it in 2009.

Music has always been part of my life. I started playing the guitar when I was six years old and when I was nine years old I went to the conservatory of music where I was trained as a classical musician. After my graduation I worked as a popular Cuban music artist in Cuba for three years. In Italy we mainly played Latin American and more specifically Cuban music. It wasn't until we moved to La Herradura that my true calling was able to come to the surface. Although I was trained to be a classical musician and subsequently became a Latin music performer I started to play more and more jazz music. It became very clear to me: *This is who I am as an artist; this is what I will be. A jazz musician.* It has of course also been a process and it was hard at times. I was searching for something positive, I had to sacrifice my health, I was artistically suffering but what I was left with in the end was indescribable satisfaction. Jazz is definitively my path.

And my inspiration? It comes to me in images. This is called synaesthesia. I can best describe it as a very intimate relationship. In classical music you repeat something that already exists to give it something personal, you have to find a way to interpret it, sometimes forcing yourself to add your personal touch. Even when I don't feel too well I know how to get myself into that space and I always do this through images. I focus on what I need to do, I focus on how I need to do it, and how I would like to do it and I then see pictures in my head and get to work. These images are musical images, not physical images. I visualise the music, I don't hear it. I see the instrumentalist with his instrument and I see what he is executing. This information is transformed into music in my brain.

Living in La Herradura I must say that I do feel music could be valued more here. I feel many people think that you don't need to study to be a musician, that you can learn it in the streets so to speak and therefore play for a few beers and a plate of food. When you are a professional musician you have to invest a lifetime of your energy and talent, your childhood and your adolescent years, but it doesn't stop there. You have to study and practice every day in order not to lose your capability, the mechanism in your hands. If you don't study enough each day you certainly notice the difference.

When you offer your art it is often not properly valued. For example, there is a plumber and he tells you that it will cost you fifteen euros an hour to get a job done. Nobody asks him why or what his studies have been. People just accept his hourly rate. But when you are a musician, lots of people don't care about what your study has been or what speciality you have to offer. They simply presume you can do your gig for a few beers and a bite to eat. Nobody seems to realise that it has been and still is the investment of a lifetime, your entire life.

To me, being a musician is having a career that will never finish, it is a way of life, it is a need, it is spiritual. The day that you don't play music or do not hear music is a day lost. Only musicians and artists can understand this, because they feel committed to their gift. First you have to have a gift and then you have to do something with it, invest in it. Your life is created around this and that will never stop, it can always become better or even different, but it never stops. I have heard someone say that a painting is never finished, it is abandoned. More or less the same happens with music.

Do I have a message? My message is a very simple one. I want to inspire. I like other people to know that it doesn't matter what your path looks like, it doesn't matter what you have to go through on your path. If you have faith and trust in yourself and focus on the outcome, like a light at the end of the tunnel, you will get there or, at least, if you haven't arrived yet, you will be on the right path. You will just know it. Whatever happens, you will find your purpose. You will understand it when you have found it, when you feel it inside you. It is like a drug. You are dependent on it and cannot live without it. The day that you don't write, you don't sing, paint or make music, is the day you lose your life.

I am currently working on an album with original themes I have created. By the time people read this book it might be finished. It is my first production of jazz music. I have produced and composed three albums before, but these were mostly children's songs and I created them with my mother in Cuba. This is my first jazz production and it will be in the most traditional style possible. It is a trio consisting of piano, contrabass and drums. The themes in themselves aren't overcomplicated. I feel that my first jazz production needs to be as sensitive as possible to the ear. This will then open a door and then, one step at a time, it will lead to my truth, but first I have to open the door, always keeping in mind that I am giving my own internal perspective. It has to leave the listener with the taste. If he or she likes that then I can give more.

This is only the overture of who I imagine being. What I very much like are orchestral compositions. So that is my objective. I am starting with the trio, drums, contrabass and piano, the traditional jazz trio, then that will grow to a slightly bigger band, for example with seven musicians. However, my ultimate goal is orchestral productions, so I am thinking of big band and symphonic jazz.

I am working on this album on my own, but I like to collaborate with other artists. When Charly Endres is in La Herradura we always play together, together with my wife Lupe, usually in El Tinao. He regularly has to travel back to Germany and Belgium, but when he is here we love to perform together. It is a musical complicity. We have that type of connection where we only have to look at each other's eyes to know what we will play and how we will play it. It was like that from the very first moment we played together. It was there right away, that special energy. When Charly is here, we just feel a need to play together, we just have to, and we always do.

What do I like about my profession? I like that I can invest the time working, say for twelve hours in a row, until I feel exhausted, but it's in a positive way, that's extremely satisfying to me. I love that I can do what I want and that I can dedicate as much time as I like to my love for music. I like that I don't have to dedicate my head to anything else. It always feels as if I don't have enough time. I can get by with only four hours sleep and that is fine. I simply have to create, create and create but I also have the time to study. I am obsessive and compulsive about studying. I have to study. So when I have a little break from creating music, because I do get tired and I do need breaks, I pick up one of my instruments and study.

The piano is very important in my life, but almost more significant to me is an instrument called the *tresaquinto,* which I invented more than ten years ago and is based on the *tres,* a Cuban instrument which is a fusion between a lute and the Spanish guitar. Originally it has six strings, like a guitar, but in pairs, like the lute. My instrument has eight strings instead of six. Just like the *tres* it has the six strings in pairs, but in addition to that it has two individual strings. It has a slightly Renaissance sound to it but it retains the flavour of the guitar.

All in all I can say that I am grateful to be where I am now, a full-time artist and father of my sons. My family is important to me. I am grateful that I came to this village even though I have been hit hard quite a few times. The first seven years were tough, but I do feel that these challenges have guided me to be the person that I am now. The more difficult the road, the more rapidly you can aim to improve things and become the person you are meant to be.

And La Herradura? I hope that La Herradura becomes more of what it already is but it needs to recognise what it has. I would like to see the many establishments appreciating and supporting the wealth of culture, music and art that is being created in the privacy of the homes of the artists, finding more ways of showing this off. La Herradura needs to respect and take its wonderful artists seriously and to celebrate them. La Herradura has great potential. I can see it becoming a cultural hotspot attracting a myriad of new appreciative tourists. I feel it has the potential to become a European cultural reference point."

Lino Díaz - www.reverbnation.com/TimbalitoStreet

Seen through a lens

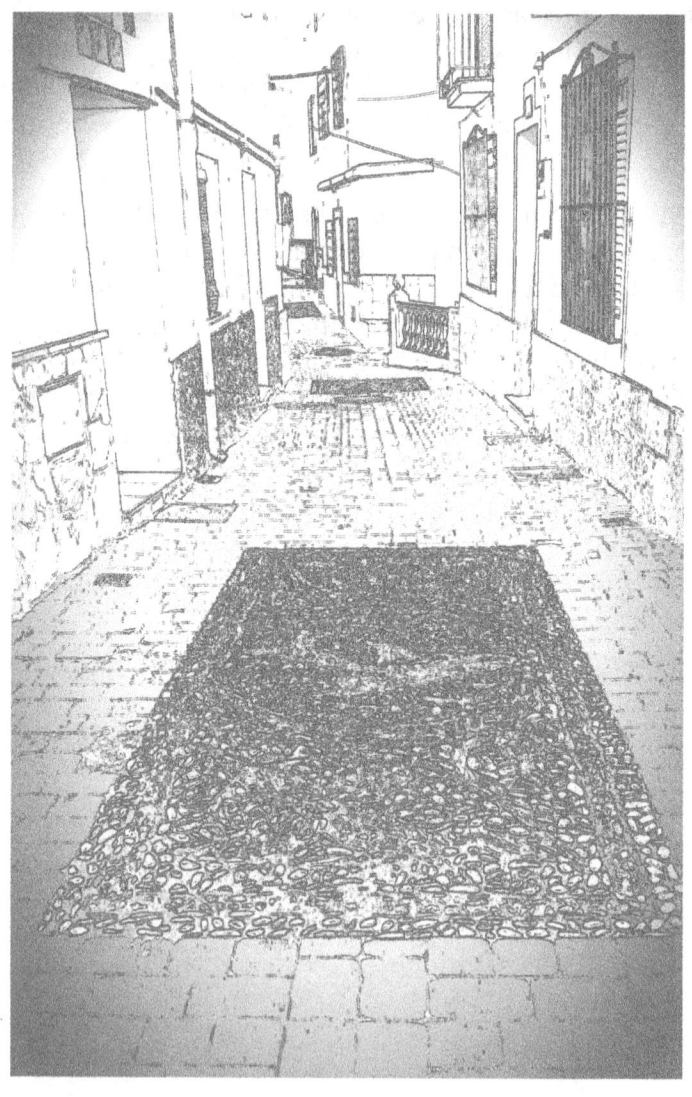

The 'Long' way south

"I am walking back home and stop for a moment on the bridge over the Río Jate. Towards the sea I overlook what is known as the *desembocadura de Rio Jate* – the place where the riverbed meets the sea. The river is dry most of the year. Sometimes there is a trickle of water in the middle, only given away by some green grasses and plants waving in the sea breeze. But in wintertime, during the occasional torrential rainfall, it rapidly grows into a full-blown river dragging dry branches and the remains of discarded household goods with it. The river gave its name to the bay and its shores in the mid-16th century, when it was known as Jate and about 3,500 years before Christ Neolithic men fused their metals, built their huts, and buried their dead on the shores and just inland at the Peña Parda. Some archaeological organisations are sad that this area of undoubted historical importance has never been thoroughly excavated archeologically, probably because of the extensive and rapid economic growth in the 1980s and subsequent urbanisation of the area. It is said that the Peña Parda was where the first human beings in this area settled. Nowadays you can still see vegetable gardens practically on the seafront, which is rather unique. I wonder how many interesting artefacts are still buried beneath the houses in the area; perhaps even beneath the place we now call our home. I live in a wonderful spot in the Peña Parda area of La Herradura with my partner Chloe and our son Pancho.

I was born in Edinburgh in Scotland, but I am only half Scottish, on my mother's side, my father was Irish. As a young boy I thought I wasn't good at anything so I worked harder than most children, and for as long as I needed in order to succeed. My father was almost illiterate and born into a very poor, large family in Dublin. He was a coal miner and the hardest worker I have known. Head down and working very hard was his and my answer to everything and that attitude hasn't changed.

I went to a military boarding school which was very strict and I wasn't doing badly, but not very well either. When I was a kid I was crap at drawing and also at music, I tried very hard, but I just wasn't any good. I was OK at sport but not great and quite frankly, in class I wasn't outstanding in anything. Then, when I was twelve years old, I discovered photography. I loved it and I found I was quite good at it. I do believe that you don't need an innate talent for photography. Talent in photography is all about having the passion and then with practice you can develop an eye for it. Photography is unique as an art because it is something that can be entirely learned if you are committed and excited enough.

There was a teacher at school who inspired and encouraged me. I still vividly remember my fascination when he developed the photos he had just taken, put them into a tank, pouring in the developer and then into a stop bath, after that into the fixer and about fifteen minutes later holding the wet negatives up to the light. I was completely enchanted. I became obsessed with photography. It was great to have found something I could be good at. Making pictures was my salvation.

So back to my story; because my father was a coal miner, there was no money but my parents were great people. They bought me a ten pound camera. I had to measure distances and guess focus, but I worked at it with a passion. I kept thinking that the only thing that held me back from taking over the world of photography was a crappy camera.

I tried to get into a Polytechnic in Central London for photography but discovered for that I needed an art O level which I wasn't able to get. I tried and tried but failed. Years later, when I was a mature student, I got in without the O level. I was horrified that the head of photography came to me to ask me how to develop a film.

The course was hugely theoretical, mainly art history and semiotics and the technical level of photography was shocking. However, I did very well and loved being a photography student; it was a licence to do everything I like. I've never been a hobby photographer except for the time that I was in school.

I ended up teaching photography in a community centre and in a prison. I also had an agent who would get me work for newspapers like the Guardian. Over the years, I have had my work exhibited in photography galleries such as The White Chapel Art Gallery and the Photographers Gallery and I've even had a one-man exhibition which toured throughout the UK and Russia. I also created a lot of feminist theatre posters, other theatrical stuff and book covers. You could say I started to make a name for myself. I was still a student and loved every minute of it. It was in the mid-seventies and if there was a heaven it was those three years at school.

I then applied to do photography at the Royal College of Art. They only took six students a year and the guy who ran it didn't like me because I had already become quite public. A friend of mine, Jo Spence, who was a famous British feminist photographer, said 'Just apply'. I ended up being accepted in the film school. When I turned up for the first day of college I met Paul Watson, a British documentary maker. He was the new professor of film at the Royal College of Art and a very straight-forward guy. There were twenty-two students present, listening to his welcome words. He said 'Welcome to the Royal College. Now say your name and tell me whether you are going to do film or television.' While they were going round I noticed that they all said they wanted to do film, so when it was my turn I said 'Bob Long, television' and that's how I ended up doing television. It never grabbed me as much as photography did, but I thought that I would continue working in prison doing photography anyway.

They then told me that I could not do that job anymore. I went to the head of arts and said, 'I don't see why I cannot do that ... I work in Holloway prison teaching photography!' I also had fallen in love with one of the inmates, had proposed to her and she had said yes. She had to be escorted out of prison for our wedding day. The marriage didn't last. I ended up losing the prison job but got a part time job teaching photography at a college. However, it was only part time and one day, when I was in a toilet, someone had a pee next to me and I asked him 'What will you do after this?' He said 'I am applying for Channel 4. They have to give all their money to independent producers.'

I formed a company and I called myself Long Shot Productions and after a year of battering the door of Channel 4, I was given £30,000, probably to get rid of me, to create a documentary about the overuse of hypnotic drugs in women's prisons, and it did well and surprised everybody. That first day of filming I had a camera crew of seven and I spoke to the camera man. I said "I have never done this before. You guys can either take the piss or you can help me." They helped me and were lovely. It was a good programme. It was the beginning of my television career. Following that I was able to do another programme about killers in prison. I then thought *I don't want to be stuck with prisons* and was approached by a guy who had never directed but who had the money. He wanted to create a documentary on AIDS. He asked me whether I would produce it and help him.

I did well in television for nine years and then spent everything I had saved in Australia in three months; I came back to London in debt. A publisher approached Charlie Richardson, a criminal and head of the Richardson gang in South London, the nearest you could get to a mafia-style gang. He told Richardson, 'I want to get your biography written by a ghost writer and then publish it.' Charlie said, 'If you want me the one and only person I will allow to do that is Bob Long'. So the publisher approached me and said the magic words. 'You will receive an advance of 15,000 and one third of it right now.' So I said yes.

One year after the initial deadline I had still not written a word. But I needed the money and convinced the publisher that I would finish the book in twelve weeks if she gave me another third of the advance. I had a job on the side and every night I would write between twelve and twenty pages, whether I was tired or not. I just had to do it, and I did it! They were pleased and when it was published I got my final payment. Writing is close to my heart and it is one of the hardest, but also most rewarding things you can do. It is funny how many people want to write. They say that everybody has got a book in them but if you ask me I think that that is where it should stay! I did write another book about the history of dog homes in Britain and maybe I would like to have another go at writing books about other people and other subjects.

During that period of writing the Charlie Richardson book I applied for a job at the BBC for a programme called Video Diaries, they had done a pilot series and it was badly done. I got the job and started working for the BBC where I stayed for fourteen years. I ended up as an executive producer and I shot about three hundred films. I was paid well and worked hard, every day from 09.00 to 10.00 pm. I never had a passion for television but I do have a passionate belief that ordinary people are capable of a lot more than society gives them credit for. We got normal people and made them into programme makers, they literally had control over the end result. From 1990 to 1995 we were riding high with Video Diaries and it was a great hit.

I met Chloe at the BBC where she was a camerawoman. During that time someone suggested to me that we work with the Police Paedophile Unit of Scotland Yard. I spent two years meeting with the police. At the first meeting I met up with the head of the unit also called Bob. I remember it was a Thursday night and we had a drink, even though I don't drink. We became friends and he thought it was a great idea. It took another two years to convince the BBC and for the contract between the BBC and the police to be signed. We finally started and Chloe was working on this with me as well. Many of the documentaries I produced did very well and I have won numerous awards including a BAFTA for 'Best Documentary'. A few years ago I also produced a documentary filmed in Iraq which was sold to the U.S., broadcast on H.B.O. and awarded an EMMY.

I started to hanker for a break after having finished two series with the cops. Chloe and I came out to Spain on my boat. Another one of my passions was boating and I restored an old wooden boat which, whenever I had some spare time, I sailed around the Channel Islands and from England to France. We decided to go to the Mediterranean and live on my boat. I remembered having heard about Sitges, just outside Barcelona at a party in the Eighties and that is why we went there. We liked it. We used it as our base as we travelled around the Mediterranean. We had saved up some money but we lived very frugally. We were able to stay in the Balearics for an entire summer and live on almost nothing. We just paid for diesel and food. In the winter of that first year we went to Thailand and lived for three months in a hut on the beach in Koh Tao, a small island, on only nine euros a day between us for food and accommodation.

The following year Chloe suggested starting a family. I had got over the yearning for a child, but I remembered the problems my ex-wife had had getting pregnant. We had tried everything including IVF. She was obsessed with it and I realised how strong that urge can be. I promised myself that if a future partner should want a child I was going to say yes. So we had our son and everything changed. He is the love of my life. I have never known such love for anybody but it was incredibly tough to live on a boat with a small child, which we did for a couple of years. We realised we could not do that forever. When he became close to school age we found out that the Catalan language is compulsory in the Barcelona area and teachers are not allowed to speak to parents in Spanish. We felt it was better for our son to grow up with a world-language instead of a language that is only spoken in a relatively small area, so we decided to move.

This coincided with the realisation that we couldn't live on land on our savings for ever. Chloe started doing some teaching and I had to start work again. I had done wedding photography throughout my early working career and decided to pick that up again. I already did wedding photography before I did television and I knew how to do it. I thought I would have to fly back and forth to the UK but then I found out that many people come over here for their weddings. The Irish especially love getting married in the Spanish sun. I don't even have to look for work as wedding planners know me and I get more than I can handle. And more importantly I love it.

Things have changed. The status of a wedding photographer has changed. In the Nineties wedding photographers were sort of low class, it wasn't considered creative, and seen as kind of a basic job, a respectable, but dull basic job. Digital photography has changed that completely as you can take so many photos and then get creative with the retouching. Apart from the family group shots, my work can incorporate landscape, food, close-up and still life photography as well as portraits and actuality. Sometimes during a wedding I feel more akin with the paparazzi.

When the bride is coming down the aisle I have to try and get people's expressions. Then you do street photography and candid photography of people together or not together. Doing the romantic portraits is like working on a fashion shoot. There is also the real bonus when you do a good job; they are delighted with it and for the next fifty years you have an audience for what you do and so it lasts for generations to come. That is very important to me. In fact wedding photography has all the creative diversity and fulfilment a photographer could wish for. I like people and portrait photography and I actually feel it is a very exciting and gratifying job. I don't necessarily think it is an easy job, as it can be stressful with its very long hours and because you cannot have a 'bad day' - that could mean you have ruined a wedding. In television it doesn't matter so much if you have a bad day one day and a good day the next. However, despite that 'stress' I am a lot happier here. It helps having a lot of sunshine, of course!

We have now been living in La Herradura since 2010. It is the right size for me. I love it here. The people are nice and as long as they don't hate me I am happy. You will always be a foreigner, but as long as we get on well that is fine. They are nice to us and we are nice to them. I never really belonged to anything. I was born working class and through a process of going to university I have become middle class in many of my values, but I still love the typical English egg and chips with loads of ketchup. All that is fine by me.

I feel comfortable in La Herradura. I have been living around the world so much that I cannot say that I am from a certain town or even country, but at the moment I am from La Herradura and when I drive down from the motorway I think *Wow, I live here!*"

Bob Long - www.spanishweddingphotos.com

Sharing reflections

We first met at a Japanese Buddhist meeting in a house in the Punta de La Mona where she lived with her partner and young son. I immediately felt a warm feeling towards her, probably because - apart from the friend who introduced me to the group - she seemed to be the most 'normal' person in the room. Now I know that's not exactly a very Buddhist thing to say, and many could argue that I am not exactly all that 'normal' myself but that's how I felt. I had come to the right place and now, four years later, we meet again at the local *Mercado municipal* in the village.

It's the indoor open market place on the *Paseo* with various fish, deli, fruit, vegetable counters and a flower stall in front of the entrance. Many Spanish towns and villages have these covered markets. However, La Herradura has a lot more to offer. There is a range of welcoming small shops to get your freshly baked bread, fresh fruit and vegetables and the other things that make life more pleasurable scattered around the village. You can find most of them in or near Av. Prieto Moreno and Calle Acera del Pilar as well as in or near Calle Alhambra and Plaza Nueva. It pays to go for a nice village walk to explore all the products that locals are offering in their shops.

But today Chloe and I make our way to the beach front to enjoy a tea and a chat at one of the beachfront cafes, where I listen to her pleasant voice as she tells her story.

"We have recently moved to the Peña Parda area and love it there. It is like a small enclave that feels like a jungle with high trees and bushes growing on and around the side. It is called El Ensueño which literally means The Dream. To me it is an enchantment. You can see the sea through the trees from our home that is sort of hidden in nature, quite rough and at the same time it has lots of light and life. We are living in the downstairs part of the house and have upstairs neighbours with whom we share a garden with a pool. It is our hideaway. We have to take a very bumpy road with lots of pot holes to get to the house but we don't mind and when I've got time I love to walk to the village. It is a wonderful walk, listening to the birds and watching the natural beauty.

I was born in El Hierro in the Canaries. My dad is French and my mum is Dutch and Swedish but she was brought up in England. My parents lived and worked in the Canaries as subsistence farmers, which is a type of farming that provides enough food for the farmer and his family but not much to sell. Our small house had no electricity or running water and the floor was made of compacted dung. We lived there till I was two years old but even when I go back now and I smell the goats it floods me with some buried nostalgia and I just start crying. I have a lot of sensory memories of the place like the smells and the sounds. When I was two years old I moved with my mum to London. I grew up both in South East England and in France.

My partner and I have a son together, Pancho, who was born in Barcelona. We were living in Sitges on a boat and we loved life there. Sitges is quite a special place and I was working as an English teacher and creating paintings for my book, and Bob, my partner, was travelling, doing freelance documentaries. But one day, one of my students, a Major in the Spanish air force, who came from a small village in the Alpujarras, told me about Andalusia. He said, 'You have to go there' and we did just that, without any good reason at all. When people asked me 'Why are you moving' I couldn't tell them, but it was the best move of my life. I feel more at home than I've ever felt anywhere else. To me Andalusia is so open and you feel so close to the earth. The people are also different from those in Catalonia. It was only because we heard that there was a great school for our son that we discovered La Herradura. We commuted to the school from Almuñécar to La Herradura for a year but then we felt drawn to come and live here. This we did in 2010.

There is definitely something special about this village. All my life I have been a bit of an outsider and I was seen as quite weird or unacceptably different in the villages and towns where I'd lived. Here people are just so into their families and their own lives that I don´t feel judged in any way. This is very remarkable to me as I have never been anywhere so unpretentious in my life. All things considered I think that Spain in general is very unpretentious, but here, it is as if people are happy to let me get on with my own thing without judging me and that gives me a sense of being accepted. Moreover it is a very peaceful place and since I can be quite manic this is good for me. One of my big lessons in life is to slow down and not feel like I need to produce so much. La Herradura has allowed me to be myself more. Being in such a beautiful place forces you to look around you and enjoy the scenery, wonderful beaches, the light …

Our lives have definitively changed. I now work with my partner covering weddings. My main task is to shoot the wedding videos, but I am also working on getting my life coaching business up and running. In addition I am trying to market the book that I've written. It is a children's story called *The Power of Me*. The illustrations are by me. It is about a boy's journey learning the power and effect that he has on his environment and on a larger scale on the whole planet. The book is in rhyme, one long poem. One day I would like to have it translated into Spanish as well. My Spanish isn't bad but I couldn't do that myself. What prompted me to write this book is the lethargy and a sense of hopelessness that I see in people around me; their feelings of impotence in the face of all the negative and overwhelming current events that are going on in the world: that, and a great desire to paint. Writing the book has given me enormous pleasure and I look forward to finding the time to write my next book as I certainly intend to write more and would love to see where the future will take me.

Communication has always been my thing. The medium is not so important. I studied contemporary media practice at university and documentary is an incredibly powerful medium to communicate with, and potentially touch millions of people in one go. It has sounds, rhythm, narrative, images and it can be quite challenging thinking of all those things at the same time when you are filming and it is very stimulating. I've been lucky enough to be able to follow my curiosity working on projects such as a photographic exhibition of the political situation in Tibet, a documentary on hostesses in Tokyo and a charity advert in Bosnia.

Before we came to Spain I worked for a BBC documentaries unit as a researcher and D.V. director in the UK. This was a very specific unit which gave contributors a great deal of power over how they were represented. The idea was to find the stories that hadn't been told about ordinary people doing extraordinary things. I met Bob there. He was the head of that unit. We realised that within the world of documentary it was getting harder and harder to make anything that wasn't driven by the lowest common denominator – that's to say – pleasing the maximum number of viewers whilst not really saying very much. Managers wanted to be assured of the success and the outcome of a documentary before it was made – no risk, whereas of course if you're really doing investigative journalism that's impossible. They were increasingly obsessed with reaching high viewing figures, and that the contributors' stories should all have happy endings – but life's not always like that and basically a watering-down process was going on. We worked very hard for a long time on a series of programmes following a specialised department of the London police force working on paedophilia and child murder. It was an incredible experience but after that we felt that it was time for a big change. So we set off into the sunset on Bob's Scottish fishing boat and sailed to Spain.

I fully intend to go back to some different form of documentary communication when my son leaves home, when I can devote proper time to it. That world of work demands so very much of a person's time and consciousness and at the moment the most important thing is for me to be a good mum. As far as documentary is concerned – and in fact any other medium, I feel strongly about using the specific 'communicative power' that is there to be able to influence people's lives in a positive way. It is very effective. Our last documentary helped change the law in the UK, making 'paedophile grooming' of children a crime. When something is put together well, it can have a life changing effect.

At the moment we mainly do wedding videos and photography. At home I work on retouching and improving the photos before they go into albums, but my work during the wedding day is making the video documentary. During my filming I try to create a family biography, documenting all the people and the feel of the day which one day will evoke priceless memories. What inspires me to work the rather long, hard days and to keep going is wanting to reflect back to people how great they are, and their unique characters, dynamic, humour and deep affections for each other. I encourage them to share their advice for a successful relationship and managing life's ups and downs – this can be very touching, I really enjoy creating relationships with them that encourage them to be uninhibited on camera. There are great opportunities for beautiful representations of the scenery thanks to the light and colours here. Filming the weddings is a way to survive financially, but it is also rewarding to put my creativity to the test. I enjoy this challenge. Potentially every shot is not only a great memory but also a beautiful image.

We can find beauty in life no matter what circumstances we find ourselves in and sometimes events can lead to an outcome you do not necessarily expect but it is either a learning process or a positive change. Everything influences and changes us and working in corporate London gave me an insight into the kind of life that wasn't healthy and that I didn't want. I have been lucky enough to have travelled quite a lot and have met people who have been through incredible hardships but bear them with such grace and wisdom that I am inspired to share with other people. It also puts my own life into perspective and makes me realise how lucky I really am.

Something that has definitively influenced me is that I have been brought up as a Buddhist. It has had a major impact on my life. Seeing the potential and the interconnectedness of everyone and everything has also influenced my book and the way I automatically respond to representing an image, making a video or a documentary. I very much believe that everything and everybody has something special and beautiful in them and that we all have a lot, not only to give, but also to learn from each other. This is more important than anything else. Buddhism teaches you to be profoundly you and use your own creativity to create the life that is right for you – this also sends out waves of benefit to those around you. As far as La Herradura is concerned … I would love for the people of La Herradura to realise that they too are special and that they have an important place in the world. And me? I am simply grateful to be part of this village."

Chloe Pettersson - www.spanishweddingphotos.com

A Dutch interpretation of Spanish beauty

"I love the view, our surroundings, with the Cerro Gordo on our doorstep and a path leading down to a dock by the water. It is a wonderful place to live with my wife and our young son. Today I make my way to the old centre of the village for an interview. I am a bit early for my appointment in Calle Real and walk up the Calle Las Flores. Then I turn into the second street to the right, Calle Granada. There are some new mosaics created with different coloured pebbles on the ground, incorporating village-related designs like an anchor or a horseshoe (herradura means horseshoe). I wander through the first section of this makeover of the old streets, including Calle Blanquita, Calle Canalejas and Calle Principe, to name but a few. Apparently this is just the first phase of the refurbishment of the old part of the village. It is summer 2015 and the renovation, which is a three-phase project, is expected to be finished in three years' time. I think it is an important addition to a village that merits appreciation from cultural tourism.

Fifteen minutes later the interview starts and I am asked to tell my story.

I was born in Weert in the province of Limburg in the Netherlands. I lived there 'til I was eighteen years old. My father was a carpenter and my mother worked in care. I had a younger brother and we were raised in a terraced house in a small village. I have nothing but good memories of my childhood, with football outside the front door and lots of friends. Also, from a very early age I had a fascination for cameras. I remember, when I was ten years old, switching off the colour of the television set to watch films in black and white because I felt the contrast was more beautiful. When I was twelve, during the Dutch Sinterklaas festival* my parents gave me a video 8 camera, a relatively expensive gift and I started shooting lots of home movies - playing Lego with my brother, off to the country side on our bikes, short theatre plays. I would point the camera at my brother and he would point the camera at me, creating simple short films and documentaries. I also had an uncle who worked for a local television station and I was able to work there as a teenager, which was great.

In those years there was a Dutch public broadcasting company called Veronica and they had a youth section. They created and broadcast rather superficial, loud youth television programmes. At one point they offered teenagers the chance to create radio, television and magazine items and to become a member of a group that would actively create television shows. After the first introduction day, I was invited to participate in a training week. I was part of a group of forty teenagers and we were taught by people in the field - professional cameramen, film directors, DJs. This was still part of the selection procedure and only five of us were selected to become part of the official television team. I was one of the successful applicants and the youngest at fifteen years of age.

All credit to my parents who gave me permission, at such a young age, to go away for the entire weekend, every weekend. Each Friday after school I took the train to Hilversum, which was quite far from my home, to create television programmes. There was half an hour airtime per month that we had to fill. We did have a supervisor, but it was still our project. We made some pretty bad programmes and many mistakes, but it was a great learning platform. On Sunday nights I took the train back home to go to school again the next day. When I finished my secondary education at eighteen, it was a logical next step to continue working for Veronica.

I was part of a team that was the breeding ground for the television world in The Netherlands. It was a wonderful experience and I was even sent to America with a camera worth 40,000 euros. I ended up living in Amsterdam and working for various television programmes. This allowed me to collaborate with fantastic professionals in all sorts of programmes such as live concerts and sports programmes. I probably would have continued working there, but Veronica went commercial and suddenly we had to make sponsored programmes and promote commercial products to the viewer. This just didn't feel right to me. I was still young and wanted to travel and study. So when I was twenty I quit my job and went to Australia to travel for six months.

On my return to Holland I wanted to study again and ended up doing film and television studies. That was a great addition to my practical television experience as I learned the history of film, film language and film aesthetics. I learned how to watch films and discovered great directors in the process. During my studies I also started a business as I still had connections in the television world and was regularly asked to direct music clips or do some camera work. I also maintained my love for travelling and whenever my studies allowed I went off to explore the world several times, backpacking.

I also took a gap year and in that year I travelled to Peru and Bolivia. This led to a totally spontaneous chain of events which actually took me to twelve different countries in South, Central and North America. Everything has a reason but I did not see that at the time. Throughout my travels I always had a camera with me and I had the idea of shooting a documentary about backpackers. I feel it is always good to pick a subject with which you have some affinity and I was a backpacker myself. Questions like why someone wants to travel backpacking could reveal some interesting stories. So during my travels I interviewed other backpackers to hear their stories. It was a year's project but it did not have any immediate priority.

In those days I also had connections with the Dutch Aviation Museum, Aviodrome. One day they rang me telling me that they were going on an exciting trip to Venezuela and asked me whether I would be interested in being their cameraman. I was already in South Africa and on their invite I flew to Bonaire where I waited for them to start the expedition. They had heard about the discovery of a crashed Fokker F8 airplane that they wanted to exhibit in their museum in The Netherlands.

We went to the jungle of Venezuela and I recorded the stories and information about the expeditions and search for the apparent wreck. It was like an adventure of Tintin in Venezuela. There were two aviation freaks, the director of the museum and a project manager. When we finally got to the wreck, situated at the end of some sort of landing strip, the plane was totally burnt out with only its frame left. It was very interesting being in stunning nature with a director who certainly would have preferred to sleep in a five-star hotel plus the rest of the team and two interpreters in search of the pilot's chair and other objects. In the end it was a fascinating story as the Indians had taken everything out of the wreck. The chief was sitting on the pilot's chair and objects like fuel and water tanks had become domestic appliances. Everything had been reused. Two years later we went back; this time with a large container and the help of the Venezuela Air Force, to collect all the remains and ship them to the museum in the Netherlands. I created two films of these two trips which were shown in the museum's cinema, to support the exhibition about the airplane. In this way people could watch the story behind recovering the wreckage.

To me travelling and filming is a great combination. After I had completed my studies I started a business with someone from my 'Veronica' past. Our first project was a four month trip to India and China, documenting these upcoming economies. We were filming street-life, everyday life in towns and in the countryside, from rich to poor. These documentaries, 'Made in China' and 'Made in India' were later picked up by an American distribution company and shown in libraries and schools as part of geography classes. This lead to our first well-paid assignment from a travel organisation and we started to specialise in travel movies. We worked for two major travel companies creating around thirty destination films. We were given free rein to shoot the atmosphere of places we went to, like Cuba or Ecuador, not as tourists but more like documentaries without a presenter.

However, the backpacking idea was still very much alive and probably the most ambitious project I have done. I interviewed fifteen people, all with the exact same questions which became an interactive CD-ROM documentary. Following this, together with a colleague, we decided to create a fiction film about backpackers. This became a five year project. I thought scriptwriting was easy and we looked for crew members and the cast on the internet. The conditions were challenging. We had no budget so twelve crew members and five actors from different countries had to go to Peru and Bolivia at their own expense to film the script. They were all young, in their early twenties, all speaking different languages and went travelling for three months to shoot this film.

Our ambition was high. Looking back I can see that I am not a scriptwriter, I am also not a fiction director. At that time I thought I was capable of doing anything but everything that could go wrong went wrong. It was confrontational. In the end, after five years it turned into a good film. It was a story about five backpackers and fourteen crew members. It documented the interactions between people including their arguments. It was a combination of fiction and 'the making of' and was turned into a ninety minute film/documentary which was shown at a number of film festivals and even shown with

Greek subtitling. This was never something that I had intended and it goes to show that your first intention is not necessarily all that important. It certainly has been a very valuable learning process.

Throughout my life there has been that link between travelling and cameras. There are always interesting people to meet and fascinating stories to tell. I like to meet new people and be creative with a camera. Sometimes it is a paid job, sometimes it is my own passion project. Currently I have a Spanish film-production company called Costamundo. For me it is all about 'moving' images. These are at the core of everything I do, in many shapes and forms. With Costamundo we work on television, film, photography, documentary and corporate film projects. I am also involved in a Dutch start-up company called The Postcard Experience which uses film and green screen techniques in a very creative way. Visitors to events or tourist places can act in front of a green screen and are edited into an animated film. These films replace the old-fashioned 'greetings from' postcards and can be shared on social media.

What fascinates me is creating a great shot. I think beautiful photography can be much more difficult than film as you have to tell a story in a single picture. In film you can add multiple shots or music to create a desired effect. I am always fascinated with the perfectly-timed shot, the perfect composition. I like to be surprised by an image. This can be the colour, the exposure or simply an image that grabs me. In a way my inspiration is the sum of what I have learned. This can be a film technique that helps me tell a story or simply the reflection on a leaf that I want to capture in the most beautiful way. I like to work quickly; I don't want to devote an entire day to one shot. This is why I am not a fiction director. I don't want to think too much. It is impulsive inspiration. Just put me on a street corner and I will see a shot.

I don't consider myself to be an artist as I do not create unconditional art. I am the commercially creative guy. I work on commission and then within that commission I try to find the freedom to be as creative as possible. However, I do have plenty of film-related ideas and ambitions. I recently finished a documentary of the Dutch guitarist Tijs Groen who also lives in La Herradura. It started with him telling me that he used to be an athletics champion and how he gave up that career to live in a van in Spain and pursue a musical career as a guitarist. This story resembles the story of many other people I meet here, even my own, slightly; giving up a secure life in your home country to start a new adventure in this beautiful coastal area in southern Spain. So I decided to follow him for a while with my camera and the story developed as we went along. The film is about Tijs but also about La Herradura and the attraction it has for so many creative people from outside of Spain. Because of this, the title of the documentary is *The Horseshoe's Happiness*. I never run out of ideas and one of them is organising a small-scale film festival. I think La Herradura would be a suitable place for this.

We came to La Herradura by accident, or was it destiny? Three years ago my wife was pregnant and wanted to get away for a week for a short vacation. She decided on a surprise trip to this area. We stayed in different towns to get to know the region. We loved it so much that we decided to book a vacation the following year. We booked an apartment online in Almuñécar but we had to go to La Herradura to pick up the key from the sister of the Dutch owner of our apartment. This sister lived in a wonderful house in La Herradura and we immediately fell in love with the bay and the house. We both thought, *Wouldn't it be wonderful to be able to live like this?* We then said, 'Let's not think about it too much, if this is what we want then we have to do it now' so we started the ball rolling. It is hard for some people to understand this. Friends and family asked us, 'Are you going to emigrate?', 'Are you not coming back?' We had discussions trying to explain it. We did not know much about La Herradura but we did like the energy, that 'turquoise feeling' and its perfect location.

We had stayed in contact with the people in La Herradura and when they went back to the Netherlands they contacted us and said 'You can perhaps take over renting the La Herradura house!'

Life is full of surprises. We can now call La Herradura our home and it is a very special place. You cannot exactly put your finger on the 'why'. Surely it is a mix of things, but one thing that struck us as really nice is that the Spanish locals, the Spanish tourists and expats with so many different backgrounds and views on life do not clash. Everything seems very harmonious. This is a mentality that the entire world should adopt and it has sharpened my priorities as well. I also keep discovering interesting facts and events which I like.

Little did we know on that visit in 2013, when we picked up the key for the Almuñécar apartment, that we would end up living in the house that we admired so much. Now we revel in our house, with the wonderful view and surroundings, with the Cerro Gordo on our doorstep and a path leading down to a dock by the water…"

Jeroen Stultiens - www.costamundo.es

* Sinterklaas is a mythical figure with legendary, historical and folkloric origins based on Saint Nicholas, a children's friend. In the Netherlands the festival is celebrated annually with the giving of gifts on the fifth of December, the day before Saint Nicholas Day.

The village photographers

Driving down into the main entrance to the village you enter Avenida Prieto Moreno named after the Spanish architect who left an architectural mark on La Herradura. There are various shops below the apartment blocks on both sides of this road that leads to the seafront. At the seafront end you can find the Civic Centre, a large light terracotta coloured building on the left. Inside, you will find a cinema, showing mostly Spanish language films, a theatre, as well as the local council and the tourist information office. The building also functions as a cultural centre with a small library, a meeting hall for pensioners and quite a few rooms offering space for many different activities, from Rumba, Tai Chi, yoga, meditation with Tibetan bells, art exhibitions as well as the local choir and flamenco dancing. The art exhibitions change regularly so it is a good idea to get into the habit of dropping in on a regular basis to perhaps discover that mind-blowing piece of art that could enhance the beauty of your home.

Some 40 metres before you reach the Civic Centre you will find a photography shop run by Jose and Nihal. You cannot miss it as brides and grooms happily stare out of the windows into the street, smiling and beaming forever, 'frozen in time' on one of the happiest days of their lives. The shop has been there for almost thirty years and Nihal and Jose are familiar faces in the village. They are not originally from La Herradura as Jose was born in Granada in Spain and Nihal in Turkey. They met many years ago during a holiday in Ibiza. At that time they were both living and studying photography in Germany, Nihal in Heidelberg and Jose in Bremen. Nihal went to live in Germany with her parents when she was only two years old. Jose received a three year scholarship to study in Bremen. Both have made their living from photography their entire lives.

Nihal started her career, in Germany, in 1977, providing

publicity photography for important companies. From 1982 till 1985 they ran a photo studio in Ibiza but found it too touristy and came to Spain looking for a better way of life. They found La Herradura more or less by accident. Jose loved the Granada province with its Sierra Nevada and the coastline so in 1986 they came down to the area in search of the right place to set up their shop and studio. The shop was not their main focus; it was the base from which to work. Driving along the coast they found La Herradura. It wasn't contaminated with a lot of tourism and felt like it had something magical that they both loved. The shop in Avenida Prieto Moreno functions mainly as an office as their photographic assignments take them to many different places in Spain as well as internationally. Apart from the usual weddings, baptisms and first communions they are also commissioned to work on a variety of other projects, for example, architectural photography, publicity for hotels and flyers for restaurants and other companies. Nihal specialises in photography and Jose in making video recordings and documentaries. Together, they form a perfect symbiosis covering all aspects of image making to create wonderful memories for their clients. Over the years they have made their name covering many important buildings and events, including publicity for the Alhambra Palace hotel in Granada, operas in Vienna, the coverage of the women´s World Ski Championship in 1994 and later the men´s World Championship in 1996. But they have also received commissioned work in La Herradura for posters for the Holy Week and for the Andres Segovia International Guitar Festival. They feel lucky to have been able to combine their love for travelling and photography in order to create a living. They are also very passionate about nature and about creating ecological documentaries, mostly for personal pleasure, not necessarily for work.

There are some older documentaries that can be seen

online, for instance, a documentary made for Polish television about the Polish writer Jerzy Pietrkiewicz who lived in La Herradura and who was famous for having translated the poems of the Polish Pope John Paul II. There is also a documentary about the village called *La Herradura, Paraiso Tropical* with lovely Spanish guitar music in the background and recent and not-so-recent images of the village and its surroundings, which paint a picture of both the past and the present.

Lately they have been embarking on shooting shorter music videos of which *Take my wave*, featuring Charly Endres and Lino Díaz is a good example (available on YouTube). Perhaps they are reinventing themselves or simply following a natural path of depicting the world in a way they know best. A world of images.... like those of brides and grooms in a village shop window.

Jose y Nihal - www.joseynihal.com

Saving the rhinos

"It is a beautiful day in May; I fancy a nice walk, just to take in the views, feeling the energy, smelling the plants, listening to the silence that becomes a symphony of nature. Searching for that Zen feeling, a moment of solitude and a desire to observe the abundance in the gifts of Mother Nature, soaking up the beauty of butterflies, the many shades of green bushes and leafy trees and plants waving in the wind, buzzing insects and birds of different song, size and shape. I walk past a few white Spanish villas enveloped in their verdant surroundings. I love walking, I love hiking. I consider this a short hike from the La Peña Parda end of the Herradura beach to the Cantarriján beach and now on my way back again. The area is part of the Cerro Gordo National Park. After a fifteen minute intense walk I stop and look out to the sea. I notice the crystal clear turquoise coloured water near the coast and more indigo coloured water further towards the horizon. I know the water in and around the caves hidden down the rocks of the Cerro Gordo is teeming with fish and occasionally attracts dolphins visiting the bay close to the beaches. I spot a group of these beautiful mammals gliding through the sea, a spectacular sight and fairly rare. Overfishing is possibly a sad reason why this has become a rather uncommon sighting. However, when going out on a sailing trip you can be lucky and enjoy the company of some of these natural wonders. Witnessing them fills me with a sense of wonder and happiness. I sit down on a rock to watch them disappear into the distance and sense a moment of being completely in the here and now. It is easy to be grateful. After a while the dolphins leave the scene and I feel myself drift away in contemplation …

My name is Charles George Jackson but people call me Charlie. I am from London, born in Paddington. When I was still a small child, my mum, my two siblings and I, left London to go and live in the countryside where my mum had bought an old Tudor cottage. My mother was a famous model and my dad was a property developer. They got divorced when I was only two years old. So I grew up on the farm, surrounded by creativity as my mum did pottery, ceramics and she also painted.

When I got older I went to prep school and I vividly remember the interesting head master of the school Mr Hooper. He used to wear starched yellow shorts and absolutely loved Kenya. He was the brother-in-law of Mr. Craig who was the owner and founder of Lewa Downs Wildlife Conservancy. The school was a lovely school that I liked very much and where the seed for my passion for wildlife was planted. After this I went to a place called Wellington College, a military type school. I left this school when I was seventeen and went to college in Winchester to study English and Art. Following my studies I moved to Fulham in London where I worked as a model for three years. I was working for *Models One*, doing really well and featured in many interesting magazines, like GQ magazine. However, it wasn't the direction that I wanted to take in life.

I left London and went to Sussex where my mum lived. She had remarried to Robin Adshead, a distant cousin and a very interesting man. He was a Gurkha, an English commissioned officer and a major in the Gurkha army (Brigade of Gurkhas is the collective term for units of the British Army composed of Nepalese soldiers). Whilst he was in the army he developed a passion for photography and became friends with Larry Burrows, who was a famous war photographer. When Robin left the army he then became a photo journalist. At a later stage Robin worked for Aviation Week and other magazines and travelled extensively. I was hugely inspired by him and when I had moved back home I changed from being a model in front of the camera to being the person on the other side. I understood how people felt in front of the camera and it gave me the necessary insight to create the right image from behind the camera. You look at a situation, at the composition and the light in the eyes. The model knows what to give and what is going to work but the photographer has to reflect that. Robin gave me my first camera, a Canon, and he taught me how to use it. We went out on many trips together.

In 2001 my mother and Robin decided to come and live in Spain. They had heard about La Herradura from a woman called Jane Roland who had a hotel in Sussex where we used to go when we were still young children and who had moved here. My mum and Robin came to visit her and loved it. Robin loved the area as it reminded him of the terraced mountains in Nepal - these and the mountain tracks are very similar to the landscape in the vicinity of La Herradura. You can find the rock steps if you go to the *Junta de los rios* or the *Caminito del Rey*, it is like being in Nepal. The bay of La Herradura also reminded Robin of the bay of Hong Kong where he had lived for a long time. Robin has had an incredible life and to this day he has a permanent exhibition of his photographic images in the military museum in Hong Kong. I moved with them to La Herradura when I was twenty-one years old.

Robin my stepfather was the most amazing man. He gave me the gifts of peace and the ability to believe in myself. I would go as far as to say that he, but also my mother, an absolute angel - who looked after me through everything, probably saved my life by standing by me in times when I could have taken the wrong path. Both Robin and my mother had a very spiritual outlook on life and that has also shaped me to a great extent. Robin sadly died in 2007. I now consider La Herradura my base as I want to be close to and look after my mother.

I dedicate much of my time to graphic design and photography and travel a lot as I have a passion for travelling and discovering beauty all around the world.

When we were young children we travelled a lot as well, to (amongst other places) Canada and France where my dad's family lived. What certainly marked my life were several trips to the *Lewa Wildlife Conservancy*, also called *Lewa Downs*, in northern Kenya, originally the oldest cattle ranch in East Africa. It has been run by the Craig family since 1922 who were great conservationists. They have always valued the wildlife that shared the land with their cattle and developed wildlife tourism as an additional activity to farming.

The late Anna Merz, a wildlife conservationist with a particular passion for rhinos, who died in 2013, felt that the only way to prevent the complete extinction of the endangered black rhino was to create high-security sanctuaries to protect them. She decided to approach David Craig in the early 1980s to ask him for his permission to build such a sanctuary on his land and together the Craigs and Anna Merz – who funded the programme – laid the foundations for what was then known as the Ngare Sergoi Rhino Sanctuary.

Anna Merz was an astonishing, feisty woman and working with the Craigs, she recruited bush pilots, game-trackers, veterinarians and others to round up animals which they tracked, captured and relocated to the refuge for breeding and safekeeping. To help the animals get used to their new environment in holding pens, apparently Anna Merz would spend hours reading Shakespeare to them, which she claimed, completely tamed them.

Since it was established in 1983, the *Ngare Sergoi Rhino Sanctuary* now known as Lewa, has gone from strength to strength and is now considered to be the pioneer private wildlife sanctuary in East Africa. It has grown into a non-profit wildlife conservancy which has gained a world-wide reputation for the protection of various endangered wildlife species, not just the rhinos. It has been visited by Prince Charles and on 19th October 2010, his son Prince

William of Wales proposed marriage to Catherine Middleton at Lewa in a year in which 13% of Kenya's rhino population lived in the conservancy.

Anna Merz known locally as *Kifaru,* Kiswahili for 'mother of the rhino', has left behind a lasting legacy and her love and passion for wildlife has inspired people around the world, including me and other members of my family. I am part of a large family as Robin, my stepfather, had two sons and my father had three children with his first wife before marrying my mother, and then having three children of their own of which I am the youngest. We are all fascinated by wildlife. Ben my full brother moved to Africa more than 20 years ago, when he was twenty-one, and has built his own company there. He lives there to this day. Before he went there we were already going to Lewa on holidays. My oldest sister Emma is married to Will Craig of *Lewa Downs.*

I have continued going there as well, taking pictures of the wildlife and of the tribes that live very close to Lewa. For example in the northern part of Kenya, close to the border with Somalia, you can find many amazing tribes like the Masai and Samburu tribes.

I have become a professional photographer shooting pictures during my trips, which include an amazing canoe adventure in Canada and a trip to Tanzania to visit *Greystoke Mahala,* a very famous chimpanzee conservation effort which was built by my brother Ben. During my travels I document my photos in a journalistic style. My work has been exhibited, amongst other places, in Copenhagen and London and of course in La Herradura. I have a website from where I sell my work, but I also sell by handing out business cards, through word of mouth, via contacts from friends and through art dealers. I am building a stock library for my work as well. I offer photo journalism, abstract landscapes, fashion, and profile photography for business promotion. Exhibitions are separate from all this.

My next trip back to Kenya is to the coast, to Malindi, north of Mombasa, to take pictures in the Indian Ocean and after that I will go to Rwanda. Ben, my brother is now working on a conservation project there. It is also one of my personal dreams to spend some time with the mountain gorillas in Rwanda. Their aura is so enormous that it will be an honour to be with them. Part of my work is to express the beauty of Africa and how much we need to conserve it. I also believe that education lies in travelling as it gives you connection with other cultures which will help you to get a better understanding of the world.

So my life is pretty intense, but my base is La Herradura. I love it here. It actually has ley lines, which are alleged alignments of ancient sites or holy places, such as stone circles, running through the village which, in my opinion, explains why it attracts a lot of artists, musicians, writers and other weird people ... interesting weird people. La Herradura is also peaceful and somewhat of a secret. When we moved here I soon met people in the local music scene and started playing with Tony Turner in a bar called Oasis which was located in Calle Real. I have been playing the guitar since I was twelve. We held jam sessions there on summer nights a few years ago. Tony mainly played folk music and I played blues and we jammed for three or four hours at a time with a lot of improvisation, which I love. All sorts of people joined in.

We didn't play for money, just because we loved it. It was brilliant, people singing, playing saxophone and guitar and bass... there was no ego involved. This then slightly changed as it became more about money, but by then the scene had been created. La Herradura is now a place with lots of live music venues and concerts. I've been playing with many musicians and my girlfriend Victoria is a fantastic singer so we are working on a gig which will also involve Charly Endres.

My life is about art to a great extent as I also like to draw. I love anything artistic, music, art, but for me photography and photo journalism are the best. You can do so many different styles and tell stories. On my website there is a black and white photo. It portrays a person calling out on his mobile for help standing on a piece of rock in the middle of some grass land, but when you look carefully you see that everything around him is on fire. When you know the information behind an image you can discover so many things. In my opinion, if any art brings out a feeling or it evokes a sensation it means it works. So you cannot say it is bad or not.

As far as my work is concerned and generally speaking I hope I can show the beauty of things and educate with what I do. You could say that there is an environmental message in my work. Take for example the rhinos. I have an absolute passion to educate people about them. They are shot and killed for such nonsensical reasons. Their horn is considered to be a fever reducer, like an aspirin, but an aspirin works better and because of its rarity the horns' worth is now higher than gold. I wish people could realise what an amazing, prehistoric animal they are putting to the edge of extinction.

If I had to describe myself as an artist I would say that I try to reflect the truth and the beauty of what I see. As a photographer I am very much influenced by David Yarrow, a great landscape photographer and Steve McCurry, an amazing portrait photographer among other things and who is famous for his photographs of the Afghanistan woman with the green eyes, both as a child and as an adult woman. My inspiration is all about where you are at a certain time. For example, the light in Africa is wonderful and it is very difficult to take a bad picture, so it is in fact about being in the right place at the right time, in dusk and dawn atmospheric light for example. So you could say that what inspires me is being in an inspiring place.

I think that my overall message to others is to keep searching because waiting for the right moment, or giving into fear can hold you back. As a famous self-help book title says, 'Feel the fear but do it anyway.' If you take that necessary step and actually do it, it usually turns out a lot easier than you think. I suggest travelling as it will change your life for the better. The beauty of what you see in my pictures or the beauty you will see in your own pictures is all part of your journey and it documents your life.

As I have travelled so much I have been fortunate enough to see many places and get to know many cultures, but I do love Spain, and particularly La Herradura. Living in this village and the surrounding area has calmed my soul. When I go away on my travels I love coming back here as it has a Zen feeling. I believe that the ley lines have both a calming and an unsettling effect and it is a constantly evolving village. People come and go, but usually very interesting people, whether artistic or pleasantly strange. The village has changed me in many ways; it has healed me and it has given me a lot of peace.

I make my way back down to the beach and ponder about my wish for the village. I would love for La Herradura to remain the secret that it still is, at the same time I would like it to be recognised for what it is, an amazing artistic haven, but I also want it to keep its charm. You know what … I am sure the ley lines will see to that!"

Charlie Jackson - www.charliegjackson.com

Flamenco passion

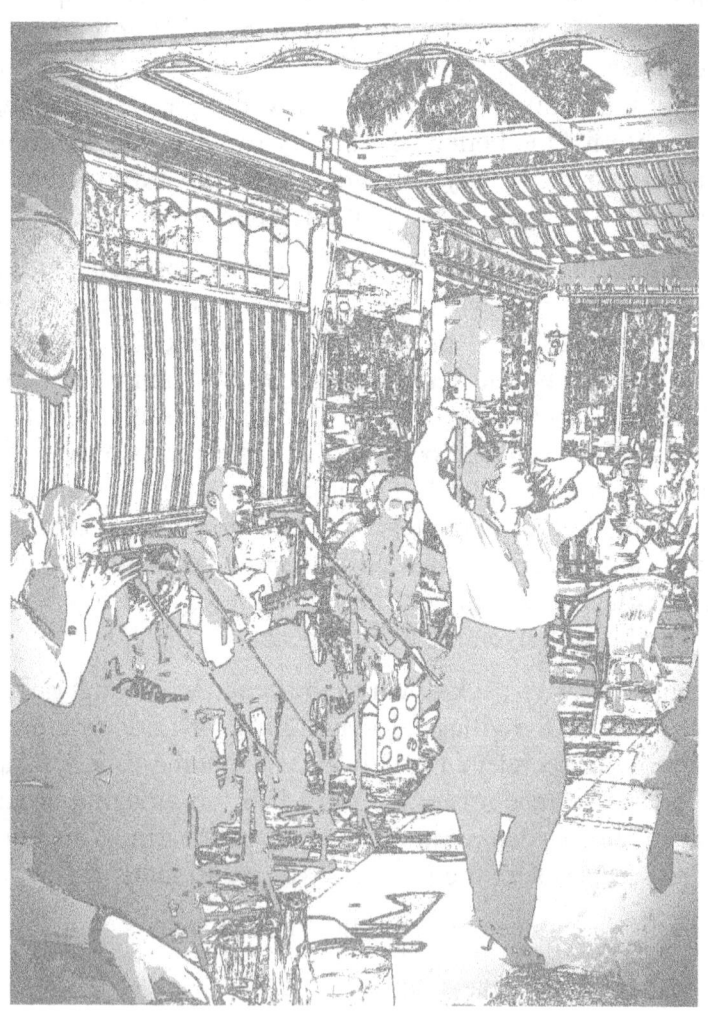

A guitar maker's dream

It was 1988. I was driving in my trusty 2 CV car, seats taken out, laden with tools and wood, crossing the Pyrenees. I had worked in Italy for a while but wanted to visit Spain in search of flamenco. I made my way to Barcelona and from there to Madrid. Then I drove down to Cordoba where I participated in a two week course with Paco Peña, a flamenco guitarist and teacher who was very well known both in and outside Spain. He had moved to London in the Sixties and was one of the top flamenco players there. It was the start of my real flamenco experience. After Cordoba I drove further south through Sevilla, then Ronda and on past Nerja and I must have driven right through La Herradura, but I have no recollection of the village then. I continued on to Salobreña and then up to the Alpujarras. From there I went right over the Sierra Nevada and stopped at the foot of the summit, parked my car and walked to the top of Mulhacén. It was extraordinary. I stood on the roof of the world in Spain and could see for miles, I could even see Africa. I drove down the other side to Granada, which was my destination; the mysterious, fabulous city of Granada, full of guitar makers with its memories of the Moors, those Arabs from Morocco who built the famous and mesmerisingly beautiful historic palace and fortress of the Alhambra. I stayed in Granada for a month and it was a very romantic experience. I met a lot of guitar makers and was inspired to really make my dream of becoming a full-time guitar maker come true. On arriving back in England I set up my workshop and started my career as a professional guitar maker.

I returned to Spain many times for holidays and was always drawn to Granada. Then the continued longing to actually work and live in Spain started to become so strong that I decided to take a life-changing step. It was 2004. My criteria were to have my base in the province of

Granada, to be by the sea, close to an international school for my son, and close to airports. La Herradura's connection to Andrés Segovia and the fact that his presence in the village had inspired a group of people to start an international guitar competition, endorsed by Segovia, made it an obvious choice. La Herradura ticked all the boxes. The guitar competition that takes place in November every year attracts world class players to the village and I knew it would be great for me to meet those guitarists. Part of the reason why this attracted me was that for a number of years I was well used to meeting great players through my work as one of the directors of the *Lewes International Guitar Festival* in the UK. All my life has been about music, it is a very important part of my life, not just flamenco music but any music that has been born out of the everyday culture of a society, whether that is Bulgarian, South American, Indian, Irish. If you go back to the original source of each country you will eventually find their musical treasure - deep expressions of the endless human struggle but also celebrations of life. This fascinates me.

When I was a child my parents had an amazing collection of world music, Greek, Mexican, Indian but also flamenco. I remember listening to Cante Jondo flamenco as a very young child - basic, proper singing and flamenco guitar. It sparked something in me and when I was eight years old I had my first classical guitar lesson. I left school when I was sixteen and immediately went working in a traditional furniture-making workshop, starting my lifelong connection with wood. I moved with my parents from London to the south of England where they started one of the first bio-organic farms in the country which was quite revolutionary in those days. It was 1976. I was surrounded by huge oak and elm trees, so beautiful. When I started working with wood I realised what was inside these wonderful trees and my love for this treasured resource began.

When I was seventeen I read information about Subud, an international organisation of people who share a spiritual experience based on human behaviour, inner force and surrender to the highest power, whether that is the divine, God, Allah, Brahman and more. My parents were involved in this organisation, but at the time I was an anarchist punk! Reading about the Subud experience seemed to awaken a need in me to follow a more spiritual path in my life and it also brought me back to music. It was a profound turning point in my life. Although I had not played the guitar for about two years, I started taking guitar lessons again. My teacher had the most beautiful classical guitar made by an English guitar maker. He used beautiful woods and inside he had his own label. I realised this guitar was built by a true artisan, made with love, passion and a deep connection with the Spanish tradition, not made in a factory. This is when I knew I wanted to build guitars. It was 1985. I participated in a couple of guitar-making courses and even worked for a violin maker in England. Around the same time I was also reintroduced to flamenco music, I heard it somewhere and it was if that music had been buried within me all along. I recognised it at a deep level and it was a very strange moment in my life, listening to music that I had heard so often when I was a child. I became completely obsessed with flamenco. By 1988 I had already built my first flamenco guitar, which I brought with me when I first came to Spain. In Spain I really began to soak up the atmosphere of the Spanish workshops. It was like a pilgrimage. The smell of cedar, cypress and rosewoods was intoxicating. The hot glue, the alcohol and French polish entered all my senses and ignited a passionate ambition to develop a workshop environment for myself. I loved the connection between the raw material and the end result.

I get my wood from Madrid or Valencia, but it originates from all over the world - the Swiss Alps, Southern India,

Brazil, Central America, Canada, Africa, even England. Different guitars ask for different types of wood. Traditionally the flamenco guitar is made of Spanish cypress on the back and sides and Alpine spruce or pine on the front, ebony from India or Africa on the fingerboards and South American cedar on the necks. It is actually rather interesting in my view that around 1850, the difference between a classical and a flamenco guitar was purely a question of economics. The gentry did not play flamenco but played transcriptions of Tarrega, music from Granada on expensive Brazilian rosewood guitars. Not the Spanish cypress and cheap pine wood of the flamenco guitar. Flamenco was the music of the poor.

I love working by hand to produce something that I consider of deep value in today's society, a musical instrument. Each guitar is different and very personal. It is signed, dated and numbered on the label. Sometimes they get names if they have inspired something particular in me during the construction. Sometimes it feels like magic. A guitar for a client is a very personal thing. It is like an arranged marriage, to receive a guitar that has been ordered a year previously and suddenly it is there, waiting for the touch of the player, who then in his or her turn can either transform that guitar to an elevated level through playing or neglect it and thus it suffers. It is a flowing process.

I believe the sound of a beautiful Spanish guitar has a unique effect on the human psyche; it evokes mystery, sadness, pain, love and also sublime joy. I am always questing after the perfect sound. My inspiration comes not only from the love of the raw material and its tonal possibilities but also directly from the player himself. The purchaser is part of my inspiration in building it. Before I start on the guitar I have a conversation with its future owner. My workshop space is like a shrine, a holy place where I can work and create. I used to work in isolation, on my own, sometimes not leaving my workshop for two days. Then, someone asked me whether I could teach him to make a guitar. It was 1993. I turned into a teacher and had my first guitar-making student. Since then my workshop has slowly developed into the European Institute of Guitar Making and teaching my craft is now an important part of what I do. I receive people from all over the world who want to have the experience of working in Spain and building their own guitar. Traditionally it can be hard to find someone who is willing to share the mysterious art of guitar making as it is usually passed on from father to son. However, my philosophy is that if I keep this art to myself then it could well die with me... I can't presume my children will take it on. I feel it is my responsibility to bring to the world the recognition of a beautiful tradition.

Through my courses I bring a lot of people to the village, they often come with their partners and love spending a month in this welcoming, beautiful village. Some of them even stay and build new lives here, usually becoming close friends with my wife and me. La Herradura has changed my life. I appreciate the Spanish way of life. It is so unhurried and lacks stress. When I first came here I spent about a year and a half working in the mountains in the tiny hamlet of El Rescate. On the old road from la Herradura in the direction of Nerja you take the Cuesta de Marchante exit to the right. A scenic rural road takes you uphill and over the mountain, a slightly hair raising journey, passing the hamlet of El Cerval where you can visit a charming tiny shrine. The natural surroundings are breath-taking. Each bend in the road treats you to numerous jewels of nature then you reach the hamlet of *La Joya de Rescate*. A few more bends later you arrive in what used to be the centre of the area, El Rescate, which is in close proximity to Peña Escrita, the peaks from which the Rio Jate (Jate River) flows down the valley.

It was an amazing experience, making contact with the few local people still living there. During the tourist boom in the Seventies and Eighties many had left, often abandoning their houses, to work in the village. I was told that during the Fifties, Sixties and Seventies it was the centre of the entire area with a shop, a bar, an olive mill - a self-sustaining community trading with the coast, bartering fish, eggs, flour, etc. People travelled down to La Herradura and across the hills to Almuñécar on mules. Life in El Rescate was rich but tough in those days. I talked to the locals about my romantic view of living in the hamlet as an artisan, wondering how anybody would give up such a perfect life for work on the seafront. They explained to me that crops sometimes failed and then they didn't have enough to eat. And the water coming down from a spring above the village would sometimes dry up during the summer and they had to go down to the Jate River to get their water. It could be harsh. I humbly realised that my romantic ideas were just that. I had no idea how hard life could be and that living in a village with running water, food in the supermarkets and work in the fields of construction or tourism was a logical choice. Interestingly though, due to the economy slowing down there is currently a resurgence of life in these mountain hamlets. Some people seem to realise what they used to have, an opportunity to work the land and to be more self-sufficient. This time life is a bit easier as most people have a 4x4 car at their disposal.

I now also have my workshop in the village. La Herradura has been good to me. Apart from setting up my workshop here I remarried and I became a father again, of a lovely little girl. We now raise four children between us. Marjolein, my wife, and I have been involved in various initiatives such as the *Starfish* project which helps to give children a chance to make music and the 'Eco Huerto' project, an educational resource for children which helps them to understand a balanced view of life, namely the ability to work with the land as well as pursuing other careers.

I also run a Guitar masters series called *Maestros de la Guitara*. We invite world-class classical guitar players to la Herradura to give concerts. I am not officially involved in the Andrés Segovia festival, but unofficially I have been in contact with almost all the players. The organisation is a very local affair and they are doing a fantastic job. However, I would like to see it grow into a bigger festival, drawing more people to the village, with masterclasses, concerts and the competition. Through contacts I've made during the *Andrés Segovia festival* I was invited to go to Moscow some years ago and I am now one of the patrons of the *Alexander Frauchi International Guitar Competition*, where the winner receives one of my guitars as part of the first prize.

I do feel that I am fulfilling my life's destiny and that is something that I would like to inspire others to do as well - find time, before it is too late, to develop the artistic side of yourself, be it music, working with your hands, anything that inspires you...and helps you to balance yourself. In my view each single person on this planet has their own unique talent and it is important to try and discover that talent even in the midst of making money, taking care of the family and tackling all the stresses and strains of modern life. Achieving balance can sometimes seem impossibly difficult as we often get stuck in the cycle of money making and all the things we have to do to survive, but we can change our values; appreciate what we have; find that moment of peace; connect with nature; find the time to talk to your neighbour and reach out to others. I think La Herradura makes this possible for people and I feel it will become more and more a village where people live from the heart and realise their dream. Like I am, living the guitar-maker's dream."
Stephen Hill - www.europeaninstituteofguitarmaking.com

In mind, body and soul

It is getting busy in the restaurant. Most of the tables have a piece of paper with the words 'Reserved' on them. The musicians are busy setting up their instruments. A tiny wooden dance floor has been put down behind the four chairs for the performing artists. It is Sunday afternoon, almost two o'clock, the usual time for the Spanish to have their lunch, and people start ordering their food. The waiters are friendly and quick. It is a fixed event, every Sunday afternoon in Las Maravillas on the seafront where Pablo Escudero and fellow musicians give a flamenco show. His partner Diana accompanies him with her singing and with *palmas* (hand-clapping). Today it is a fusion session with a talented violinist. Pablo is singing and playing the guitar whilst a pretty girl in a typical flamenco outfit seems ready to dance her way into the hearts of the captive audience. 'Olé'

Pablo's story

"My love for flamenco music came from my grandfather, Manolo Escudero. He was a successful flamenco singer and has five records to his name which he recorded with an important Spanish label. He played with well-known flamenco singers, for example, Juanito Valderama, Lola Flores and Argentina Imperio. My grandfather made his living as a singer. He was famous and also appeared on television, but I was personally never allowed to go to his shows as he had divorced my grandmother before I was even born. However, he was the reason why I got into flamenco music. He left a guitar for me in the house of my grandmother. Had he left a piano or another instrument, perhaps my life would have looked different. But he didn't and it did get my interest in flamenco going. Possibly you could also say that it is in my blood, in the blood of my family. I am now passing on this love of music to my daughter of a previous marriage who is a very good singer at only nine years of age. I seriously started playing the guitar when I was ten years old. I was taught by great teachers, among whom was Juan Maya Marote. When I was slightly older I became part of a group of singers that was fairly well-known in Granada with Iván Vallejo. At a later stage I participated in a project with the Town Hall of Motril that gave special opportunities to children in schools in different poorer districts by providing them with dance classes, singing classes and music classes like percussion and guitar. I chose the guitar. I was fourteen years old. It was a great experience and at some point the most advanced students of three or four districts were formed into a group. I was in that group for about three years and I learned a lot about flamenco, how to accompany others and how to play or sing in the background. This refers to playing with someone who is dancing. They say that if a singer knows how to be the lead singer, he also needs to be capable of being a background singer. This is actually more difficult as you depend on the dancer. The dancer is the one who decides. You need to take the rhythm from the dancer. If you are good at playing and singing in the background then you also know how to be the lead singer. I love playing the guitar but I predominantly consider myself to be a singer because I have done a lot more singing. Flamenco has been a dominant factor throughout my life. I was always listening to it and I remember that, at twelve or thirteen years old, I fell asleep with a record still playing.

Since I have come to live in La Herradura my life has become even more about flamenco music. This village is inspiring. I was born in Motril but my current partner, Diana is from La Herradura and she is the reason I came here. The village has taken me in in every respect. Apart from the fact that I love living close to the beach and being able to go fishing with a friend, there is a large group of musicians to meet and play with, all with their own particular and distinctive styles of music. They are

Dutch, Spanish, English, German, Cuban... you name it. This variety and level of talent is very unusual for such a small village. Of critical importance here is the fact that we are allowed to play live music in bars and restaurants, not just in the discotheques and music halls. This support by the local government for art in all its forms really caught my attention and it makes it easy to live as a musician and to meet and play with others.

Thanks to La Herradura I have been able to live my dream. Before I came here I had to do other jobs on the side to survive, and I worked as a plumber. Music could only be my hobby. Now I can dedicate all my time to my passion - flamenco! I am a full-time musician! Over the last years my capacity to play the guitar, as well as my singing, have gone through a fantastic evolution and I feel I have grown as an artist. With the help of Diana I am always involved in organising or participating in flamenco spectacles. The village has given me many opportunities and I am very happy and grateful for that.

It is easy to feel inspired here with the beautiful light, the clean air and the pleasant temperature, but also because of its legacy of Manuel 'El Ruso'. Originally people from flamenco circles in Granada did not take much notice of the flamenco singers on the coast. 'El Ruso' certainly played a big role in changing that. He won many competitions throughout Andalusia and was highly esteemed and respected in the flamenco scene. He sang in the style of Malagueña Granadino but also performed some typical La Herradura fandangos. I never met him personally but every year there is a special homage event to 'El Ruso' in the village and I have participated in that. Many young people these days are more involved in the rumba and the *flamenquito* styles which are more modern, but I like to conserve the *flamenco puro* in the style of 'El Ruso' and only want to concentrate on that. I like the *solea, el canto puro* and the *malagueña* and I intend to hand that on so it doesn't get lost. There are about fifty different *palos* in flamenco, but then you also have the style of the performer and geographical influences on styles. When you add all this up there are about two hundred distinctive styles. Learning them all would take a lifetime and so you can never stop learning.

Flamenco contains so much more history than many perceive and most people when they think of flamenco immediately think of gypsies. In Spain they are called *gitanos*, and it is indeed very much part of the gipsy or *gitano* culture. Flamenco was first mentioned in 1774, but because it came from the poorer social classes, and people in those times were largely illiterate, the tradition has been passed on vocally. It is thought that flamenco dance originates from a Hindu tribe in India. Apparently, during wartime, they fled the area and split up. Some of the tribe ended up in northern Europe; including Romania, Bulgaria, France and Germany where they developed a music style that featured a lot of violins; another group went to Africa and from there they ended up in Spain. Apparently *gitano* is a word that means a person who comes from Egypt. Spain at that time was a very religious country and the *gitanos* were persecuted. During the seventeenth and eighteenth century there were already a lot of *gitanos* in Andalusia, many of whom took refuge in the caves in the mountains. They were very poor and mingled with other poor minorities like Muslims, Christians and Jews. They lived peacefully together for 200 or 300 years and influences from other types of music, including Gregorian and Jewish music, changed those original sounds. In Spain flamenco also developed into a combination of singing, guitar music and dance. The mixing of cultures greatly influenced flamenco, but mostly it was a song of protest. The songs were very much from the heart and different *palos* developed. For example, the *martinete* and the *seguiriya* are songs that were mainly sung in prison and lyrics could be about a mother that was unable to visit her son in jail. They were songs against society and against oppression. At a later stage flamenco was also influenced by folk songs typical of people who were working the land, and from mountainous areas and these songs tend to be about love and about pain, the themes of the poor and of *gitanos*.

We are now working on a show called *Trascendencia del Flamenco* and it is about the evolution of flamenco in which people will be introduced to its history through *palos* that we will play in chronological order. In this latest show we can also count on the participation of a great singer, Juan Penilla who is an authority in the flamenco world.

Although flamenco puro is my thing, I also like fusion music a lot. Currently I am working with other musicians on another show that is a mixture of Arab and flamenco music called *Mestizaje Andalusí* and includes instruments such as the violin. It still contains a lot of my favourite types of flamenco music, it could not be any different and I am really happy that, in 2015, we were able to participate in the Jazz Lagos Series, a well-known Jazz Festival in Nigeria. You could say that flamenco lives in my soul, my body and my mind."

Violin music now joins the singing strings of the guitar. Pablo's voice is mesmerising the audience. People listen and watch in fascination. The music gets more intense, the fast movement of the dancer's feet on the wooden floor are hypnotic and the atmosphere is radiant and electric. Pablo's voice fills the pavement café area of the restaurant, and beyond. Passers-by stop and listen to the flamenco spectacle as the wind takes his voice and music to neighbouring establishments. Rhythmic hand clapping, rapid movements of the strings of the guitar and the graceful swirls of the colourful flamenco dress accompany the intriguing violin music... then wind down to a slow dance, very controlled and restrained but full of strength and passion which, after some magical long-lasting minutes, grows into an accelerating rhythm again, ending in a joyful musical climax of song, dance and music…Olé

Pablo Escudero -
https://www.facebook.com/pablo.bravo.9022

My life is flamenco

I am on my way to Plaza Nueva, the main square in the village to meet up with Olga Rodriguéz Garciolo. I enter Calle Las Flores and turn right immediately, passing the guitar-making workshop of Stephen Hill. A few blocks ahead I smile at the ceramic flowers, made by Rosario Gonzalez Torres, below the statue of Pepe Gámez in Calle Canalejos. About ten metres further to the right a few steps down lead to the central square of the village. It is a fairly large open space with a permanent stone stage and surrounded by modern apartment blocks and shops. During the day it can feel somewhat abandoned but on Sundays and during the summer months there is a real buzz in the mornings in front of the tiny *churros* stall. *Churros* are fried-dough pastry snacks and are much loved in Spain. Many dunk them into hot chocolate for that extra bit of sweetness. Throughout the year the plaza comes to life during the evenings when the village mothers come out for a chat and their children can safely run and play on the square. The stage is also used a lot for local festivities, concerts and spectacles. Every Friday there is a weekly market here too which, although it can be reduced to just three or four stalls during the winter, livens up in the summer months when the village bustles with (mainly Spanish) tourists. In July and August the plaza is lit up with lots of artisan stalls exhibiting their often hand-crafted items during the evening hours.

Olga is a young, very pretty, La Herradura born girl who has a passion for dancing. She remembers that she was already dancing when she was three years old. Her mother used to dance a lot and Olga was certainly influenced by that. She attended dance classes with a flamenco dance teacher till she was about sixteen years old and then she went to a dance academy in Almuñécar. On top of that Olga attended many courses all over the region. For quite some years now she has been a dance teacher. In order to do this she has created an association in La Herradura and four days a week she gives classes in the civic centre to children from three years old as well as to adults. Her oldest student is seventy years old. Olga teaches a variety of dances, not limited to just *flamenco puro*. She teaches *sevillana, alegría, tango, bulerías, guajiras, solear*, you name it, including *fandangos, tanguillos and farucas*. She has formed an adult dance group called Alma Flamenca which has already given performances in, for example Barcelona and Morocco as well as in many other towns and villages. This group also performs in large hotels, at local festivals and at private parties. There are thirty girls in the group, but not all of them perform. Some only come to the classes because they like to learn how to dance. Apart from performing to a live audience the group still continues its flamenco training in Malaga. Olga absolutely loves what she does. Dancing gives her complete happiness and seeing little children who are picking up that passion for flamenco is a real joy. "It's as if we are one big family" says Olga. There also are foreign children in the classes and they integrate really well. They might not continue for many years, but some foreign families, who have lived here for a few years, when they come over for a holiday, ask her whether she can give some flamenco dance classes to their children. I ask her where she gets the clothes for the flamenco performances from. "A dressmaker helps us create the dresses for the performances. I tell her what we need, like trousers or dresses and she then makes them" she says. Every year, in April or May, there is a day of performances by all the students that come to the classes, the little ones and the adults. This is always a big event and much loved by everybody. In La Herradura there is not a great history of flamenco dancing, it was mostly singing and El Ruso is a great example of this. During festivities people did dance, but this was usually the *fandango cortijero* which is a type of *sevillana* dance for both adult women and men. It is not flamenco, but it does bear some similarities.

Olga also likes to sing and is learning how to improve her guitar playing skills. She is part of a group called La Chirigota. This is a group formed by musicians and singers that performs during carnival - mainly singing in in the streets and offering humorous *coplas* to the villagers. During the carnival period there is also a singing contest for these types of choirs. La Chirigota always participates but there are also other groups from other towns and villages. When I ask Olga where she gets her inspiration from she tells me that she is always watching programs about dance and people who dance in general. She goes to spectacles and spends hours on YouTube to see what is happening in this field all over the world. She is fascinated by flamenco and finds immense joy in passing this on in her classes. She feels fulfilled in her life, but she does not see her dance career as her full-time profession. She loves children and teaching children how to dance is certainly giving her much fulfilment, but she is studying to be able to work in the field of child education. She explains how teaching children in general gives her back so much more than she could possible put in. The dance group and the classes are part of an association so Olga is not making a living out of it. She is a hairdresser as well and works in one of the local hairdressers. However, it is her dream, after her studies are completed, to be able to combine working in a nursery with offering dance classes and taking part in performances. She hopes that one day there will be an official dance school in La Herradura, not simply an association.

She has to rush off as she is a busy bee. Another dance class to teach, smiles to put on the children's faces, and on the faces of the proud mothers watching their little ones. Her enthusiasm has been contagious and there is a little dance in my step as I make my way back home through the narrow back streets of La Herradura.

Olga Rodriguéz Garciolo

Flamenco, a family passion

Everybody has a story to tell and first appearances might not always reflect the interesting life journeys of fellow human beings. I had seen her many times, in the La Herradura streets and in the herbalist shop behind the colourful children's playground. Ana Maria Aneas is a woman with a story and a passion, which she reveals when she starts talking …

"I have been coming to La Herradura since I was a little baby as my grandmother was from here and my grandfather from Almuñécar and although they had lived in many places they always returned to La Herradura. In the mid Sixties my parents built a house in the village. My grandmother loved it so much here that she used to cry when she had to return to Madrid. Then, when she was 90 years old, she decided she was going to stay here, and there was no way they could convince her to go back to the city.

The village has always had an important place in the lives of my family. I lived here from 1997 to 2001, first I worked as a journalist for Almuñécar television and then I created a centre of educational and environmental activities in La Herradura, from where we organised conservation awareness campaigns on the beaches of La Herradura, Cantarijan and Marina del Este in collaboration with the Town Hall. We also organised educational workshops and walking routes to create environmental awareness. The theme of nature conservation has always been close to my heart."

Ana studied journalism, specialising in audio visual communication, and worked in the communication field, always alongside her passion, the flamenco. She started studying Spanish dance when she was nine years old at school, but soon went to specific dance academies and later at at the international choreography centre *Amor de*

Dios in Madrid. She has had the privilege to have been taught by great teachers such as Manolete from Granada, Merches Esmeralda from Cádíz, Paco Fernández at the conservatory in Madrid, and attended courses with Antonio Canales from Seville, to name but a few.

Her aunt, Ana Esmeralda, a famous dancer and actress inspired Ana a lot. She had her own company and performed in major theatres all over the world, including England, Russia, Brazil, Persia … As an actress she appeared as the main character in about thirteen movies, including *El Amor Brujo*, *Bronce y Luna* and *La Casa de la Troya*. Mario Audra, a Brazilian film producer fell in love with her and pursued her on her tours until she said 'yes' to his proposal of marriage. Ana Esmeralda created a culture and flamenco art association and has helped to spread the Spanish flamenco culture into various countries. Paz, Ana's mother who loved art, literature and architecture awoke an interest for culture in Ana from when she was a small child.

Art and in particular the flamenco took up an important part of Ana's life and she has always worked in fields that were related to art, music and culture, such as the INAEM (National Institute for Scenic Art and Music) in Madrid. As a journalist, she also submitted many reports and articles about dance and flamenco.

"My interest in the flamenco dance started at a very young age. I remember feeling fascinated when I admired all those photos and flamenco paintings of my aunt. Her enormous dressing room was a dream for a little girl like me. Not only that, my father used to listen to a lot of flamenco music in the house; very profound flamenco music by great flamenco musicians. Above all I remember being touched by the guitar music of Paco de Lucia during a live concert when I was only eleven or twelve years old.

When I started studying the flamenco I wanted to find out

more about its origins. For quite some time I went to many soirees in Sacromonte in Granada because I wanted to immerse myself in the flamenco in one of its cradles. I was also fortunate to assist in flamenco soirees in the Candela in Madrid with great masters like Rafael Requeni, Duquende and more. It is so special to go to a live performance to see new creations in music, singing and dancing."

Andalusia - the cradle of the flamenco with cities like Granada, Cádiz, Jerez and Seville, to name but a few, is steeped in flamenco history. Madrid also has a large flamenco community and, as in Andalusia, you can find many *tablaos,* where you can indulge yourself in the spectacle of the powerful and colourful flamenco culture whilst having a meal and a drink. Also well-known and popular in the flamenco world are the so-called *peñas*, which are spaces where flamenco lovers get together and where flamenco artists promote themselves. They are not commercial places but more like cultural clubs where rental costs are shared by the artists and sometimes they get help from the government in promoting flamenco. Shows are organised with both famous and young, promising artists, that can sometimes last till the early morning hours. Another important aspect of the *peñas* is organising flamenco contests. Some of these contests are very highly respected with important prizes and many artists have, in this way, been able to make a name for themselves within the flamenco world, including 'El Ruso', the famous flamenco singer from La Herradura.

Flamenco has developed in many different ways and it is often depicted as a tree with a lot of branches, like a family tree. These branches are called *palos* - the *buleria*, the *alegría*, the *soleá*, the fandango, the taranta and many more. An important part of these songs is the hand clapping. As such, in the *bulerías, alegrías, soleá, seguiriya*, etc., the movements are different in each choreography and artist, although they have common structures such as the way of singing, the shoe tapping, the closing, etc. - The 4 sevillanas on the other hand are more or less the same wherever you go, for this reason they are very popular, however they are not considered to be flamenco puro. A performance can, for example, start with an *alegría*, which is lively music with handclapping, then it continues with the *baile*, which is the part where the dancer moves elegantly to the rhythm of the music, then there is the *silencio*, which is a lot slower and spiritual, followed by the *zapateado* (shoe tapping) which then converts into the *rosa*, with a more joyful rhythm and then it all ends with a *bulería*, with its faster and more energetic pace.

The *palos* find their origins in different towns and cities like the *malagueña* from Málaga, the *granaína* from Granada, the *bulería* from Jerez, the *soleá* from Seville, etc. In La Herradura they sing the *fandango cortijero*, which originates from the farmsteads in the coastal mountains. The folkloric music of this area has been stylised and elevated by evolving into a deep and pure flamenco. Flamenco, like jazz music, is very well suited to improvisation while one is playing, singing or dancing, like a conversation in different voices.

The flamenco was always present in La Herradura. 'El Ruso' was great performer of the *fandango cortijero* and also of the best known *palos*. He was a man of the land and had his roots here. His parents sang as well and he learned from great flamenco masters. Ana knew him personally, the first time when she saw him perform, she was still a young girl and she was very impressed listening to his voice with the sounds of the sea in the background. She can still feel the emotion of that moment. Another great flamenco singer who lives between La Herradura and Almuñécar is Rafael Muñuz, with a long artistic career who has also won a lot of important prizes.

Ana formed a flamenco group in La Herradura together with Carmen Lara, a singer and dancer, and Rafael Hoces, a guitarist. Later she was also part of a fusion called *Flamencos en La Herradura*, with Graham Emes and Stephen Hill, who composed their own themes and Ana contributed with music and words. She has also danced professionally in various groups, including the dance company of María Velázquez and Ana Esmeralda; most of her professional life has been related to communication, culture and the flamenco.

"In 2007 we settled in La Herradura with our priority to raise our son, to dedicate the necessary time to him and to give him the benefit of a natural surrounding. We opened a health-food shop, which is the type of business that ties in with my principles of sustainability.

My life is still about flamenco, but I also have a strong interest in the social side of life. I have interviewed people for a documentary in the city of Granada. I was able to see the poverty and the ravages of drug abuse in some marginal parts of the city. This had a major impact on me and made me want to fight for social justice, to create a more fair society. I always had a strong sense of wanting to make things better in the world.

La Herradura is a nice place to live and not just because of the marks great artists have left on the village. One of the artists who has done a lot for the village is José Luis Merino. He had a house in the Cerra Gordo and directed a theatre group in La Herradura. He is well-known as a cinema director and writer who, amongst others, directed *El Vagabundo y La Estrella* with Ana Esmeralda in the leading role.

My dream for La Herradura is to get a real flamenco school up and running, with singing, dancing, percussion and guitar classes as well as cinema, flamenco books and magazines. In this way people can have easy access to this information and our children and the youth of the village can be involved. A very lively school with flamenco shows and theatre that even can become known outside Spain, I would love to be part of that.

Flamenco is part of this village; it has been for many years and will continue to be so. La Herradura has attracted many artists over the years, both from Spain and abroad and this will not stop. It deserves to be known for its beauty, its cultural and historical legacies and its future potential."

Ana Maria Aneas

Living the dream in colour

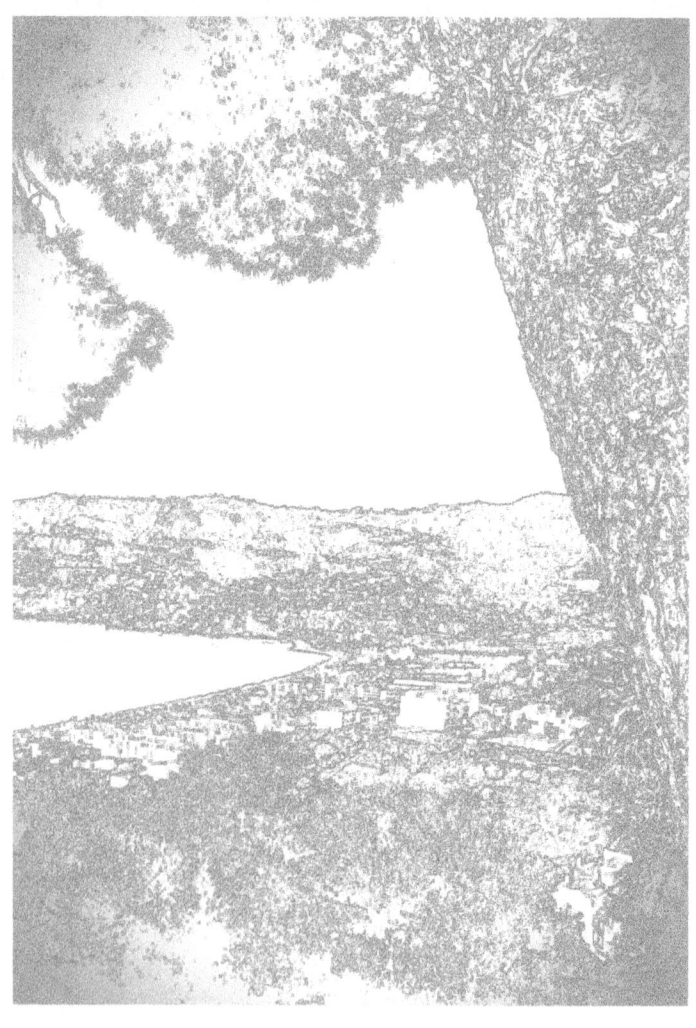

American politics

She lives near the cemetery, a wonderful place of peace and quiet. A place where Spanish people pay tribute to loved ones no longer with them and where foreigners can marvel at its tranquillity, its beauty and the unusual way of putting to rest those who have passed away. For here, in walled rows there are slotted holes just big enough in which to place a coffin. When someone dies the coffin is put into one of these spaces and then closed with cement and plaster. A tomb stone plate with the name of the deceased and their date of birth and date of death are placed on the sealed tomb. Families of the deceased create little shrines of remembrance in front of the tombstones, mostly with a photo, some artificial or fresh flowers or sometimes with a specific object. It is a humbling experience to visit the cemetery. The deceased seem to speak through their faded pictures, a moment back in time.

Anna DiGesu smiles when we meet. She is an inspiring lady and well known in the village. Not that she mingles a lot. She needs her peace and privacy to be able to paint. It's her passion and her life's choice. Each day, you can find her riding her bike through the village to get some shopping or simply to get a fresh breeze of air in her stunning, expressive, story-telling face. We sit down at a pavement cafe with its lovely view to the sea. It is a calm and sunny winter's day. We order a tea and a coffee and Anna starts talking.

"I was born in Long Island in the United States, the daughter of Italian-American immigrants. In the mid-Sixties I was in a bad mental state. The political situation in the United States really got to me. I very much disliked the path America was taking, having developed its power through the military. The Vietnamese war and the deaths of the Kennedy brothers had been adding to my worries. It was heart breaking. I thought "I just need to get out of here!" One evening I was watching television and saw this programme about a man, dressed up to the nines with a shiny grey flamenco hat and he was dancing. His body didn't move, only his feet, incredibly fast and so skilled. He was in his seventies and amazingly fit, he looked so vibrant, so full of life. Then a woman dressed in a traditional flamenco dress started dancing as well, using her castanets. They also sang lyrical songs and I was fascinated. I realised: *That is where I will go!*

I came to Almuñécar in the province of Granada in 1967 and I stayed for twenty two years. I felt the sea was talking to me, the leaves on the trees were whispering to me... *we live here, we die here and we will be born again.* The sky was inviting and welcoming, the Mediterranean light was inspiring. The years from the late Sixties to the Nineties had a wonderful atmosphere and the excitement of very valuable change. When a country is advancing from a very low level of development there is an energy, a vitality, which is palpable. I loved it. I felt its history, its present and its hope for the future. I also loved the people - they were so compassionate. They bent over backwards to make me feel at home with their 'my home is your home' philosophy. These were the most joyous years of my life.

It was a boom time for my art as well. I caught on to a style of naïve painting that was liked by everybody, from peasants to university-schooled people. My works of art were selling like hot cakes. I lived a happy, successful life and earned enough to build myself a beautiful house with a big studio. It was fantastic. Then an old friend came to visit me and loved it so much here that he decided to stay, but he got seriously ill and as he had nobody to look after him I decided to take care of him, because of that, I didn't have time to paint anymore and in the end I had to sell my house to take care of all the bills. I still miss that house. Being a full time caregiver changed my life dramatically.

Not being able to make any money was difficult for me. The times had also changed. A new administration in Almuñécar decided to cut down lots of trees in the name of progress, in my view destroying the soul of the place I had called my home for so many years.

After twenty-two years I decided to go back to America. My mother had fallen ill and I went back to take care of her and to try and make some money. I was also able to catch up with my sister and my son and grandchildren, still living in America. Over the years we had been able to visit each other regularly, but it was nice to spend some more time with them. I stayed in the States for six years but I did not like it. It is a harsh place with no healthcare. I tried to live in various states, but the government was led by cruel Republicans. It just didn't feel right for me and my longing to return to Spain became more intense. No matter what's happening in Spain, it is far better than in the US in my opinion.

The man I had taken care of before I left Almuñécar six years before, used to live in La Herradura, this is how I got to know it. So when I came back to Spain I settled in this lovely seaside village. The year was 1996. It took a little while for the locals to get to know me, but once they accepted me I was welcomed with open arms. I have been living here ever since. I find the people in La Herradura jovial, hospitable, resilient and very accepting. What I very much like about the Spanish, generally speaking, is that they adapt to their circumstances. Since the Euro has been introduced, life has become more difficult for many, more expensive. It has for me as well, but I still love being here. Just being grateful for what I have and not thinking about what I've lost or could have had, had times been different.

It is an absolute joy living in La Herradura. It just is so very beautiful, you have the sea right there and whilst you are swimming you can look at the mountains on the other side. I thank my lucky stars for being able to live here, with its beauty and lovely people, including many different nationalities that live in the area. All this has really broadened my horizons. It inspires me to do what I love most - painting. My style has developed and I no longer paint naïvely. I feel inspired by painters like Matisse and Chagall, but I now have my own style. I always seem to get back to painting the female figure in expressive colours and images. I love the human figure and, together with some other painting enthusiasts, we come together one day a week to draw from a live model.

I often ask myself why I do what I do for a living. I find being an artist one of the most difficult vocations. You constantly have to shell out money to buy your materials and it takes a year to create a show, but it is just something I have to do. An urge. If I am not doing it I feel miserable. Creating art is a fantastic process. I usually put on some classical music. Painting with this music in the background transports me to another plane, into another life, almost reaching God. It doesn't always happen like this. When a failure occurs this can be very frustrating, but I see it as a learning process, but when it all flows, and a painting that I am working on comes together and works, it is worth all the trouble having to survive as an artist. In fact it is a very gratifying, rewarding feeling. Pure happiness. Then, when I get some positive feedback; someone likes my work and gives me a compliment, or even better, buys one of my works, I feel spiritually nourished for a long time.

I do hope, generally speaking, that my work will bring some joy into people's lives. For this reason I never paint anything didactic or dreary. If there is a message in what I do I believe it is that if you really love what you are doing it makes life worth living. La Herradura has helped me to see that as well. In comparison with for example, the United States, where people are judged on their income and worldly possessions, people here are not always thinking of the monetary value of things. They appreciate the inner character of all their acquaintances and family members. I feel that life here is far more compassionate and open. Living here has even changed my personality. It has made me a lot happier, a lot more amusing and more jokey. It has certainly turned me into a more rounded and, hopefully, more understanding person. Seeing how the Spanish accept people's idiosyncrasies has helped me see that this is a good way to be. So thank you, La Herradura!" Anna smiles...

Anna DiGesu - www.annadigesufineart.com

An important address

I could not sleep. It was three o'clock and dark and cold outside. He told me he would go out for a cycle ride earlier that evening. My heart sank as I knew what this meant. Always hoping for the best and that he would come back fit and healthy and optimistic. But he did not come home. I tried to sleep and not worry but that was impossible. Early in the morning, at seven o'clock I heard the key in the door. He could barely walk, tried to pretend he was fine with a fake smile, went into the bedroom and fell down on the bed with his clothes still on, a thick, strong smell of alcohol hanging around him. Our relationship was extremely fragile. His alcohol addiction and my inability to deal with it did not make things easier.

During the good moments, and there were plenty, we dreamed about leaving the Netherlands to start a new life in Spain. Already approaching middle age and given our situation this sounded like madness to my family and friends, but there was a strong longing - I had an incredible urge and faith that this is what I had to do. I decided to leave Holland to go to Spain, following an intuition so powerful that it would have been madness not to. I had done it before, giving up my 'secure life' to live abroad. I was only 18 when my horizons expanded during a six-month stay as a volunteer in a kibbutz in Israel. Getting to know so many fascinating young people from all over the world flocking there to do voluntary work was a great way to become a world citizen; and thanks to many excursions I had felt blessed to discover this amazing and controversial country. It changed my views on life, politically and personally, and made me want to leave Holland forever, so I immigrated to New Zealand, on my own, when I was only 21 years old. It turned out to be an interesting and educational experience, but I did not feel at home in New Zealand, beautiful as it is, and I returned to the Netherlands, only to follow another strong desire to leave my home country six years later. This time I went to Italy where I lived for five wonderful years. It was in Italy where I became a full-time artist. Circumstances took me back to the Netherlands again where I continued my artistic career, taking up sculpting and developing my writing skills in a more serious way. Then I reached the pivotal age of forty. My mother had just passed away by means of euthanasia, choosing to end a terrible illness which would have left her with no control of her body and having to die choking. It was a release to see her freed from the body that had become her prison, but I needed a change of scene. I went to England for a writing holiday and met my then partner.

"Go to La Herradura!" said the gallery owner in Amsterdam, three years later. "A good friend of mine is setting up a group with other artists to give workshops and organise art holidays; here is her address." I told him thanks but my current partner and I had decided to go to the Barcelona area to try and set up a new life. My partner went ahead by plane to look for work as an English teacher, for which he was highly qualified. He found a job in Logroño in La Rioja and one month later I followed him by car, filled with all the belongings I could possibly cram into it. Spain suited us. My partner, a so-called functioning, binge-drinking alcoholic, who only drank at weekends and holidays, thrived in his job. The weekdays together were great, holidays and weekends were full of drama.

I was offered a part-time job as an English teacher and life was good. During the summer months, when his excessive drinking completely took over our lives, we saw an online advertisement that requested translators from Dutch into English. I applied for the job, which was in Torre del Mar in the south of Spain and got hired. So was my partner who could start working as a proof-reader. The next year was a happy one with the alcoholism of my partner not totally dominating our lives. At weekends we took out the car to visit surrounding areas and during one of those first trips we went to La Herradura to see if we could find the group with the aforementioned Dutch artist.

For me it was love at first sight as soon as I set foot in La Herradura. It's an intangible and inexpressible feeling. Rolling down the hill right after entering the village at the traffic lights it felt like the sea front embraced me with a magical energy. Although a little rough around the edges with a mismatch of architectural styles and without a sleek boulevard to roller-skate along it felt a bit grubby, but in a charming and attractive way. The bay ringed with stony beaches and palm trees and charming beach bars rose in front of me and I knew immediately ... *this is where I want to live.* My path, however, took me on an emotional journey for years to come.

I never met the Dutch artist as she had moved on and so did we, from Torre del Mar to Alcaucin and then to Rubite, whilst continuing working from home for the same translation company. At that point my partner's addiction started to completely overtake our lives and we had to split up while maintaining a very close and intense friendship. I rented a house in Alcaucin again and subsequently moved to Cajiz and then to Torrox. Then I joined a writing club in Nerja and I was inspired to translate my first book into English and publish it.

I kept dreaming about living in La Herradura but the rents were simply too high. However, I regularly returned to soak in its energy, relax on the beach and visit the local Nexus art gallery where I had some of my artwork on permanent exhibition. I got to know the village little by little. La Herradura has a unique blend of untouched ethnicity and a laid back cosmopolitan air. I loved the fact that it has a predominantly Spanish feel to it, even though there are no less than twenty two different nationalities in the local primary school. Most foreigners who live here make a serious effort to master the Spanish language and are keen to practice it in the local shops and markets. I personally feel this is important out of respect to the Spanish who welcome us without hesitation while allowing us to live our own lives. I wanted to call this my home.

Two years later I finally had a lucky break when I found an affordable penthouse apartment in Calle Rambla del Espinar. I was so happy; my heart sang when I drove up in my car full of boxes on moving day, entering the Rambla, just opposite the iron statue on the beach. This is the street that I love so much with its riverbed to the left, dressed up by palm trees and tropical plants on the side of the road. From my penthouse terrace I was offered a view to the row of palm trees, ficus trees and oleander shrubs along the dry riverbed. I finally felt the peace inside me to write the book that needed to be written.

Early in the mornings I walked my dog and then sat down at one of the sea front pavement cafés with a milky coffee to do some writing. I like to write outside whilst enjoying the sea view and listening to the morning sounds of the awakening village. For me it was therapy but it was also a scream for attention, not so much for me but for the many people who were still in that same situation from which I had managed to free myself. Two in every five people experience the negative effects of alcohol abuse in their lives and I wanted to reflect the human being behind these often heart breaking stories. I interviewed partners, children and parents of alcoholics as well as alcoholics and addiction care workers throughout Europe and told their stories in *Cheers, the Hidden Voices of Alcoholism.* My ex-partner had returned to England and publishing Cheers was the end of an era and a new beginning for me. I was relieved and proud to find out that people were actually helped by reading my book, a humbling experience. Now I had to focus on surviving - with the worldwide recession unfolding. Making a living from art was practically impossible and the translation business was disappearing, so my monthly income had reduced dramatically. But still I felt liberated, happy and full of hope.

Then I saw him. *Gosh he is gorgeous, probably married, but that smile...omg!* I thought. I had recently joined a Buddhist chanting group in Almuñécar and was far beyond believing in coincidences. Reading *SynchroDestiny* by one of my favourite writers Deepak Chopra just confirmed what I believed. This gorgeous guy popped up everywhere; passing me by in the car, or walking his puppy dog; always smiling, always greeting me. I saw him when I did not expect to, in situations that were not logical for me to see him. I fell in love but was the synchronicity to become my destiny? "Why don't you join Tai Chi?" said a friend from my Buddhism group. "Really, Tai Chi? Here in La Herradura? I have always wanted to learn that!" I replied. I went along and there he was again, a passionate Tai Chi practitioner, and here it was again. Synchronicity. I was introduced to Miguel (for that was is his name) and we became friends. I found a cheaper place to live and he helped me move; he helped me with various exhibitions that I had during that period and a few months into the friendship we became a couple.

Meanwhile my artistic life continued, creating mandalas, and painting flamenco dancers with a twist. I presume you could call my art style figurative and expressionistic as I like to use figures in my work, recognisable but not overly realistic with some surreal and abstract touches. The best way to describe my work in one word is colourful. I just love colours. I also started working on a new series of seven books which contain visualisations and images of my mandalas.

Looking back I can see that La Herradura has had a profound healing effect on me. I feel calmer, more blessed and more grateful than I have ever felt before and my artistic and writing adventures are booming. It is a need in me. I feel inspired by the sea, by things I hear or read and by passers-by. I am inspired by stories I observe in the streets. When I paint or write I sense a deep happiness. I feel very much alive and yet on another planet as if I don´t exist, like in a meditative state. It is who I am and what I was meant to do. The pictures I paint with words and the stories I tell with my pictures do not need much explanation - whatever one reads into it is their truth and that is fine. I simply hope that my paintings, my mandalas* and my books have a healing effect and induce happiness in others through giving insight, understanding, or just providing some relaxation.

I also have a dream, for La Herradura to become a vibrant little village with art and culture bursting out of its seams and attracting cultural tourism and thus creating a future for its young people while totally preserving its Spanish feel and quietude. On a personal note, La Herradura also had more magic for me in store. Miguel and I embarked on a new journey together and started renovating his old family home that had previously been rented out to a local carpenter, who, in 2003, had lived there with his then - Dutch partner, an artist. Miguel and I got married in June of 2014 and moved into our new home … at the exact same address I was given eleven years prior by the Dutch gallery owner. Synchro-Destiny.

Renate van Nijen - www.renatevannijen.com

* A mandala is a powerful symbol that can be found in many cultures. It is a design in a circle and usually made with colours, symbols and patterns. It is said that mandalas contain specific energy. They are for example used for meditation and for healing purposes.

A nomadic lifestyle

"Nowadays I just want to follow my heart and be honest to others, but also to myself. I feel good as I am sitting on the tiny Playa la Caleta beach just below the Calle Ctra. de la Playa that winds its way up the Punta de La Mona. It feels like a very private area of the beach, sheltered by rocks. I enjoy coming here a lot because it allows me some detachment from the village whilst still being part of it. I watch the majestic rocks of the Punta that have fallen into the sea, keeping the sea separate from the land for so many years, with so many stories to tell. Here it feels so silent, quiet and tranquil, despite the sound of the breaking waves on the pebbled beach and the rocks in the sea, the wind in the shrubs behind me and a lonely seagull trying to shout above the wind. It is cold so I am wearing black gloves and a thick white knitted jumper that I bought in the local cancer charity shop situated on the side of the municipal market building. I didn't expect it to be this chilly on the Costa Tropical, but I am not complaining. It is winter and this is the type of winter that I came here for - ample sunshine, beautiful views and the peace and quiet I need to write, paint and reflect.

My mind drifts back to the moment I arrived here. I was invited by my friend, Renate van Nijen, who told me about the artists, musicians, guitar-makers and other interesting things going on in and around La Herradura. I immediately felt warmed by the idea and decided to come.

During the first year, which was in 2012, I stayed for a month. The following year I also stayed for a month and this year I have come to stay for four months. I know I will be back next year. It begins to feel a bit like home, even though I lead a quite a nomadic life at the moment, living on a boat and resident in the Netherlands, visiting family in Devon and spending part of the winter in La Herradura. I feel warm and at home in all these places.

I am British and was born in Ripon, Yorkshire. My father was a navigator in the Royal Air Force so we moved every two or three years. My first memory of travelling was with my parents going to Singapore, where we lived from when I was seven to about nine-and-a-half years old. Growing up in this way had a huge influence on my creative energy. It wasn't immediately obvious that I would have a career as an artist because I preferred subjects like mathematics and sports when I was at school. After I had finished school I worked in a bank until I became a mother. However, I had always enjoyed drawing. Someone who saw my drawings suggested that I should go to Art College and a seed was planted. However, the seed didn't grow until a few years later when I was divorced and a single mother. I decided to go back to college in Doncaster, where I was allowed to attend two colleges, one of which was an art college. By then I was in my mid-twenties. I passed all my exams with good results gaining a great sense of freedom at being able to express myself in an artistic way ... I knew art would now be my chosen profession.

Shortly after finishing my studies I met my second partner who was offered a job in the Netherlands so eventually my son and I moved there as well. After this relationship ended I decided to stay in the Netherlands and have now been living there for thirty years. I have an art room/studio in a beautiful part of the Netherlands, on the edge of the national forest and I have a permanent exhibition there. It is also a very nice place to work. My artwork varies from sculpting to painting and printmaking, but I mainly paint in acrylics. I also write and some of my poems are on my website, but I have yet to try and get my stories published.

Usually I go through phases of painting in one style or another. I am always tranquil when I paint and never feel stuck for ideas. I must be picking up ideas on the wind with images spontaneously coming when I need them. My inspiration also comes from my study of various philosophies such as Buddhism and listening to people like Mooji and Eckhart Tolle. The art of being still and quiet allows for inspiration. I think we are all inspired by something even if it flows from our subconscious.

I do not make many sketches before I create a painting, if I do it is just a quick, simple sketch. The process is very spontaneous and difficult to put into words. It is basically a feeling, as effervescent as the wind. I cannot see it but I feel it and then transform these feelings into images. What comes out of me feels like something that is going through me and then goes outwards. It is not easy to explain and maybe explanations are not necessary. If I am asked to interpret my paintings I am aware that I like in some way to show that all things are connected physically and harmonically. Often it becomes a conversation about my philosophy, but if necessary I leave people to interpret my paintings themselves so that they can find their own sensations and message in my work, which is not necessarily my interpretation.

I do believe I was born happy and therefore in most situations I find myself in, even the very difficult ones, I can find a way not to submerge myself into sadness and continue with an uplifted spirit. And I have been challenged. One of the biggest turning points in my life was the death of my son, twenty years ago and four years after that the death of one of my brothers; both died in tragic accidents. These events stopped me from painting for many years, but they also propelled me into a world of helping other people and in doing so helping myself.

When my son died I was in Almuñécar on holiday with my-then partner who was hang-gliding in the area. Ending up enjoying an environment only five kilometres away from the place where I heard the most tragic news of my life seems ironic. However, it has also led to another avenue of healing. The first year I came to La Herradura I spent time in Almuñécar wandering on the beach, close to the place where I heard the very sad news of my son's death... working through feelings and memories that caused and still cause some anxiety about the place. Healing for me means: to be surrounded by peace and quiet; knowing that learning to live in the present is important and to be the pilot of my own journey and La Herradura is certainly part of that journey and will continue to be so. The village has given me the opportunity to be on my own as much as I want, but also to enjoy being with many other creative and inspiring people. It is a special place to be and not just for one reason but a combination of things. If I have to sum it up in a few words I would say that you can feel it but cannot totally find the words to express it. Wherever I go I get gut feelings, which are not pleasant, or heart felt feelings, which are pleasant. I have a heart feeling when I am in La Herradura, sitting here on this 'special' stretch of beach while listening to my 'favourite music' - the sounds of nature, like the wind in the trees, people laughing in the distance, birds singing their song, the waves of the sea breaking on the pebbled beach..."

Kerry Broomhead Brown www.kerry-bb.nl

The past is shaping the future

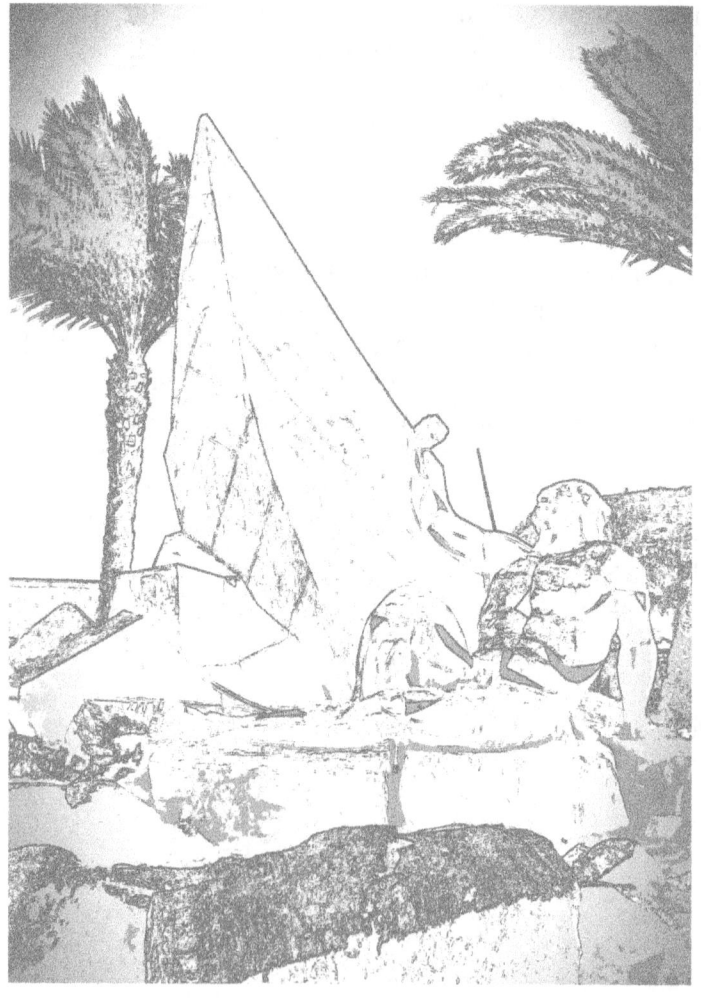

Discovering Andalusia

I only have to cross one of the last few courtyards left in the Calle Ramblas del Espinar. Most of the old houses are now replaced by modern apartment blocks in these erstwhile corrals. Crossing the patio I take in the so-familiar view of the sapodilla tree and lush green plants in many smaller and bigger plant pots and a narrow section of soil on one side of the patio. The other side of the patio that used to offer space to cows and chickens is now filled with three houses to accommodate the family. I am a *guiri* (a term often used in Spain to indicate a foreigner who rather obviously isn't a local), but I married into a Spanish family. Although my husband is a farmer, in my extended family there are definitely some creative people. Rosario González Torres, the local ceramicist, is my sister-in-law; Reinaldo Jimenez, a poet is one of my brother's-in-law; and I am on my way to interview my other brother in law, Juan Franco Quiros, a retired teacher and writer.

Juan, born in Almuñécar, has been living in La Herradura since 1995. He knew La Herradura from when he was a young boy when he used to walk to the village along the coastline to play a game of football. He now lives on a permanent basis in La Herradura because he likes the village and his wife, Mari Carmen, has a house in the patio.

For 30 years Juan worked as a geography and history teacher and talks about his working life with a lot of passion. His first job was as a geography teacher at the University College in Jaén, where his children were born; from 1979 to 2003 he worked in Malaga and his final years as a teacher were in Fuente Vaqueros, the place of birth of the famous poet Federico Garcia Lorca. Now, since his retirement, he lives in La Herradura.

His passion for history and geography becomes even

more evident when I ask him to explain certain historical facts to use in this La Herradura book. Not only do I receive an adept explanation but also an interesting story around the facts. I ask him about the cane production in La Herradura, and he explains that the main cane production was in the valleys of Salobreña-Motril and Almuñécar-La Herradura; in those days cane was also cultivated in Torre del Mar-Velez Malaga, Nerja-Maro and even Malaga in the area where the airport is now located. When Juan was a young lad between the ages of ten and twelve years old, he worked in the Almuñécar and Salobreña cane fields. His job was taking water, food and cigarettes to the workers. It was hard work for the labourers, the produce had to be taken by donkeys and mules from the fields to the nearest road where it was loaded onto a truck and then taken to the sugar cane factory to be ground and converted into sugar.

Cane cultivation was introduced in the area by the Arabs and was important in the 10th century. Widespread cane cultivation continued until around 1960 but then production costs became too expensive. However, there was still some cane cultivation in the Salobreña area till the early years of 2000. These days there is no cane cultivation left but there is still a rum factory that uses imported sugar cane for its production. Life changed and so did the agricultural landscape. It was only from the mid-twentieth century that the commercial cultivation of *chirimoyas* started. *Nispero* trees had already been around for much longer but were cultivated more intensively and avocados were introduced during the Eighties. Commercial mango cultivation started much later.

Juan also explains an interesting fact that I had not heard before. He speaks about an underground natural sweet water *acuifero* (water reservoir) that still exists today beneath the valley of the Rio Jate; in wet years it sometimes floods basements and in dry years the reservoir can get salinated, which creates huge problems for the fruit tree-cultivation. The water comes from the limestone mountain barrier which rises to the North and accumulates on the impermeable rocks which extend below the valley and meet the threshold that separates them from marine waters. In periods of continuing drought if the water is still extracted from the wells a vacuum is created that leads to the intrusion of sea water, so-called *intrusión marina*. Water is of course a valuable resource, especially in summer when lack of natural water supply by rain and the influx of tourists can wreak havoc in the underground reservoirs.

I am fascinated about all this, but today we are talking about Juan. A special moment turned his life around. He was a twelve year old boy when he came home from a day's work during the Motril-Salobreña cane harvest. It was Wednesday evening when Juan and other children were taken to catechism class by their school teacher. The young priest suggested that he should go and study at the Seminario de Diocesanos de Granada. He stayed there for ten years, studying Latin and philosophy. Later he received his Bachelor in Arts, Geography and History at Granada University.

That priest changed his life as Juan was born into a poor family with many children, seven in total. Indirectly the priest had made it possible for Juan to dedicate his life to what he loves most, teaching. Over the years Juan was the coordinator and co-author of the book *La vida en el Seminario* (life in the seminar). He was a teacher for thirty-six years and even two of his three children have followed in his footsteps, dedicating their life to teaching and apart from being a teacher Juan has dedicated time to writing.

His interest in exploring and writing about Andalusia had already started with his Bachelor degree's thesis *Modos de vida agrarios en el bajo Río Verde* (Almuñécar-Jete) which is about ways of agricultural living. He also wrote a series of articles about Jaén, where he had his first job, articles about the city and the Linares mines (amongst other things) as well as various articles about teaching geography and history in secondary education.

Since his retirement he has been able to write considerably more and at the time of our interview he has written and co-written many books.

He tells me that he has collaborated with Antonio Guzman in creating a series of nine books all set in the province of Jaen. These books, called *Viajeros por Jaen,* contain a total of 36 routes through the province of Alto Guadalquivir. Juan and Antonio would travel to the place of interest and then spend three days a week exploring the area, talking with people, taking photos to add to the information in the series, and making notes. Then they would spend four days writing. This process took an entire year.

Together with Antonio Guzman and Antonio Salgero he has also written a book called *El Viajero Romántico y La Ciudad Industrial.* (The Romantic Traveller and the Industrial City) It is a book about Málaga in the 1900s and is suitable for both adults and children. The drawings in these books are by Antonio Salgero. The book also contains the English translation, which was done by a close friend of Juan, Janet Henshall, who used to live in La Herradura, but sadly passed away in 2015.

But Juan's writing doesn't stop here as he has written various articles about the Alpujarra region and the Moors and is currently working on *El viajero morisco y la ciudad de la Alhambra* (The Moorish traveller and the city of the Alhambra) which is a guide book about Granada and has a similar structure as the 'Malaga book'. This traveller is not a romantic Englishman who comes to Málaga in search of Muslim patrimony but finds an industrial town. Instead, this book is about a Moor from

Granada, who, after the Spanish conquest, has to leave his land because he is not permitted to practice his own culture and he writes about this to remember the land and to remind his descendants of their roots.

Together with his colleague Antonio Guzmán he is also working on a study about the exploitation, processing and transformation of natural resources in the Malaga region of the Axarquía. The duo have published various articles and are now working on the heritage of and water use in the basin of the river Veléz. They have been collecting information about the grapes used to create muscatel wine, about the exploitation of minerals, lime quarries and coal furnaces, and they have interviewed elderly people who told them about the oil and flour mills, the factories and the sugar production of the area. They are also gathering all the graphic information they can find about the land as well as publications about the rural industry.

I ask Juan what he likes about writing these types of books and he tells me that it is at the root of his profession. He always enjoyed preparing texts for his students, not just following the official books, and he simply loves visiting interesting towns and villages and talking to the people who live in them, in an anthropological way.

The books about the travellers are particularly close to Juan's heart as he has lived for many years in Jaén, Málaga and Granada, where he continues to go every week, on Mondays and Tuesdays, to meet up with friends for a walk and a chat and also to work as a volunteer at the CIS. This is a social integration centre linked to the provincial prison of Granada.

Juan has a very socially inclusive view on life, and says that the greatest values in life are liberty, solidarity and equality. But he also has another passion. Together with his wife you can often find him working on a vegetable plot called El Pago del Zapo with stunning views over the bay of La Herradura.

We wrap up the interview and Juan, also an excellent cook, gets up to create one of the best gazpachos that you could wish for, made from fresh tomatoes carefully grown on the Zapo hillside. I consider myself lucky as I get to eat it for lunch, before I make my way back through the green patio.

Juan Franco Quiros

Story telling pictures from the past

"I haven't written anything and have no intention of doing so. Neither am I a professional photographer. I am a retired carpenter who loves to compile old village photos. I have contributed village photos for a book about La Herradura, called *La Herradura en blanco y negro* (La Herradura in black and white) which has been created in collaboration with the local council. I feel it is a very interesting book. I have already collaborated in two other books published some years ago – *Recuerdos del posado* (Memories of the Past), printed in May 1991 in collaboration with Jan Kruse and the second book was ten years ago in collaboration with Jan Kruse and Jean Louis Andreck , -*Almuñécar y La Herradura, Cien Años de Fotografía.* (Almuñécar and La Herradura, A Hundred Years of Photography) I supplied some of the photos in these books."

Paco Alaminos talks with enthusiasm about the collection he has put together and points out some of the photos just next to the old fountain in the Chorrillo de Casa Fuerte, just across the road more or less opposite the El Chorrillo bar. More than ten years ago Paco was asked to supply some of the photos for a compilation showing life in the old days. All the photos are related to a time when the fountain was more than a village monument; it was a working fountain with two taps which provided the villagers with water. It used to be the centre of the village with the Casa Fuerte right next to it. This was a large antique house and part of a group of buildings that housed people working for the *Guardia Civil*. In those days people had no running water in their homes and so had to come to the fountain as it was the sole source for their water. Sometimes there would be lots of people waiting to get water. Any superfluous water went into a water trough for the horses and mules. The name *chorrillo* comes from *chorro de agua* which means fountain of water. Above the fountain's basin (which has just a single tap nowadays), there are some tiles with the La Herradura coat of arms and an inscription saying 'Chorrillo de Casa Fuerte año de 1922'. These days, it is a relatively peaceful tiny square, with a large ficus tree surrounded by a cement bench that gives some welcoming shade and situated between the entrance and exit roads to the village. "Unfortunately the 'Casa Fuerte' was taken down and with it a piece of La Herradura's history" says Paco.

He continues "I was born in La Herradura, apparently on the 17th of February but in my ID card it says 20 February 1945. I have an old family book which says that I was born on the 17th but my dad went to register me on the 20thth. Everybody in the village knows me. I have witnessed many changes in the village, some for better, some for worst but I am still very proud and fond of it. It offers a wonderful environment and atmosphere. I started working as a carpenter when I was twelve years old. You can still find me in the workshop that is now run by my son in Calle Las Palomas, a side street located opposite the Civic Centre.

I just love the smell of the wood and seeing what's been created. I started carpentry in a cousin's workshop. This workshop was situated near where you can now find the *El Copo* beach bar on the sea front. My cousin had a farm and had also opened a carpentry business. He took me in to work for him. At a later stage the workshop moved next to where you can now find the Hotel Almijara. I have an old black and white picture from 1957 of that shop. I do not consider myself an artist, but I am creative which is necessary when you are a carpenter. I have completed a lot of work in my long career of fifty-seven years, everything from windows and doors to wooden furniture which I have designed myself. I have always loved working with wood, mainly imported wood, but also some native wood, in particular from Soria and Galicia in the north of Spain.

I have a real affection for the past. Looking at the photos I have accumulated I feel some nostalgia for those long gone days when life was so much simpler. You might wonder how I managed to compile such a large collection of old village photos. It began in 1984. Jose Manuel Lopez, the owner of the campsite in the Peña Parda area of the village, was always talking about these old village photos and he sparked an interest in me. There were some of these old photos hanging on the walls in a bar that used to be on the sea-front where you can now find the BMN bank. It was called Las Flores. This bar is seen in many of the old photos. It was during one of the summer festivals in August when José Manuel told me 'you are going to put together an exhibition of photos of La Herradura'. So the first exhibition took place in 1984. The location of the exhibition has changed several times, but it is still an annual event in August.

By the year 1986 I already had a large collection of photos, mostly black and white, but also a few colour photographs. Quite a few people from the village who came to the exhibition told me "I also have an old photo" and they then gave it to me to make copies. This is still happening to this day. I guess I have always been fascinated by photos. I did not always have a camera and remember buying my first one during a trip to Ceuta in Morocco. Since then I've had various good quality cameras and of course these days, with everything being digital, things have become a lot easier. I love taking pictures of my family and especially of my lovely granddaughters. The photo collection with the photos of the village has now grown to around 400 pictures and I keep them on a CD. Sometimes we combine the photo exhibition with an exhibition of art works by local artists, as in the summer of 2015.

I also appear in a film made by the local village

photographers in which I read from the book *Cien años de fotografía de la Herradura y Almuñécar.* (One Hundred Years of Photography in La Herradura and Almuñécar) The film shows many of the pictures as well and is called *La Herradura Tropical Paradise* by Joseph and Nihal Sofia Perez Abay and can be seen on YouTube. I also extend my immense gratitude, without naming anybody specifically, to all the people who have shared their photos (and there are many) in the books and videos where these beautiful images can be seen, as well as all those who have helped me to ensure all these photos from the past can now be enjoyed by many people.

Contributing to various books hasn't turned me into a writer, nor into a photographer, but I love telling a story with pictures, the pictures of my village. By doing that I can keep the history of La Herradura during the early and mid-1900s alive for many generations to come."

Paco Alaminos

A passion for history

"You could actually walk it and many avid walkers do, but today I am taking my car. As I turn left on the roundabout leaving the village in the direction of Nerja via the old coastal road I look forward to a moment of contemplation at one of the best viewpoints in the village - one of my favourite spots. Passing the exit to the urbanisation of San Antonio I see the sign *Paraje Natural Acantilados de Maro Cerro Gordo*, a natural park. Just before the Cerra Gordo tunnel I turn right following the sign to Cerro Gordo. The road meanders up the mountain and not long after that I reach the restaurant *El Mirador* where I park my car. Doing what I always do I walk to the right to gaze over the sea in the direction of Nerja. I look at some villas almost hidden from my view by a green, protective cover of surrounding trees. The sea is calm and serene and has a relaxing effect on me. A few cars drive past and a couple of cyclists park their bikes in front of the restaurant. They walk up the steps and sit down at one of the tables on the pavement café area. I walk back to the other side of the restaurant to take in the view over the La Herradura bay. The village where I was born and raised looks peaceful in the distance with a turquoise sea touching its beach. I follow the path up to the old watchtower, now a favourite belvedere for many tourists and villagers alike. Arriving at the top I touch the old exterior of this proud building and breathe in its history. I imagine everything the tower has witnessed over the years. It reminds me of my passion for history, one of the reasons I studied archaeology at university in Granada. I was only a ten year old boy when I got to read a book at school. I think it was called *Nacho y sus amigos* (Nacho and his friends). It was an adventure story about a group of children who entered a very old tower. It really got my attention. In the tower they met an archaeologist who had found some human bones. I very much liked the story and since then I wanted to become an archaeologist. Just goes to show how important education can be.

Archaeology is my profession, but in Spain this is something that you have to consider as a hobby. There are few who are able to make a living as an archaeologist. I have had to take other jobs to survive like working in bars and restaurants as a waiter or in the construction business. From 1995 to 2000 I lived in Ibiza, working in an office. Beautiful as it is over there I was always longing for my beloved Cerro Gordo, I missed it. My wife, who is from Ibiza, is a teacher and speaks very good English, so it was fairly easy for her to be transferred to this region. I became a stay-at-home dad to look after our two children with an occasional job on the side if and when an opportunity arose. I have written three books and three articles about archaeology in La Herradura. One of these books, *Šāṭ - Jate, La Herradura. Aportación a su studio histórico* (contribution to a historic study), written in collaboration with Carmen Molina Poveda, my wife, contains a lot of the information that we gathered when we first started investigating La Herradura. I sometimes felt like Neil Armstrong, the first person to walk on the moon, because I understood the huge importance of the history of my beloved village. I realised there are so many things still to be discovered, so many stories that have not been told. Areas that could hold important information have now been built over and historic buildings have been replaced with not necessarily attractive buildings to cater for the tourists. That saddens me.

It has been a fascinating process writing my books and articles. I obtained a lot of the information from visits to local people who then showed me the artefacts that they or their families had found over the years whilst working the land; objects that were kept in the family. These objects allowed us to trace the history of La Herradura way back to the Chalcolithic or Copper Age and we discovered an evolutionary line of cultures that have inhabited the area. Then there was of course the shipwreck in 1562. Interestingly, after the tragedy, all the documents refer to the bay of La Herradura as a very dangerous place to use for shelter, because of the unpredictable changes of wind direction, however with no mention of the shipwreck. This continued to be the case till the 1900s. We also know from documents that, before that horrific event – in the times of the Arabs, and even before, La Herradura was used as a harbour and a place to shelter from bad weather. They came here to clean and repair their ships with wood from the trees in the vicinity. All this history fascinates me and I would like more people to be able to get to know these interesting facts. I very much hope that one day the castle itself, an object of archaeological importance, will become a museum where people can come to immerse themselves in a journey of discovery about this area's rich historical and cultural legacy.

The more recent history of the village is also very interesting with its current Spanish population, for the greater part descended from an Italian family called Garziolo that came from the more northern parts of Italy to the south-coast of Spain, settling down in La Herradura. A book that shows this more recent history is a book that I wrote in collaboration with Paco Alaminos and Francisco Barbero Domingo. Paco Alaminos has collected an enormous amount of photographs, mostly black and white, and these photos also depict a very interesting story of the recent past. The book contains mostly pictures but there is also some written information. I was in charge of finding this written information - for example, a piece of writing from 1953 that talks about the history of the village, written by a teacher who worked in La Herradura. His name was Eduardo Palomares. This teacher talked about stories that had supposedly happened. One is the story of a witch who took a boat every night only to return in the early morning hours. One day, one of the fishermen cut a piece of her dress without her noticing it. The following day they found out that the witch was a woman from the village. However, I soon discovered that these were simply legends that were told in many villages and towns. Eduardo also wrote about the Italian families but he thought they had arrived here in 1812. As it turns out they arrived quite a few years later as we know from a birth certificate of one of that first group of people that came here, a man who died in La Herradura, which stated that he was born in Noli in Italy in 1917. The book also contains some of these interesting stories of village characters that have left an impression for future generations. The photos are of the village, its natural surroundings, the land being cultivated and also of the sea and people. It has been a pleasure to have been part of this.

I really like investigating and finding out the true story behind a man-made object, for example, the tower of the Cerro Gordo where I now watch the sun going down, creating a bright orange spectacle on the horizon. I wonder how many have witnessed a similar view..."

Jose Angel Ruiz Moralez

Arty objects

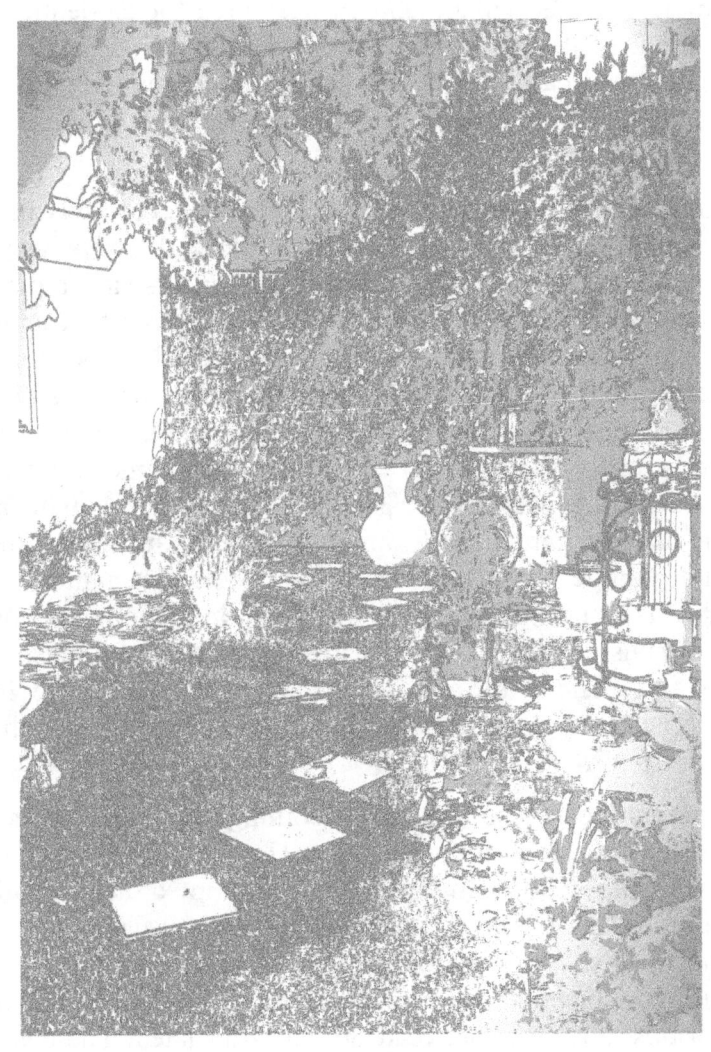

Artistic adventure in an enchanting garden

Big colourful ceramic roses attached to the wall, ceramic flowers on stalks and a painted fish pond with some ceramic fish bring to life the small front garden of her studio near the village church. Her love for gardening is evident in the many large pots holding various types of plants well cared for by Rosario. A hand-painted sign on the gate helps you to gain access to *Estudio Rosario Gonzalez*.

Rosi, as her friends call her, welcomes everybody with a friendly smile. It is like stepping into a different world when you enter her studio. It's a wonderful space, a place many artists can only dream of. You are free to wander around and admire the many styles of painting and Rosi's ceramic art. She also sells the art of other artists so her studio has turned into a colourful, interesting experience. Perla, one of her friendly cats might even come and greet you. At the back of the studio a door leads you to an enchanting garden with, amongst others, an orange tree and a large berry tree. Here more ceramic statues and objects can be found on the walls and, in the middle, more generously planted pots with lots of greenery and seasonal flowers. There are also some tables offering space for people to work at during the ceramic or art classes that Rosario provides.

The garden is also used for a coming together of poetry lovers, four or five times a year. Her love for poetry and friendship with many poets has prompted her to help organise these events. The meetings are usually held in the Spanish language but every now and then there is a bilingual meeting in Spanish and English where poems in various languages are read out and translated. The chairs are set out in a row in the lovely garden, creating an intimate wonderful atmosphere, and poets and poetry lovers recite their beloved poems in front of a loyal audience. Afterwards people can socialise whilst enjoying a tapa and a drink.

These regular meetings began to celebrate the one hundred year anniversary of Miguel Hernández followed by the famous poet Federico García Lorca. Poetry by well-known poets, both from the past and contemporary such as Tomás Hernandez and Reinaldo Jimenez are recited. Rosario was born and raised in La Herradura where she still lives with her son, above her wonderful studio. "I wasn't always a ceramicist", says Rosario. "I used to work in an office as an administrative employee. Then the company I worked for had to close down and I was made redundant. I had had enough of working with my head and felt an intense longing to work with my hands. As long as I can remember I have been fascinated by art, both paintings and sculptures. I love watching it, understanding it and, if I can, buying it. I bought quite a few paintings of the late Pepe Gámez, the village artist and a close friend of mine. I totally admire his abstract paintings. Pepe used to work in my studio; he came every morning at eleven o'clock when I open my studio doors to the public and stayed till two. He went home when the studio closed at lunch time to then return again at four o'clock, usually not going home until the early hours of the evening. He worked on his paintings or statues with a never fading enthusiasm. His palette of colours was one of the best I have ever known. He was a master of colour and a gentle soul who loved working in my studio, usually accompanied by classical music. He was really funny too, and could talk for hours on end, recounting interesting and humorous facts that had taken place in the village during his lifetime. In his later years he was still a beautiful man with his clear coloured eyes and an abundance of grey wavy hair. He was a big man, as he liked his food and a good glass of wine.

One day, as I was working on a ceramic portrait of him, he accidentally knocked it over with his body. Luckily the clay was still wet and the work landed on the back of his head, so little damage was done. He was very sorry for this, so we laughed and he kept making jokes about how he now had a damaged head. It is the portrait that is now placed on a column in Calle Canalejas in remembrance of Pepe. I miss him very much.

After my redundancy I started studying ceramic art in Motril. I loved every minute of it. I was fortunate as there weren't many pupils in the class so it was almost like private tutoring. I studied there for two years and then continued taking private classes with my favourite teacher for another year. I participated in many more courses and do so up to the present day as I believe you can never stop learning. After my studies I was lucky to be offered a job at Felicia Hall's art gallery in the village. That was a very nice period in my life and it was great meeting interesting people, setting up shows for talented artists and helping out in the gallery.

Unfortunately, due to the recession, the gallery had to close down. That is when I decided to use the space beneath my home as a ceramic studio. I invited other artists to show their work here as well so that people can still have a gallery experience in the village. Although I love admiring the work of other artists I am not particularly inspired by a specific theme or style. I just create whatever comes up as I start working. The clay talks to me and ideas just seem to pop up. I have a passion for using existing objects - an old pram, an old door, an iron fence, anything of that nature. Sometimes I just spot something in the streets, thrown away by people, or at a boot fair. I like visiting these markets full of stuff that people no longer want, or unusual objects. These objects then seem to call me. Often I am not sure what to do with something I have found or purchased but I just feel attracted to it. Once at my studio it can simply stand in a corner for weeks without being touched by me. But then, out of nowhere, ideas sprout from my brain. I like that inspirational process very much.

Creating ceramic wall objects or fusing existing objects, such as old doors, with ceramic is something that I do more and more. I am now a full time ceramic artist and also give classes to adults and children. I find working with children in particular very gratifying. They are so creative and full of ideas. Some of my students are as young as three or four years old and usually active little people but they can sit down for hours on end, fascinated by the texture of the clay; their tiny hands moulding their fantasy into reality. It is a fulfilling existence.

Apart from ceramic art and art in general I have a passion for literature and cinema, to be more specific... Spanish films. There is a small theatre in the village and they usually play interesting movies that I love to watch. It is a shame that not many seem to know about this as there are often only a handful of viewers. I hope this will change and that more people will make an effort to read the information outside the tourist office about films that will be shown and then actually go and see them. People sometimes tell me they didn't even know about the existence of this facility. It would be such a shame if La Herradura lost its little cinema due to lack of interest.

Being born and raised here I have a natural love for my village but I also like the fact that it attracts many foreigners. It is nice to mingle with other cultures and tourism is good for the village economy. Cultural tourism would of course be even better. Sometimes life takes you on a journey that you might not have predicted. Having started my adult working career in an office I never had a specific wish to become a professional ceramicist. But now I am really happy to be able to share my work and that of other artists with the public. I like it that others can enjoy and perhaps even learn to appreciate art, as in my opinion art can make you more sensitive and less angry. It can calm your senses. I have always loved art, but I guess that you could say that circumstances in my life have turned me into the artist I now love to be."

Rosario Gonzalez Torres - www.rosariogonzalez.com

The Jewellery of crop circles

"I like to come here with my son. I feel relaxed, a slight breeze from the sea taking the edge off the heat of the early summer sunshine. To get here I just walk past the Marina Playa beach bar in the direction of the rocks. At the end of the beach a pathway leads to the open space. It is fairly close to where I live at the moment in the Marina del Este. I appreciate living in this part of La Herradura with its fresh air, its quietude and thanks to the mountain range, its spectacular sunsets.

Sirio, my son is trying to get higher and higher on the swing. There are quite a few people on the beach but not here. The open space with a wooden railing overlooking the Ensenada de los Berengueles beach doesn't usually attract many people. The occasional dog walker, a mother with a child, me ... enjoying the calm whilst remembering the past, contemplating the future or simply being in the now. I am a dreamer.

I was born in Brindisi, which is a small town in the south of Italy. Although I certainly had an interest in the artistic and creative side of life I wasn't encouraged by my parents. Even before I could have contemplated going to art school my parents would have said no. There was no support for a creative career. I left my hometown when I was twenty years old because I had to join the army which was compulsory at that time. After my military service I went back home, but four months later I could not stand it there anymore. I wasn't doing anything, I wasn't studying and I wasn't working, so I flew to London in England where I found a job as a waiter in an Italian restaurant. Whilst I worked in a number of different restaurants I also studied English. A couple of years later I managed to get a job working for an Italian airline in Heathrow airport and ended up working in the tourist industry for two more years which made it possible for me to go to Spain where I found a job in the hotel industry in Barcelona. I was twenty-five years old.

I have worked in many different jobs - selling apartments, providing language courses, setting up ADSL home connections, I've even been a hotel receptionist. None of these jobs was related to the world of art. I always started with enthusiasm, learning everything there was to learn and then I'd change jobs again. I never felt the need to specialise. Life was good; I was in a comfortable situation, but after six years, when I was thirty-two years old I left Barcelona. I was longing for a change of scene, a different life.

I enrolled for a diving-instructor course in Asia but ran out of savings before I could finish the whole programme, so when I got my assistant instructor certificate (it's a certificate recognised throughout the world) I went to Menorca in Spain for a job as a diving instructor at a dive centre. I didn't like it there and after a month I looked online for diving jobs and found what was to be my second job as a diving instructor assistant in the Puerto Deportivo de Marina del Este in La Herradura at the beginning of the summer. And that is how I discovered La Herradura. It was a wonderful summer, I loved it. I loved my job and I loved my colleagues. I didn't know anything about the village, but I certainly knew I liked it. However, the decision to stay and live in La Herradura wasn't taken in a split second. It was taken gradually.

At the end of that great summer I met Elisa, the mother of my son. We were seeing each other whilst I was working the winter season in the ski resort in the Sierra Nevada, only about an hour's drive from La Herradura. After this we stayed in the Cabo de Gata area in Andalusia for a year and then we decided to go to Asia where I wanted to end my training and certify as a dive instructor. After my training we went travelling throughout Asia looking for a diving instructor job, but because of the monsoon it was a very bad time of the year for diving tourism and there wasn't a lot of work around. We decided to go travelling in Thailand, Myanmar, Malaysia and Indonesia instead.

The second day we were in Indonesia, in Sumatra, I met an artisan silversmith. He did some amazing, very authentic filigree work. I was fascinated by this and felt the desire to learn how to do it myself, but that had to wait as we were quite fixed on the idea of going to Bali in order to find a diving job for me. Our visas were limited so we decided to continue travelling. We covered about two thousand kilometres but I did not succeed in finding a job. By this time Elisa's visa had expired but I still had ten days left on mine.

So when Elisa returned to Spain I decided to phone the silversmith in Sumatra to ask him whether he would be willing to teach me his craft. We reached an agreement and I went back to see him for eight days learning as much as I could about this filigree work, a particularly fine, very detailed type of silver craft. In such a limited time you can only learn so much and my teacher only managed to teach me the basics. Although I loved the technique, actually I did not continue to use it. The most valuable aspect of my apprentice experience was that it filled me with enthusiasm for working with silver. I returned to Italy to find a job to earn some money and then, after three months, I returned to La Herradura, where Elisa was living.

I realised that as a silversmith your direction is also dictated by what the market is asking for. I had already started to gather every little bit of information that I could find about the different tools, techniques and for example about whether to use chemicals instead of natural products. I thought of Iwan, my teacher in Sumatra. Apart from buying the silver, he didn't have to buy any other products. He only used natural products that were easy to come by in his nearby surroundings, such as the fruit of a specific tree, but those materials were hard to find in

Europe. I was very eager to make silversmithing my profession, even without really knowing or discerning any specific technique and my challenge was how to implement what I had learned with different techniques and tools. I was hoping to find someone with the same passion to pass on the trade like Iwan but could not find such a person, so I learned everything from information I found on the internet. Iwan told me in his broken English: 'If you succeed, you call me, if you don't succeed, don't call me!' He also said, 'When something does not work, stay calm, take it easy, get up and watch a bit of television, relax and then come back to it.' I kept this in mind and I have now found my own, very specific way of working.

At the moment I use some chemicals in my work because I can get hold of them easily. One day I would like to work without them and that takes time and more research. I will then use techniques that allow me to bypass the chemicals and only work with natural products and then teach others how to do this. In the meantime I have to prioritise the marketing of my art.

The chemicals are not indispensable. The information and tricks on how to do this is not easy to find as most jewellers do not share their secrets and knowledge on YouTube. The people I met in Indonesia do not use the internet so it will be a time consuming project and will need plenty of resources. It is one of the many projects I dream of doing. I want to give more of myself. I have many ideas, many things in my head, but I have to put them in a drawer until I have the time to do it. At the moment I need to concentrate on expanding what I am working on now.

Meeting Elisa has definitively changed my life. Having a close relationship with somebody who works with esotericism has given me the opportunity to get an in-depth insight in the esoteric world and how energy works and this has definitively influenced both my art and the person that I am. I used to be someone who was mainly thinking of having things, making money, a rather selfish way of thinking, but that has totally changed.

I also use this esoteric approach in my art. The creation of my jewellery is like a form of meditation. It is a moment of connection with the universe. The more authentic and spontaneous this connection is, the more it is a work of art. The less the fluidity of the creation is polluted with the need of making money out of a piece of jewellery, the closer I am to the perfect expression of art. It is a big challenge to be able to devote yourself to your art without having to think about money. But of course as an artist you also have to survive. Apart from my bespoke and unique pieces, I have started larger scale production to appeal to a more commercial market. It starts with an original draft or design that has been cast into a mould for 'industrial' production. However, even creating the moulds is a very artisanal process. Each piece is made in clay, each time by hand, so authentically handmade. They are always part of a limited edition of one-hundred and one, so they are fairly unique and not one of those fifty cents worth items made in China. This 'industrial' production allows me to lower my costs and make my work available to a larger audience. So I sell these, wooden jewellery pieces and my handcrafted designs.

Clients can also give me a specification of what they would like. What is important though is that all my pieces are made with a total awareness of that connection with the universe. I actually meditate on that connection so it will bring good energy and love, compassion, prosperity, peace and joy. I channel these types of energy into the silver when it is still liquid, with the idea that the qualities of the electrons will keep those powers on the inside of the piece which then can transmit these positive energies through vibration.

I am inspired by the schools of thought of scientists like Masaru Emoto who have had the courage to challenge the scientific community with new discoveries of metaphysics unveiling very revealing realities. This fascinated me and my interest in metaphysics was born. I call it 'the alchemy with love'. The idea of channelling specific positive energies into my work comes from the experiments of Masaru Emoto who experimented with water. The results were very impressive. The crystals in the water samples that had been put in a freezer had completely changed when a word or a powerful message was written on the bottle. That gave me the idea of channelling a powerful message into my art creations when it is still in its liquid state.

I also like to use symbolism in my work, such as crop circles, sacred geometric shapes that have an interaction with the environment and supposedly have a positive influence on the harmony of the space where they are. I feel I am on the path that is right for me at this moment in my life. I feel that I have found myself but what I like today might not be so attractive to me tomorrow and that is fine. I have no regrets. Everything that I have done in my life has led me to where I am now and I love what I am doing. This doesn't mean that this is what I will be doing for the rest of my life; I don't really want to limit myself as I like to create new things. Having said that, in my previous working career I used to get bored after some time but I do feel that with jewellery this is different. When a client wants a specific piece it puts me into a fascinating place. I have to find the way to create what they want. I might not make lots of money with this but it does give me a sense of life and it is certainly worth doing it.

If I have to describe my art I will say that it has something to do with the transmission of power, in an esoteric sense and also in the sense of the forms that have the ability to transmit vibrations. It is surely this. Also, in my personal artistic expression, I like an avant-garde appearance. I like to create jewellery with a futuristic touch, which fascinates me. It is difficult to define my art in a few words because I do so many different things, I do what people ask me to do although I will always try and give it my personal touch and fundamentally always relate it to esotericism. I feel it is important to be connected to the whole and to not worry about anything as everything is going to be alright. The key concept behind my art is the interaction of you creating your own reality. If you can think and act with a positive attitude you will get good feedback in life.

My life as a professional artist is pretty good at the moment. I enjoy doing what I do and as I can organise my own time I can create time for the two things that are also very important to me. One is spending time with my son who has showed me for the first time in my life that you can give unconditional love, a very intense and beautiful feeling and in my view it is one of the most beautiful things life can give you. It makes you want to carry on. The second thing that is very important to me is dreaming. I need to dream. I like dreaming, just as I'm doing here and now, watching my son having a good time on the swing, whilst contemplating my life.

I am a dreamer.

Paolo Sgura

The smell of leather

They live above their workshop and shop in one of the oldest buildings in La Herradura in Calle Príncipe. A wooden sign with the words: 'Lilian Urquieta' marks the shop entrance. I open the door, noticing a vague smell of leather as I do, and go inside. The workshop is at the back of the inviting retail space which is filled with leather articles, jewellery and some clothing. The house is about a hundred years old. The workshop is now situated in what used to be a stable area for animals such as donkeys and mules. There are some old photos of the street which show that it hasn't changed much. You can still conjure up a sense of that bygone atmosphere and tradition, especially during local festivals like *Las Cruces* and *El Dia del Señor* (see festival chapter). Calle Príncipe is just around the corner from the Hotel Almijaras in Calle Acera del Pilar. For the interview I have agreed to meet up in the shop as Lilian and Iñaki are preparing for a design market and have to meet a strict deadline. They cannot leave the shop for an interview. Iñaki is busy in the workshop and Lilian sits behind her table next to the shop counter. A bright light shines on the white wedding shoes that she is handcrafting with a themed design on the request of a bride-to-be. Lilian cannot stop working and even during the interview she continues painting. Lilian is the designer and Iñaki is the craftsman. They themselves create the jewellery and the leather bags and other items in the shop. Lilian keeps reinventing herself. She loves trying out new things and painting on shoes is one of them.

A creative lady, Lilian is not from la Herradura. Her father is from Chile and her mother from Leon in Spain, but they moved to Denmark where Lilian was born. Her parents decided to return to Spain in 1989. They came to La Herradura because her mother's sister, Helena, is the director of the local school. Iñaki was born in Madrid and used to work as an assistant cameraman. He came to La Herradura in the year 2000 for the summer and he fell in love with the village. He decided to stay and started working as a waiter. They met in the village, in Marina del Este where Iñaki was working. Lilian was studying jewellery making in Cordoba at the time and came down to visit her family. It was 2007. She and Iñaki first became friends but their friendship blossomed into a love affair that was sealed with a marriage certificate in 2015. When they got together they went to Madrid where Iñaki started working for television again, but a few months later this was no longer possible because of the recession. They returned to La Herradura where they set up a shop. Initially they sold clothes, hand-made jewellery and some bags and this has now grown into a successful business. Lilian likes to work and keeps getting new ideas that she then translates into wonderful accessories and designs. They love working and living in La Herradura, although as they have now developed their business with clients all over the world it probably would be more logical to be based in Madrid or another big city. But they love the atmosphere and the tranquillity of the village. It is the quality of life that keeps them here, it feels like a homely nest and they both love living near the sea; they need that to feel free to be creative. They take their work on a regular basis to important designer markets in places like Madrid and Barcelona to reach their clients. La Herradura is the base and with Granada and Malaga so close by it is their perfect spot. Contacts are made via the internet which is the open door to the world. Their work has already been featured in magazines such as Vogue and Elle and they can count famous Spanish people as their clients. They were able to extend their market thanks to social media. It is however, a 24/7 job as after a day of designing and creating they still have to spend a lot of time on the internet to stay in touch with existing clients and find new ones to promote their products. Lilian explains that their work is more than a full-time job as they have to do everything themselves, the communication, the marketing, the sales, taking photographs of their creations to put on the web… the list, she says, is endless, but they feel privileged nevertheless.

Lilian gets her inspiration from whatever she sees in her immediate surroundings. Sometimes she wakes up with the design of a bag in her head, which she then rapidly transfers onto paper. When she finds some time to relax, for example, during a concert or a theatre performance then lots of ideas come to her. She was only four years old when she came to La Herradura and remembers that she used to make necklaces from stones from the beach. She hand-painted these stones with lots of colours. There was a time she felt she had to find her vocation in life and went to a school to learn chiro-massage in Granada, but it didn't give her much satisfaction so she decided to study jewellery design – first in Granada where she passed her medium level and then in Cordoba for the second level of jewellery making.

When she met Iñaki he started helping her with the jewellery and they began introducing leather. It was a logical next step to then think of bags. They bought a professional sewing machine and learned through experience. It was a personal and professional evolution. They are now proud that many people have bought their bags and it was fantastic news when their work first appeared in a magazine, Vogue no less, which recommended one of their bags. People who have visited La Herradura sometimes go on to buy their products online. Some of these clients, including a few well-known actors, have now become good friends. In order to protect their privacy Lilian prefers not to mention their names. Their clientele is a mixture of people mainly from Madrid and foreigners who visit the village. They have a stall to promote and sell their designs in the Mercado Central de Diseño in Madrid. Not everybody is accepted there and it is not an artisan market but only for designers of all sorts. Lamps, furniture, bags, you name it. They still have to pay for the stall and plan to go there once a month. It is a fantastic opportunity to extend their market yet remain living in the village they love, surrounded by like-minded friends.

Lilian doesn't like to repeat herself so she is constantly looking for new ideas and hopes she will soon be able to combine her love for travelling with work, for instance, buying fabrics in India and stones in Thailand. She feels that their work transmits a way of life, a natural way to live. The materials they use are all as natural as possible and hardly treated. When they use a pearl they use a Baroque pearl, which is irregular. They only use Spanish leathers, usually cow leather. Spanish leather is of a very good quality. They either buy the closures or they collaborate with designers of closures to create bespoke design that is unique to them. Sometimes they find antique closures of very high quality in markets. It feels fantastic, she says, when they make such a find, which they can then incorporate into their designs. Their style and brand is about always trying to create something special. Lilian likes following fashion and keeping up with new trends. The next step will be a new collection every six months. She seems to have an unstoppable energy and I am surprised at how well she could answer all my questions without taking her eyes off the assignment which is now almost finished. I thank her for the interview and we say goodbye. As I make my way to the door I no longer notice the smell of leather, but I do feel inspired to reinvent myself thanks to a talented couple.

Lilian Urquieta - www.lilianurquieta.com

A different approach

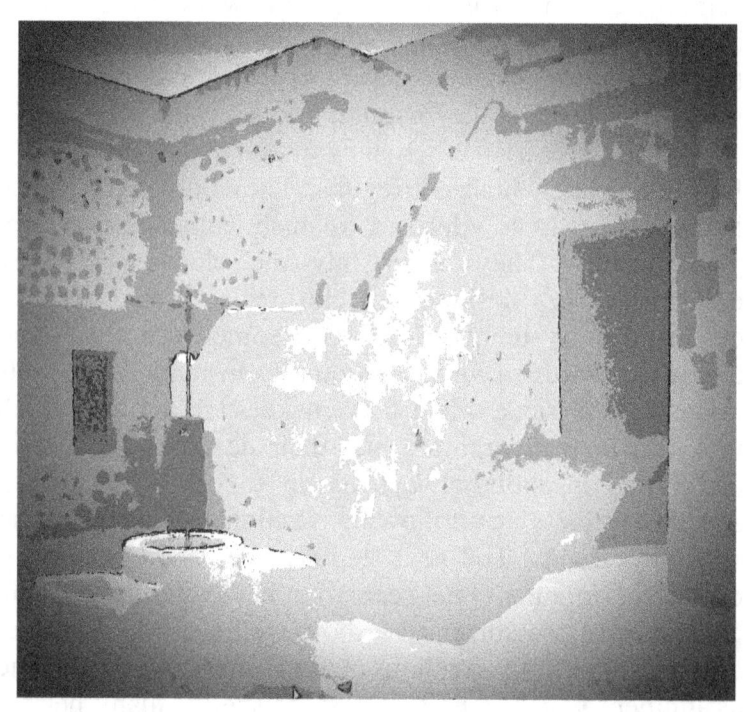

Cult, religion and art

A strong wind seems to push us forward as we walk through the narrow street of Calle las Palomas to visit the old plant nursery situated close to the sea. As I'm propelled along, I hear the high-pitched voices of school kids in the nearby playground and the sounds of seagulls, waves and shifting Mediterranean shells on the beach. The old nursery, which opened to the public many years ago, used to produce and sell ornamental plants which gave work to several people in the village. These days its function is very different, as it is now the studio where Juan Manuel Calvache develops his artistic creations.

Mario Alguilar is accompanying me to my interview. As we arrive Juan Manuel comes out and asks us to wait for a few minutes. He is in the middle of one of his artworks and he doesn't want anybody to see it yet. His studio is a private studio and not open to the public as Juan Manuel needs peace and solitude to produce his work. At his invitation we enter the large plastic structure which still shows signs of the horticultural space it used to be, with ornaments, plant pots and garden furniture here and there. As we walk in, I notice an immediate change in atmosphere. The sense of dereliction disappears completely as I notice some of Juan Manuel's amazing art works. The wind that rattles the plastic structure, is shouting down the pleasant classical background music coming from the direction of the old shop counter.

I have seen Juan Manuel many times as he walks down Calle Real on his way to the nursery. A remarkable figure with his round sunglasses, an oriental looking fez type hat and a sleeveless vest with interesting embroidery and small trinkets, carefully applied by Juan Manuel himself. I introduce myself and I am welcomed with a warm smile both in his bright blue eyes and face. We sit down in the middle of some of his artworks 'in progress'.

Juan Manuel lives in Almuñécar but every morning he walks from Almuñécar to La Herradura to create his artwork in the old nursery that has now become his art studio, and in the evening he walks all the way back home. It is a meditative walk during which he also contemplates his next artwork, feeling inspired by what he encounters.

Juan Manuel's creative story starts when he was a little boy. Born into a normal Spanish family without any special interest in arts or theatre, creativity wasn't evident in his genes, but it definitely was in him. From a very young age he loved to differentiate himself and organise theatrical events. He was always creating theatre acts, in his home and if he could in the streets. He would ask the other kids in the neighbourhood, "Shall we create a theatre play?" Usually they preferred to play football, however, come Semana Santa Juan Manuel would create images with whatever material he could find and they would build exhibitions.

"They say that Lorca, when he was a young boy, was impressed and inspired by seeing a puppet theatre and the same thing happened to me" says Juan Manuel. "My fascination led me to ending up working in children's puppet and marionette shows and eventually I became a professional member of various theatrical bodies. He also became a close friend of Robert Lenton, a classical musician, painter and puppeteer who came all the way from the United States, Philadelphia to be precise, where he ran a puppet theatre called Lenton's Puppets.

"I met Robert Lenton thanks to his love of the works of Federico García Lorca, whose work I also admire. Working with Robert, as one of his puppeteers was like working with a fabulous and magical prodigy – it felt like a trip out of this world and reality."

Juan Manuel's work is also very much related to religion. I ask him what fascinates him about religion and why he feels attracted to it. He explains that it is a matter of aesthetics of the image. It has nothing to do with faith. He is not religious and doesn't go to church and feels that he has his own religion. He talks about a friend who was fascinated by the world of the Vatican. He loved it as if it were a theatre play. For Juan Manuel it is mostly aesthetic, he sees art. Magnificent art. He loves the Catholic images but for his own art he transforms them with paint and collages. His works are in continuous progress as he keeps adding and replacing parts of the artwork.

He explains: "I intend to make things even more colourful but all with respect. I mainly do collages and I use a lot of gold and sequins. My inspiration just comes up, not from a particular place or person. But there are things that give me ideas, like the *femme fatales* in cinema - the sinfulness, religion but with some provocation, the forbidden and the fatal, all very colourful. It is transformational art. Something already exists, like a statue of the Virgin Mary which I then paint and I add specific materials. It is a mixture of pop art and kitsch. I consider myself a versatile, self-taught artist, but it is all very Andalusian. When I worked in theatres throughout my life I would usually do costume work and decoration. I love the process of transformation you get when you alter clothes and objects. I create my art because I just love the creative process with a piece of art as the end result and, although I like giving people a pleasant image to look at, I create it mainly for myself."

At this stage of his life he feels that he finds everything he could possibly want here. What he was looking for all his life - inner peace that is - has come to him in Almuñécar and La Herradura. He has travelled a lot in search of that special feeling, always searching for that perfect location, and never realising, until now, that the perfect place was the place where he was born.

When Juan Manuel's mother died, the family home was left to him and his sisters. As Juan had the means to buy out his sisters he decided to go and live in the house and turn it into a type of artistic story, like a museum, a museum that will not get any publicity. It doesn't need any publicity. During the summer months the windows and doors might be open and people can be invited to come in. Invited by Juan Manuel, when it suits him. It is his world, his life story. It is a compilation of all he has lived, like an album created in the form of statues, pictures and collages. He explains what the house means to him, "I am sitting in my living room, in the dark, without light, just the golden glow of streetlights filtering in through the windows. I am sitting in my chair, with a glass of red wine, watching my surroundings and it is like watching a mirror. An internal mirror. I am surrounded by my life; it is a story and a cabaret."

La Herradura is his studio, where he creates his art, but even before the artwork is ready, he already knows where it will go in the house, in his private museum. Manuel explains that when he starts a work he has the theme in mind but he doesn't know what the end result will be. I ask him when he knows that a work is finished. He says that it is something he feels, but it is very possible that once it is in its place in the house he feels he needs to add something. It is like an on-going project. Juan Manuel recycles everything. He finds his materials in rubbish bins, at car boot fairs and when people leave things out in the streets to be picked up by the local council at specified hours. He has a special route that he takes on his daily walk from Almuñécar to La Herradura. He finds all sorts of things, like old shop mannequins and torsos which he then transforms. He is never in a rush because neither his artwork, nor his house-museum will ever be complete. Both are in continuous evolution. They are alive.

Juan Manuel feels he is even helped by a strange force to

find the things that he needs. He explains, "When I think of something I need, I visualise it in my head, I imagine working on it and I then always find it in the streets. For example, I had created a character, a feudal gentleman, sitting in his chair. But I needed something to support his feet. I was thinking about that and planned to go to the Sunday boot fair in Almuñécar in search of that missing piece. A few days prior to that I was going for a walk in Almuñécar and planning to go my usual route. For some reason that day I decided to take a different route. I had never taken this route before and then, at the bottom of a big skip, I found the perfect little stool. It was exactly how I had pictured it in my mind. This happens quite often to me, and to be honest, it also scares me a little bit."

Juan Manuel smiles and says a similar moment happened when he needed some decoration for one of the rooms in his house, which is dedicated to Mexico. He is fascinated by Mexican culture. That particular Sunday he went to the Sunday boot fair and there it was. The very first stall had exactly what he needed: a piece of cloth with dramatic flowers. He picked it up and looked at the back. It said Mexico! He still finds these moments hard to believe but welcomes them all the same.

The house also came about thanks to one of those moments. Juan Manuel lived in an apartment in Almuñécar and had no desire whatsoever to buy his parental house. One night on his walk back from La Herradura to Almuñécar he was watching the full moon and not watching where he was going. He tripped and hurt himself. The next morning he could hardly get up and his sister said, "Why don't you stay in our parents' house which will be easier for you?" He did what she suggested and stayed the night in the bedroom where his mother used to sleep. It was as if she was talking to him. The next morning he woke up and it was totally clear to him, *I am going to buy this house* and so he did. He speaks with love about his mother and the special energy in the house. It was a radical change for him but one that he is happy to have made. He feels protected by his mother and likes to talk to her.

Juan Manuel is at peace and happy with his house, his art and his life. He describes his house as inspired by Visconti, with a sense of baroque and lots of candelabra, ornate curtains and rugs. It is a special project: an interaction and a theatrical installation, the story of his life.

When he talks about la Herradura it is also with love, but he likes to think back to the old days. When the horses were still led to the water at the old Chorrillo fountain beneath the shallow light of the street lanterns, it was very pretty, very authentic and Juan Manuel says, "I would like La Herradura to go back to these times, but that is, of course, impossible. There is no reality in that, but I have my own reality when I take a sip from an excellent glass of red wine, illuminated by the glitter and golden shine of my life laid out in collages, as life is, a layering of experiences, caught and brought to existence by the yellow street lights in front of my home."

Juan Manuel Calvache (Tito)

A colourful castle

Friendly eyes, a contagious laugh, sensible words flowing like a waterfall followed by an effortless stream of thought provoking ideas, not always so easy to comprehend. Softly spoken, gentle, witty and sometimes what I can only describe as somewhat transcendental as if from another world, wrapped in a meditative flow or, who knows, perhaps on an astral voyage. Somehow it all makes sense and yet nothing does. Currently he is about waves…. energy waves, sound waves, quantum waves invisible to the human eye, visual waves and the micro and the macro, everything is captured happily on the modern medium of YouTube where his presence is ever growing. His interests and prolific body of work paints a fascinating picture of the artist who has somehow lost his website but doesn't care. You only have to add his name to a search engine and you will be presented with a sea of choices to find out about Manuel Lecrin. He sits down and takes a sip of his *anise* tea.

Manuel Lecrin explains that he was born in Durcal in the Valle de Lecrin. Hence his name, which is not his birth name, it is his artistic name. Everybody knows him as Manual Lecrin and for the past sixteen years he even bears this name on his driving license. Durcal is the capital of the Valle de Lecrin and is one of the major towns. The valley is referred to as *Valle de la Alegría del Arabe* (Valley of Arab joy) and is known for its orange trees, almond trees and for its mountains and rivers.

Manuel has been coming to La Herradura from when he was born as his parents used to come to the village to spend their holidays. They loved the place. His parents liked the beach and the sea. They actually thought about settling in the village but ended up buying a house in Torre Nueva. However, every year they came to spend three or four months in the summer and every weekend in the Almuñécar and La Herradura area, spending time with friends and during the summer, Manuel went fishing with his father and they ate *chumbos** with delight when they were in season . It was a great time for tourism as it was the very beginning of Spain opening up to the world.

Manuel says: "I grew up in the country side around Durcal and Marchena, but I went to Granada for my studies, a Fine Art preparation. I was twenty-two years old when I decided to start a gallery. I just loved art and had always painted and was doing creative things from when I was a small child. The gallery was in a space in Almuñécar behind the Town Hall. It was a place for exhibitions and art fairs but it was also my studio, where I created my art. Juan Calvache was one of the first artists who had an exhibition in this gallery. I have known him for thirty-two years, since when I first came to the village. He was doing marionette shows. The art scene was interesting in those days and from 1985 to 1990 we organised an international art fair each year. I helped with the mounting and the installations. It was in that same period that the annual Jazz Festival started in the Majuelo Park in Almuñécar. The jazz festival coincided with the art fair and there were also many cultural shows.

In 1987 I opened a gallery in the Marina del Este in La Herradura. Jorge Graver, a German man who used to have an art gallery in Freiburg, Germany helped me out when I was travelling. He died quite a few years ago but had become a good friend. Over the years the gallery has seen many really good artists, quite a few have sadly past away already. It was a great time and a good space in the marina. There was always movement and many activities going on, cultural activities. In 1991 I also opened my art studio in Marina del Este.

I am now taking a different route. I am hoping to be able to move around with exhibitions of other artists to create a type of museum with different cultural spaces. At the moment I am involved in discussions about installations, new alternatives and new ideas with a group of artists in Granada."

Manuel also has signed a contract with the local council to use parts of the Castle in La Herradura to exhibit art. Initially the contract was for one year, but this has now been given to him on a more or less permanent basis so Manuel's work can be viewed when visiting the castle.

El Castillo (the castle) was built as part of a defence strategy on the coast by the ancient Kingdom of Granada during the reign of Carlos III. Its original name was *Batería para cuatro cañones de La Herradura* (battery for four cannons) and was completed in 1771. It is situated approximately 120 meters from the beach, and intentionally placed to better protect the mouth of the Jate River. At the beginning of 2005 the castle was acquired by the Almuñécar Town Hall in order to restore it and dedicate it to cultural events. The castle had not suffered any major military actions and it had been used as the Guardia Civil station. For this reason regular maintenance had taken place and thanks to this it was in a fairly good state. The first phase of the restoration started in March 2007 and during the excavations the old cannons were recovered. As a cultural centre the castle is very flexible (it hosts a blues festival and other events in the summer months) and adapts to the characteristics of the building. Manual Lecrin's work is part of this.

"I am currently creating a lot of digital art. This is sold by means of a disc or via email, from where people can click on a link to the artwork, as if it were a real painting, which can be projected onto a wall. It is a motion picture and I am interested in giving them a lot of movement with aesthetics as its main purpose. So it does not contain information. These artworks are simply for the pleasure of contemplation, the pleasure of the technique, an explosion of colour, a world that can envelop you. It's also an attractive decoration that can be purchased for little money via the internet and thus enjoyed by many. It is like buying a CD with music or a film on DVD, but instead you buy a CD with art.

I have so many ideas that it sometimes becomes confusing. I want to paint, I want to do digital art, I want to check things on the internet. You have to keep up with modern media like YouTube and Facebook. I want to do so much but I cannot be in all places at the same time. You have to organise yourself as there are so many interesting things and possibilities out there. In fact I have to eliminate many ideas or let them go for different reasons, but I do intend to communicate something.

I am always investigating my origin; it is a game that I like to play. I like doing what I do. I have to fall in love with each work, each collection. I am very interested in playful art and I usually create a new collection every four years and am always exploring new trends. I feel that the grace of art is the imperfection, nobody is perfect. Art is not perfect. Grace also creates spontaneity, and small defects can be charming, it is human. This is different to industrial products. A cup or a mug has to be perfect. We are now living in more technological times, and we are all becoming little androids, with our WhatsApp posts. Parts of all this is great, but it is about finding the balance in my opinion, the Yin and Yang.

Balance is very important to me. I do yoga every day. I also do health exercises. I like to keep my mind and body healthy. I do classic gym and have a cold shower daily. After that I do some relaxation and meditation. I find this all very interesting and incorporate it into my work. We artists visualise a lot. We need this to create a scene or an atmosphere. I consider myself a synaesthetic.

What is also very important in my opinion is breathing, being conscious of your breathing. Oxygen feeds all the cells of your body. This is what I like about Hatha Yoga. You have to learn how to concentrate and when you are good at this you can even go on an astral voyage. It is free infinite travel..." Manuel laughs and admits that not everyone is interested in this topic and not everybody needs it. But he does feel that people should dedicate time to relax, that it is important. Breathing correctly is part of this, according to Manuel, "We need fresh air, we need to breathe and this earth plane is all that we have. If you only go 5000 metres up the mountain most people cannot breathe anymore. We only have five kilometres of breathing air and we should be more conscious of that.

I believe that everything is related," he continues, "The stars and the micro and the macro. I use that a lot in my work. It is all about energy. We are all energy and everything that is surrounding us is energy. I also love plants and birds and the colours of flowers, the smell of fruit. These things can awaken a sensitivity in a person. I have many plants in my house and have always loved living in the countryside. I like to create a Noah's ark for plants. I also have strong views on conservation and feel sad that so many animal species and plants have already become extinct. Humanism is very important to me and I think that will shine through in my work and personality. I like to be original and futuristic.

Primarily the message in my art is to invoke beauty and I currently do that by interrelating the micro and the macro that I spoke about before. The collection that I am working on is about the invisible waves. Everything moves by waves, our voices, images, light, sound, television, you name it. I'm playing these waves aesthetically, always looking for the beauty. The message is the relationship that can be seen between the visible world and the invisible world and the realisation that both these worlds are intelligent. I'm working with cells and with planets, with galaxies, and with the infinite mind, because the mind is infinite. I am searching for infinite ways of seeing art because I feel that the concept of art has changed since the 1970s. Today everything can be art. The art of storytelling, theatre, the art of cooking, the art of moving. Everything has a form of art ... film, architecture and botany for example, as even to create a garden you need special sensibility. I am a pantheist, I believe that everything is part of the divine and everything is interrelated.

The project that I am working on at the moment is trying to intervene with architects, designers and decorators in order to create a team. With this team we then have to find venues where people can interact with different arts, each with their own specialty. I feel it would be good if architects collaborated more with artists, because with the same materials, the same cements and the same colours you can either create a beautiful 'picture' or a less beautiful 'picture'. We are talking about creating a more harmonic and interesting world.

Although I am in Granada a lot, my heart is still very much in La Herradura and Almuñécar, where I have my home. I have always done things in La Herradura and have this image of a place where people will live forever and where people protect artists; where stress is removed and where everybody is protected by the rivers and the mountains - a paradise. And wouldn't it be nice to be able to create a cultural centre with a contemporary flavour, a space to enjoy art and also to enjoy a cup of coffee?'

It feels easy to agree. I thank Manuel for the interview and walk him to the front door where we end with a "*nice to have met you*" goodbye kiss. Then there is that charming laughter again.

Manuel Lecrin

* chumbos: very prickly cactus fruit with a delicious, sweet taste

Life is theatre, theatre is life

"I live in beautiful La Herradura, but I was born in Bilbao in the north of Spain. My name is a bit of a giveaway. Josune is a Basque name and is the female equivalent of the Spanish name Jesús. My full name is Josune Sáinz Santana. Since 2004, I have been living in La Herradura with my daughter, who is now almost an adult. We live in an ordinary house with fantastic views to the sea. It is a very tranquil area, just a 20 minute walk from the centre of the village, and I love it there. La Herradura has several urbanised areas in its outskirts among which are: San Antonio, on the west side in the Cerro Gordo part of the village, San Nicolas in the middle and San Carlos on the east side with several little clusters of houses in between. Tranquillity is the norm in these neighbourhoods with houses in the typical southern Spanish style beautifully placed to get the most of the views of both the sea and the nearby mountains. Lots of greenery, gardens and pots with plants and trees create an idyllic atmosphere.

La Herradura, in my opinion, has a very special energy. I know people who do not like it at all, but there are others who fall in love with it at first sight, just like I did. Some come here for a month and stay here for years. To begin with I didn't know how long I would stay here, but the village has embraced me. During my travels throughout South America and after that through Europe I met someone from the south of Spain and decided to go and live in Andalusia. I lived in Cadiz for three years and in the Alpujarras for five years. I knew the area of La Herradura because I had friends in Almuñécar who were dedicating their lives to theatre. During that same time I also started to attend some theatre classes in Almuñécar and about two years later I realised that theatre was an important part of my life. From then on, together with some other theatre enthusiasts, we rented a place and I joined an association called 'Comunicarte'. By that time I was clear about what I wanted and had decided to dedicate the bigger part of my life to theatre. I had already moved to Almuñécar some time prior to that. Almuñécar to this day is important to me, both workwise and culturally, but I really enjoy living in La Herradura. It offers me everything I could wish for and it has been the perfect place to raise my child who was only six years old when we came here. There are a lot of children in the village including many of different nationalities. I like that and it has given my child the opportunity to get to know other cultures, which I feel, is important. The peaceful life of living in a small village and the amenities of larger towns nearby are really great as well.

My life continues to be about theatre. I am currently part of another association called *Dionisio Theatre*, which is a theatre group in Almuñécar. My teaching continues as well; I give theatre classes to children and adults in La Herradura. I have a weak spot for children though, I love working with them. The first course I attended was a clown course with the aim to being able to work with children. I have since done many clown and animation courses after which I went on to get theatrical training. I lived for about four years with a theatre group from Madrid, the members of which all lived in Las Alpujarras, but were giving performances all over Spain. Working with them taught me an incredible amount as they were all very professional. We did many different things including dancing and clown performances. In the beginning my acting work consisted of a lot of street theatre, but these days I mainly work in theatres. However, the type of theatre I do is often improvisation and so it constantly changes. I sometimes write theatre plays with the children; as a collaborative project. They give suggestions that I then write down and in just a few days we will have a play ready. Often I use an existing theatre play, for example by Reinaldo Jimenez Morales, a poet and children's theatre playwright from the village. I also transform his children's stories into theatre plays.

The classes I run for children are for four to twelve year olds and I currently have three groups. They all take place in the Civic Centre of La Herradura. Since I have lived here I have been involved in many projects and have also worked in after-school activities doing crafts and theatre. The City Council makes it possible for me to offer free theatre classes. The Almuñécar cultural department, which La Herradura is part of, gives great opportunities, in my view, to music, theatre, art, etc.

There is a profound theatrical tradition in La Herradura, and a good example is Carnival. People are introduced to it at a very young age and lots of detail goes into its preparation. As an artist I would say that I love to transform and transmit something to people. That is theatre. It is a game and I like to 'play' in the theatre. It is something that I try to convey to the children, getting rid of your fears and play, play, play. It is a bit like life, but on top of that you can be any character you wish to be. Once you are standing on the stage, in your role, together with other actors, you become a medium of expression and every bit of fear drops away. I always say this to the children ... 'when you prepare yourself well, even if you are a little nervous, during the play you will forget yourself and get into character, it is then no longer really you. Then all will go well and it becomes very enjoyable'.

Once a year we present the works of the oldest children's theatre groups during the Almuñécar theatre contest called the Certamen Martín Recuerda (Martín Recuerda competition). This is always in the month of May. The stage decoration and the costumes are designed by me with the help of some of the parents. I try to involve the parents as much as possible but I always save everything from previous performances so I have a large collection to choose from. I keep it all in my house, which is, as you can imagine, full of trunks and bulging cupboards.

Sometimes I chance upon something I had forgotten I had, which can be a pleasant surprise.

After this contest, usually at the end of May, we hold the 'end of course' presentations of the three La Herradura groups. In the morning this is performed for the schoolchildren of the local school and then in the evening for the parents. Locally I am always active and also like doing street theatre, often for a good cause. For example, we gave street performances on promenades and beaches with the aim to make people aware of not consuming fish that are too small. We were dressed up as fish. For this we collaborated with companies and with biologists who informed us about this theme - the different forms of fishing and what to do and what not to do. We were a group of six or seven people. I was the reporter and interviewed people. I like this type of assertive work.

I also help out during the annual Carnival and school events. I guess you could say that theatre is my life even though I am quite a shy person at heart, for this reason it is also a challenge for me, a fantastic, magical challenge. Life offered it to me and it is deep in my heart. I have had the pleasure of working with people who also live theatre from their hearts, who carry it in their skin. Some of my teachers have dedicated forty years of their lives to theatre. Even when they had become less active as actors they still wanted to pass this love of the theatre on and so they became teachers.

Although I am now a professional theatre person my life did not start out like that. I have a degree in technical design and graphic art. This also serves me well as I can design our own theatre backdrops. I have always loved working with my hands and have done all sorts of workshops in this field, like working with wood and leather. In fact, from when I was seventeen until I was about thirty years old I made my living creating things from leather - little objects and jewellery that I then sold at medieval fairs and summer markets. In a way I feel that everything is related. I can shape an object that tells a story with my hands, or tell a story with my body and with my voice. Nowadays my art study still comes in handy when times are a bit rough, like in times of economic crisis. I can create pieces of artisan jewellery and other nice gifts to sell in markets. During the summer months when the theatre work quietens down I work in the summer school in the mornings, I have a stall at the craft market every evening in La Herradura in Plaza Nueva.

Life seems pretty special to me, every moment of it. I am grateful for that. From when I was a young girl I always watched my parents work extremely hard in jobs that were not their dream job. I decided that I would always only do work that I liked. That is why I have chosen this path, that is why I am doing theatre and artisan work on the side. It's a bonus to get that really nice feeling when someone likes something that I have created. I am not specifically trying to convey a message with what I do, but when I work with children I do try to be very objective. That is not always easy.

I love working with children, teaching them what I know and transmitting my love for theatre. My approach is always teamwork and letting go of judgements. It is about removing fears and everyone respecting everyone else. Everybody has an important role in a theatre play, not just the leading character. In the group, everyone is equal and important. You are all in it together and you have to work together, which in my view is a valuable life lesson. All this is very satisfying.

I think La Herradura already is, but could be even more of a wonderfully inspiring place where people can come to experience art, culture, literature, music and theatre, where artists can come together and collaborate. For me personally... I love my work. I love my life and I love

where I live, in beautiful La Herradura."
Josune Sáinz Santana

An artistic chameleon

It is like walking into a work of art, this unique bar with an Eastern touch and lots of warm colours embracing you in warm and welcoming feelings. There is an abundance of objects that might seem mismatched but here it all works wonderfully. An old suit of armour overlooks wildlife themed walls with colourful leopard prints. A few tables and chairs grace the small stage which plays host to wonderful live music. From here you can look out of the window and enjoy the sea that is framed between two sets of palm trees proudly towering into the sky.

Every little inch of the bar is full of artistic curiosities. A large birdcage with Asian puppets, a tiny disco figure on a dark wooden bedside table and an art work made of coloured glass all complement each other. There are astonishing Indian, Indonesian and Arab touches everywhere.

At the end of the bar there is an enchanting courtyard garden that is equally artistic, with arty and kitsch objects treating the eye to an exceptional experience.

Colourful cement benches, as well as plastic, wooden, iron and wicker chairs and tables sit harmoniously together just like the mix of different types of people that visit the establishment. Hippies, politicians, businessmen, young and old, everybody is welcome to La Cochera. It's one of the best-known bars in La Herradura and famous for its exceptional musical offerings particularly at the weekends. It is well-loved by locals and tourists alike and has been for many years. "It even featured in some scenes in a famous comic magazine from the eighties called La Vibra", says the charismatic owner Antonio.

Antonio grew up in La Herradura and talks fondly of the Sixties and Seventies in the village where he was born. He remembers that he was still a young kid when he and his friend went to Calle Real to soak up the strange and wonderful atmosphere of El Sombrero, a bar that was situated where there is now a little supermarket. At three o'clock in the morning the women in the street were still sitting outside – on their doorsteps - to get some fresh air. El Sombrero used to be an old house where they kept mules before it was turned into a bar. Antonio and his friend at ages four and five hid in the doorway to peek at the foreigners and listen to the music.

La Herradura was very much ahead of its time and it attracted many interesting people. During the Sixties, Seventies and Eighties more *chiringuitos* were created. Antonio in particular remembers the Pelillera Antiguo, opened by a Swedish man called Sven. By this time, Antonio was about fourteen years old and impressed by this 'new world' created mainly by people from Madrid, Paris and other places. Tourism peaked during the summer months. June, July and August was a time to meet other French, Dutch, German and English children who came for summer holidays with their families. In those days the families in the village were poor and many rented out rooms to foreign holiday makers. These were great and happy times for Antonio, but come September, the exotic visitors had all gone and it made him feel sad.

As a young boy Antonio was always drawing and he particularly liked figure drawing. He wasn't a keen student, but his parents wanted him to study outside La Herradura and forced him to go and study technical drawing in Granada. He wasn't really interested in that, but did it out of obligation. He was only 17 years old when his parents let him live there on his own. He then found a partner in Granada, a man who was considerably older than Antonio and who introduced him to bars with live music. He remembers a bar called Grenache where they had live jazz music and it was this special ambience that Antonio fell in love with.

La Cochera was opened thirty years ago in an unused

garage space to recreate the special ambience of mixing all sorts of people having fun and listening to great music, including live music during weekends. Antonio was inspired by what he had seen in Granada so many years before, but he always liked the hospitality trade and running a bar suited him. His creativity shines through in what he has created. Apart from his life-time love for drawing he also paints, but that remains a hobby. Whenever he has created an artwork, there has always been someone who likes it and he then simply gives it away. However, Antonio is an artist who has created a work of art in La Cochera.

Thirty years ago the decoration was in the same vein as it is now, but it has been changing continuously. Antonio's palette comes from life itself, from meeting people, travelling and getting to know other cultures. He gets inspired and then just uses ideas that he likes. Although the whole concept is not unique, it is uniquely put together. Sometimes things are everyday items that people have given and are then given a new lease of life. However, he does feel that he could not have done it without the help he has received - the cement benches that have been painted by creative friends, as well as the inside of the bar. He has been given many things as well and the decor is in fact a 'work' of many people.

Antonio particularly likes that he was able to create such a unique bar with such a liberal attitude. There is no prejudgement. Everybody is welcome and this is symbolised by the flag that he put on the roof of the bar on the opening day. This indicated that this would not be a bar specifically for gay people, but a bar open to everyone. It gives him a lot of satisfaction that he has been able to realise that. Everybody is welcome as long as they are happy to respect others. It's a rule that works, which you will notice as you experience its unique atmosphere whilst enjoying a drink amidst several generations of people listening to the same music and sharing the same space. It perfectly reflects Antonio's view on life as he says: 'We all have to live together and we therefore have to respect each other'.

La Cochera is like a chameleon that always changes. Things keep being moved around and replaced. So from one week to the next its artistic beauty and quirkiness might have changed. It is an organic, never ending artwork in constant progress that might or might not disappear into non-existence. La Cochera lives in the now whilst showing a past put together by its charismatic owner Antonio. There is beauty in the chameleon as it continually recreates the mystery of the unknown and leaves one guessing whether this will become an artistic memory or form a continuing part of this art and musical attraction in the ever magical evolution of the village of La Herradura.

Antonio Cochera -
https://www.facebook.com/lacochera.laherradura

Attraction and inspiration

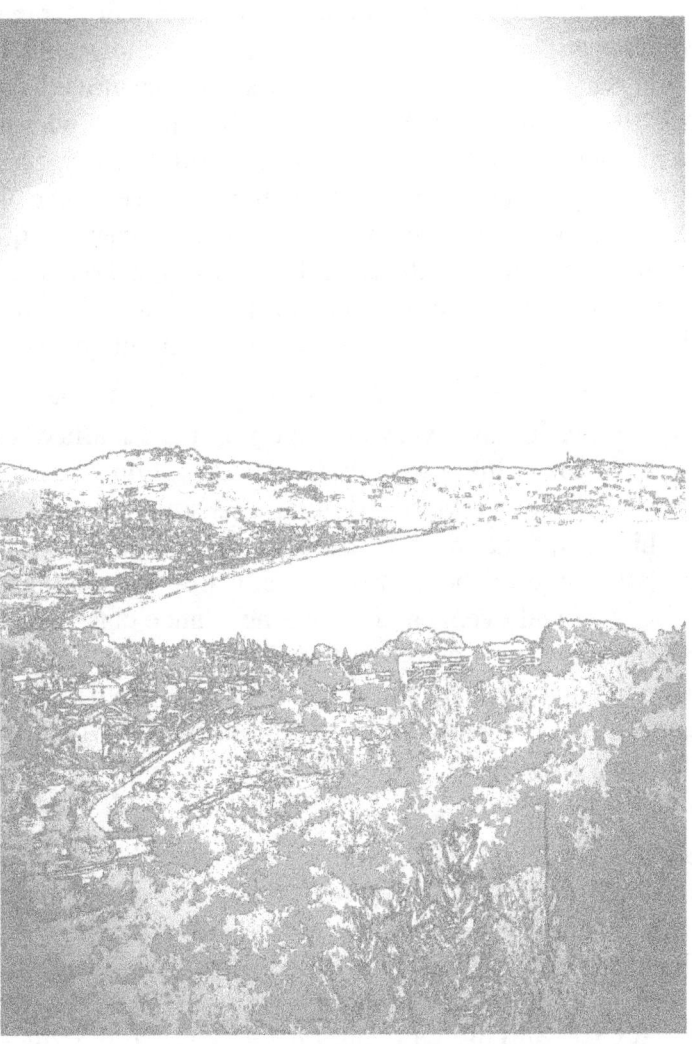

Dreaming big - La Herradura, a major cultural space

"I was born in Paris but my parents are from Andalusia. I have known the area of La Herradura since I was a small boy as my parents and I regularly came here by car, all the way from Paris. My mother was born in Granada province and we came to the seaside area to spend our holidays. When I was twelve years old we moved from Paris to Madrid. I met Fabiana who became my wife and the mother of our two children in Madrid in 1998. She is from Uruguay but came to live in Spain when she was twenty-six years old. In Madrid it is very easy to meet people from other cultures. I feel that is a bonus as it changes your perspectives on life through learning about other people's habits, arts, and way of living in general.

I worked for Antena 3 for many years in a television programme. It was a very creative job and I learned a lot about many things, including decoration." As he continues his story Mario Alguilar puts some brown sugar into his coffee that has just been served by the waitress in La Califa, one of the seafront bars. Califa has regular art shows, musical events and sometimes dance classes in the winter. Apart from enjoying the sea view whilst having a chat with a friend on the outside terrace, you might be treated to live music events in this local bar which, just like many other bars in the village, likes to create an arty stage for its visitors.

"So how did you end up in La Herradura?" I ask and Mario continues. "Throughout my years in Madrid I always dreamed of coming to live in a quiet seaside village in Andalusia to start different projects in the field of art and culture for children and young people. Over fifteen years ago my wife and I came down to the town of Almuñécar for a holiday. We both fell in love with it and when our daughter was born we decided to make the move and come to live here. My wife's mother also came over to help look after the baby while I went to Madrid for work during the week. After eight months it turned out to be too difficult for us to be apart and Fabiana and our daughter Julia returned to live with me in Madrid. My mother in law stayed in Almuñécar and we kept returning for our holidays. My wife was offered a job in a health-food shop and started developing a great love for natural medicine and natural food, which started a life path for her that she never intends to leave again. She developed an interest in Tibetan bowl sound healing and started studying both in Madrid and Serra de Grego Diafanum to become a meditation teacher and sound healer – using, amongst other things, Tibetan and quartz singing bowls - and a fitotherapist.

But then, in 2011, 'destiny' struck. The economic recession resulted in my television programme being taken off-air and I became unemployed; being nearly fifty years old made this extremely worrying and stressful for me. We tried to make ends meet in Madrid, moving to a cheaper house, but it was still too expensive a place for us to live. Then our son was born and we decided to move back to the coast, found a lovely apartment in La Herradura and both fell in love with this quirky seaside village.

Losing my job was very hard and when it happened my entire existence was shaken, but every cloud has a silver lining. La Herradura opened up doors for my wife enabling her to develop her sound healing work. She gives meditation classes and healing treatments. She also gives meditative concerts with a wide range of ancestral instruments, either as a soloist or accompanied by different musicians from the east and the west and I help her organise these events.

I have lived most of my adult life in big cities and being born in Paris to Spanish parents I feel fortunate to have received an abundant cultural upbringing with a wonderful mixture of two great cultures, Spanish and French. I am aware of being French, but also of being Spanish and very much of being Andalusian. The Andalusian culture is very rich. On the one hand it is very religious and at the same time very liberal - a mixture of the hidden and the vulgar, the modest and the extravagant. It is also a very welcoming culture. Having to live in a small village did require some adjustment and a change of mentality, which was not necessarily a bad thing. Life is so much calmer down here, people are more relaxed, but it is also harder to innovate. I think the fact that my parents are Andalusian has helped me to integrate. I understand the Mediterranean mentality and its special humour. To me La Herradura holds the essence of a typical Andalusian village with its white-washed houses, the narrow streets, the Mediterranean landscape and the character of the people. Apart from the natural beauty surrounding the village it has a very special atmosphere with its blend of mainly Spanish inhabitants and tourists and a significant number of non-Spanish people who have settled here.

I feel it is an ideal place to plant seeds for various ideas that will have a chance to germinate and turn into something valuable for the village. It is my dream to share my cultural knowledge and life-experience in this field with the youngsters in this village. So far I have made many contacts and planted a lot of seeds that I hope will flourish some day in the near future. I have set up an association to help me realise this dream. It is an association with cultural and social development ideas. The name of the association is *La Hoja Viva* (The Living Leaf). The name was inspired by a French poem by Jacques Prevert that I like very much, called *Les Feuilles Mortes* (The Dead Leaves). *La Hoja Viva* means the opposite and to me feels inspiring, alive and hopeful. Since living in La Herradura I have organised various cultural projects and now within the association we organise the concerts that my wife is giving both solo and with other musicians. Giving lectures at secondary schools is also part of the project. Both the La Herradura and Almuñécar administrations have been very accommodating and have helped where they can. What I also like about La Herradura is that I have met quite a few people, both foreigners and Spanish who are passionate about supporting positive change and helping to turn this village into a shining example of development based on cultural and environmental approaches. This approach will undoubtedly create a healthier economy and a future for the young people of the village.

If I hadn't met these people in this alternative atmosphere, I probably would not have stayed here. These people inspire me with the energy to do things. Life is still a challenge as the seeds that have been planted take time to germinate and some might get lost in the process. Meanwhile we have to survive and raise our children, which means that I also have to accept odd jobs both abroad and in Madrid to try to make ends meet. My dream is to have a permanent venue for cultural activities where people can participate in workshops in all forms of art and help them to learn and widen their horizons. It would be a place to learn in a pleasurable way with perhaps photography, painting or music workshops etc. It would also be a place to hold presentations of books by local writers and facilitate talks about documentaries or books etc. without political agendas.

The intention of the association is to democratise art and to inspire all kinds of artistic endeavours. I would like children to understand contemporary art and to get in touch with music, art and literature from other cultures. *La Hoja Viva* has already attracted people to the village through their attendance at our musical events from all parts of the world. For people from the village and tourists alike, I very much believe that La Herradura can be a lot more special than it already is as it has so many brilliant artists living and working here and its history is fascinating. The idea is to reawaken the love of the Herradura people for their village and its history and for people from outside to get to know it through interesting art shows, musical events and perhaps guided, historical walks while enjoying some of the excellent hospitality in one of the many bars and restaurants.

I feel blessed as I was introduced to culture, art and literature from a young age. I was also lucky to meet many different cultures in Madrid - from Uruguay, Argentina and Columbia. Here in La Herradura I have met many lovely people from other parts of Europe - Dutch, Irish, Italian, British, German, Swiss, Swedish etc. as well as people from further afield, with a real appreciation for this lovely place. To me this is incredibly enriching and something I would like to share, especially with children. I am not saying that I think that people should stop being Andalusian or Spanish at all, but rather open themselves up to other ways of thinking that could help to change their lives for the better.

Part of my heart will always stay in Madrid, but I no longer like to live there. La Herradura has something that is difficult to describe and now I want to be here. If one day, my dream to have a cultural space will come true, everything is ready to start as I have already developed various projects, all ready to go. I like organising theme parties, events and concerts, all with the aim of putting La Herradura on the map culturally. It's one step at a time, perhaps even just baby steps, but we'll surely get there eventually. La Herradura is a unique place and its art, culture and literature can make you happy. I can, and hopefully will, make La Herradura 'happy' by attracting more culturally aware people, thus helping the social and economic situation of this enchanting bay."

Mario Alguilar

Creating an interest

"I guess this is what I am about to a great extent, creating an interest in others in what interests me. I hope that doesn't sound presumptuous as it certainly is not intended that way. I am passionate about things that matter in my view and I like to pass that on. Whether that is looking after your body; giving underprivileged kids a chance to make music; introducing people to different ways of approaching life or appreciating classical music.

My life is about many things, amongst which is being a mother. I am married to Stephen Hill and together we have four children, two from my previous relationship, one from his and the child we had together. Stephen is English and I am Dutch. I was born in The Hague in the Netherlands but circumstances led me to La Herradura. The relationship with the father of my two young children wasn't perfect and I needed some space to clear my head and decided to take some time out with the children. I also wanted to learn Spanish and a friend of mine recommended La Herradura where she had been six years earlier. I didn't want to end up in a big city so living in a seaside village where childcare was available sounded perfect. So we came here in August of 2006. Initially I had planned to go on some sort of a world tour with the children for eight or ten months, Portugal before Spain and then either Asia or Australia, however, I didn't get that far, as I decided to stay here. I realised that the lack of social integration with children of their own age would not be good for my kids so I decided it would be better to stay for eight months in La Herradura. Their father agreed. I needed some distance from him to get my head clear and find out whether our relationship could be saved. He also came over to Spain to talk in November but he didn't feel it could work anymore. By January he had a new partner and I decided to stay in La Herradura. Shortly after that I met Stephen.

It was 2007, an eventful year for me, a year of many changes. Somehow that first year in Spain had been sort of a catalyst year as it was here that I found the freedom to think about how I wanted to live my life. I realised I wanted to get off the treadmill in Holland that everybody seems to be on - imprisoned by mortgages and jobs, dominated by rushing and running; a life ruled by obligations, diaries full of appointments, everything overly organised and where stay-at-home mums were frowned upon. I needed to find a different life for myself and my children.

In the summer of 2007 I went to Switzerland for a two week retreat with Tulku Lobsang, a Tibetan monk. Getting to know Tulku has had an important impact on me. It has helped to shape my views and ideas about life, about the earth. It's like a framework, a life philosophy. Shortly after the workshop in Switzerland my father died after a long battle with a brain tumour. I was very close to him and it was almost as if he had waited for me to find 'my path'. He used to be a civil engineer and was not much in touch with his spiritual side but his illness made him reflect on his life. He decided that he wanted to make the best of the time he had left and he wanted to get back in touch with the spiritual side that he felt he had lost. He took up meditation and art, making things out of wood. Towards the end of his dying process that lasted six years he was at peace, as if in touch with 'the Light' or the other side. This was palpable when I was with him. I knew he was happy that I had found a new direction in life and that meditation was part of that. Over the years that followed I became a professional Tibetan Lu Jong yoga teacher and I became a mother once again, to a lovely baby girl. Stephen and I were very happy and decided to get married.

We love living in this village as there are so many like-minded people. It feels like being part of one great, big family here. All the people who have moved here are looking for a new life; a way of life where you can live your own freedom, fill in your life the way you think is best and also work together for a better world through various projects and activities. It is also great for the children to grow up without too many of the distractions of modern culture such as electronic equipment while being in contact with nature and in balance with oneself and the earth. I also believe it is beneficial that they are exposed, on a daily basis, to such a great variety of cultures.

We also found a wonderful house to live and raise our children in, on the Punta de La Mona. Every day when I drive back home after dropping off the kids or a yoga class I feel a little spark of gratitude in my heart, taking the exit for the Punta de la Mona and driving straight on past the Iron flower sculpture by Feliciano Hernandez and down into the heart of the Punta. It is like being sucked into a fairy-tale reality. Large green pine trees, apparently the oldest trees in the village, embrace the street, giving it a magical feel. At the roundabout I go left in the direction of the Marina and then immediately with a sharp curve to the right into Camino de la Ermita that we now call our neighbourhood. A few hundred metres down the road lies the Hermitage of the Punta, designed by architect Prieto Moreno who had a good relationship with a priest of a Catholic congregation in Madrid. The chapel was created to allow for Catholic masses to be held in the summer. This religious sanctuary is unusually modern on the outside and inside. A beautiful iron sculpture, made in 1992 also by Feliciano Hernandez is a reminder of the vision of Prieto Moreno who was an architect and politician who lived from 1906 'til 1985, and who fell in love with La Herradura. He was behind the urbanisation of the Punta de La Mona. His vision was to create a beautiful area with houses with plenty of green spaces. He was adamantly against overbuilding on the Punta, as is the case in so many parts of the Spanish coasts. Stepping inside the hermitage you feel like going back into a fairly recent past. A modern pillar with an abstract white cross and a beautiful, wall mosaic depicting Mother Mary with baby Jesus, watched over by two angels, are the obvious signs that this is a religious sanctuary. The sunken section of white stone benches with blue fabric cushions seats those who come for weekend masses during holiday periods very comfortably and has a distinct Seventies 'feel'. Large windows treat you to a wonderful panoramic view over the sea in the direction of Almuñécar. From the hermitage a woodland path takes you to the lighthouse where you can take in a breath-taking view.

We both love living in this area of La Herradura. Apart from sharing similar views on life, Stephen and I also share a love of music. I play the piano myself, not very well but I enjoy it. I also love singing and have taken some singing classes. We used to organise a project called 'Starfish' to provide an opportunity for young people to make music together. It was actually my husband Stephen Hill's idea, as he had set up a similar project in Lewes, a town in the United Kingdom that hosted the Lewes International Guitar Festival, also created by Stephen. He felt inspired to do this because of his son who was drumming. The association Starfish was created to be able to provide practice space for young people to play instruments, to organise concerts and to promote bands. I was involved in the organisation together with my husband and a few more music lovers and musicians. We had a number of successful concerts and a group of musicians also went round to local schools to do spontaneous music classes. Thirty people in a class would have a jam session with instruments. It was extraordinary and very demanding on the musicians but it was very rewarding to see youngsters who had never had the experience of spontaneously making music together and bringing music to life. It left everybody with an incredible buzz. Unfortunately the project was put on hold due to lack of practice space - we lost the space we initially had. We were then unable to find a cost effective place that could be made soundproof and have proper supervision so that young people could practice there. But we very much hope we can pick this up again someday and continue Starfish.

Stephen also runs a series of concerts called 'Maestros de la Guitarra'. I help him organise these concerts. We bring classical guitar players to the village as part of the cultural life of La Herradura. They usually love to come here and feel inspired because of the connection with Andrés Segovia. They feel it is a great honour to play here in the presence of Segovia's legacy and they can count on an appreciative audience. I quite enjoy organising events and I am also proud that I was able to invite Tulku Lobsang to the village twice so that other people can get to know his views on life. The Tibetan yoga that I've learned from him has become an important part of my life. In my opinion yoga is very good for body and mind and has a healing effect. This healing effect is something that interests me greatly as well and it was a logical next step for me to study reflexology. This is pressing specific points using the reflective zones on the hands and feet. These points are believed to correspond with specific organs and systems in the body and this pressure then promotes self-healing.

I feel that living consciously and healthily is important. Stephen and I were also involved in the 'Eco Huerto' project - introducing children to the experience of growing their own food responsibly and in harmony with nature without using chemicals. We felt it was a great project and we hope we can continue it someday. The land we used was originally given for free but the owner subsequently found a paying client which meant we had to put the project on hold until we hopefully find a new plot to restart it. The local school, Las Gaviotas, was involved as well and the Eco Huerto project ran for two years. From the parents viewpoint there was an understandable division of interest. Some parents loved it - those who grew up in towns or cities valued the contact with nature approach. However, some parents from the area could not see the point of their children losing school time over this project. These parents had family members who had had to work the land to survive. These parents did not want to go back to that life and want their children to become doctors, lawyers, etc. For them education is strongly associated with the mind and they want their children to be successful. They want their children to be who they never were. It's a reasonable point of view but I feel it would be nice if there was a balance. There are so many projects and amazing things happening in my life and all here in la Herradura. I love that and I like to share it with whoever wants to hear it! That is what I am about, I guess, creating an interest..."

Marjolein Lu Jong www.in-spira.info

A village of festivals

An integral part of living in Spain is the many *fiestas*. In many villages, towns and cities it is the custom for every single *barrio* (neighbourhood) to throw a party at least once a year. It is also customary to mark most national holidays with some sort of a fiesta. Each village, town and city has its own Saint's day, which is then also celebrated with a fair and musical events where people stay out and dance into the early morning hours. Barbecued tapas and drinks are served in the streets and from empty shops and or garages.

Also very common in Spain is that in the event a national holiday falls on a Thursday or Tuesday, people will also take the Friday or Monday off. They call this a *Puente* (bridge). Many take a mini-break to celebrate a Puente.

La Herradura is still a very Spanish village with, especially in summer, mainly Spanish tourists. Many of the apartments and houses have Spanish owners who travel from cities such as Madrid and Granada and who come to the village to spend their holidays. They love the peace and tranquillity of the village, its 'laidbackness' and also the wide range of sea sports and the excellent entertainment in the bars and restaurants. They love strolling around on summer nights meeting and greeting old friends.

Local holidays, national holiday and fairs

January 1 - New Year's Day - National Holiday

January 6 - Epifanía del Señor y los Reyes Magos - National Holiday

The *Epifanía* which literally means 'manifestation' is one of the oldest religion-based celebrations in Spain and refers to Jesus coming down to the earth in a human form. In Egypt and other Arab countries it marked the celebration of the winter solstice and its earliest mentioning was in the year 361 BC.

Now this date is used to commemorate the birth of the baby Jesus and, in particular, by the three men (kings) who came to Bethlehem to worship Him and to offer their symbolic gifts of gold, frankincense and myrrh. In some countries it is tradition to give gifts to children on this day. In La Herradura this is always celebrated with wonderful spectacle. As soon as dark falls on the night of the 5th January a colourful procession of beautifully dressed floats containing the exquisitely adorned Three Kings and their accompanying Queens sets out from the Castle and moves towards the village surrounded by adults and children dressed up for the occasion. As they proceed they shower the children with sweets which the excited little ones collect in bags. Other local children dance at intervals in the procession representing various cultures. This colourful parade eventually arrives at the Plaza Nueva where the three Kings and Queens take their seats on the stage on their elaborate thrones. As their names are called out, local children come up to the podium to receive their gifts from the Kings amidst great excitement.

February 2 - La Candelaria

The *Fiesta de Nuestra Señora de la Candelaria*, (Presentation of Jesus at the Temple, Candlemas), is a popular holiday celebrated in honour of the Virgin of Candelaria. Particularly important in Tenerife (Canary Islands) where the Virgin of Candelaria is believed to have appeared in the 15th century, it is also celebrated throughout the rest of Spain, usually with parades and in seaside villages with small campfires on the beach.

Carnival – dates vary

In La Herradura Carnival is celebrated and people prepare for the event throughout the year. Various associations dedicate their time to turn it into an annual spectacle worth visiting. Usually there is a Carnival parade by the children, accompanied by their parents, showing off their costumes and heading for the civic centre to enjoy the party with music and theatre.

But Carnival in the village is not just for the kids. Every year there is a so-called *chirigotas* competition. *Chirigota* is a genre of Spanish choral folksong, satirical in nature, and predominantly performed in the streets during the annual carnival. The singers are all dressed up and sing about political, local or moral issues.

February 28 - Día de Andalucía – An Andalusian holiday marking the recognition of Andalusia as an autonomous community in 1981.

March 19 - San Jose. This is the major festival in La Herradura to honour the Patron Saint of the village. There is a religious procession in the old part of the village and there are various celebratory events like the horses "ribbon racing" on the beach on the final day. The fiesta is always extended over four days, and a big catering tent on the Plaza Nueva hosts live music and sports demonstrations every evening. During the fiesta there is a fair on the sea front. Street barbecues offer food and drinks to visitors and there is always a genuine, happy buzz wherever you go. On the last evening of the *fiesta* people go to the beach to admire a beautiful Firework display.

Easter Week (dates vary) – *Semana Santa*. Arguably the most important holiday in the calendar is *Semana Santa* a week-long celebration starting from Palm Sunday till Easter Sunday. The *Semana Santa* is famous for the many processions taking place during the entire week, in remembrance of the Crucifixion and the Resurrection of Christ. It is a week of very moving spectacle. Brotherhoods solemnly parade through the streets for hours carrying large, heavy wooden thrones adorned with elaborate decoration and various statues of Jesus and his mother. The statues set out from different churches on set routes at various times throughout the day (and sometimes into the early hours of the morning) in a highly coordinated programme. In these processions there are also penitents wearing hooded robes, bearing candles and religious objects as well as people dressed up in Roman soldier garb and women and girls with candles and long mantillas. Town and village bands play appropriate stirring music to accompany these processions. When the statues meet each other the thrones are raised by the bearers with one hand and the statues salute each other in a unique and moving form of dance.

Viernes Santo (Good Friday) when the death of Jesus Christ of Nazareth is remembered. This is a national holiday.

May 1 - El Dia del Trabajo (Labour Day). National holiday celebrating workers' rights.

May 3 - Dia de la Cruz – Usually celebrated from 1 – 3 May. One of the most popular Spanish *fiestas*. Religiously, the festival refers to the search by the Byzantine Empress Saint Helena for the cross on which Jesus died. However, popular traditions connected to the festival originate from pagan traditions brought to Spain by the Roman Empire, of which May Day is an example.

Locals create elaborate crucifixes which are decorated with flowers and shawls and even incorporate household implements and kitchen utensils. Old traditions such as displaying an apple with a pair of scissors on the table in front of the crucifix are still preserved, used as a warning that one should not criticise a *Cruz* decoration.

June 23-24 - San Juan. Also known as *Noche de San Juan* celebrates the birth of John the Baptist as well as the Summer Solstice and it symbolises change. In tourist regions it also marks the start of the summer holiday season. In seaside towns and villages it is the only night during the year when people can officially light fires and have barbecues on the beach. Groups of friends and families gather and set up their tents on the beach during the day and at night the barbecues and bonfires are lit. The fires are used to symbolically burn old memories and mark a new start. According to tradition, people have to jump a bonfire three times in order to be cleansed and purified and for their problems to be burned away. Some people write a wish on a small piece of paper which they then throw into the fire. It is then customary, at midnight, for people to either jump into the sea or wash their faces in the sea water, which is believed to create luck and to help see the future with more clarity. Food and drinks are shared, guitar music is never far away and the celebrations continue into the early morning hours. It can be a truly magical experience.

Corpo Cristi - Dia del Señor. Dates vary. A church celebration during which the children who have just had their first communion go to various barrios in the village, where people have created a cross and where flowers are scattered in the street.

July 16 - Fiesta for Virgen del Carmen This fiesta is well celebrated in La Herradura and Almuñécar. Virgen del Carmen is the patron saint of mariners. On the 15th of July the statue of the Virgin del Carmen is carried from the church down to the beach accompanied by band music. She is then taken on a boat to sail around the rocks of the bay escorted by a small armada, to arrive back on land. This is then followed by a truly amazing firework display from the beach. After the fireworks people go back to the feria to eat and drink and dance to live music on the Plaza Nueva.

Every last weekend of August - La Herradura Blues Festival – This features national and international blues musicians playing live music in front of an audience. The festival usually takes place in the local castle.

October, 1st week – Sea Festival – A festival to raise awareness of current marine environmental concerns. A variety of festivities for the schoolchildren, live music and interesting sea activities for adults.

November 1 - All Saints Day or Day of the Dead. More of a date for locals, but those staying in town may notice a mass exodus to the cemetery on the road to Jete, where the graves are decorated with flowers and ones relatives are both discussed and remembered with friends & family. Also a National Holiday.

November, 3rd Week - Certamen Internacional de Guitarra Clásica Andrés Segovia - Andrés Segovia International Guitar Competition. Five days of the very best Spanish guitar music from all over the world, held in La Herradura. The heats can be attended for free but entry to the finals is by ticket only.

December 6 - Spanish Constitution Day. National holiday

December 8 - Día de La Inmaculada Concepción. National holiday marking the immaculate conception of the Virgin Mary.

December 25 - Natividad del Señor - Christmas National Holiday

December 28 - Dia de los Inocentes (Day of the Innocents) also called *Dia de la Zorra* where people go out on an excursion to the Cerro Gordo to share food such as pork, game and stews.

Note from the author

Writing this book has been an incredibly interesting journey. A journey of gathering and then sharing the amazing and inspirational stories told by some of the locals and some of the many artists who have found their way to the village of La Herradura. Naturally, there are more artists, writers and other creative people that have either once lived in the village or that still live here than I've been able to include in this book. I simply could not include everybody. All the interviewees have received a copy of their own story for approval before publication. Most stories required a few minor changes; a few people took out and added paragraphs, all in line with my style and the idea of the book. Tomás Hernández Molina chose to completely rewrite his story which might explain a difference in style.

Having finished the interviews and written the book, what shines through for me is the overall passion of the artists not only for their own work (they all were fantastic examples of following your heart's desire and your soul's purpose) but also the true and enduring love everyone has for La Herradura, itself.

I can totally understand their passion. It was my personal love for La Herradura that prompted me to take this journey. I hope when you read this book you will dive into the history and the evolution of La Herradura, as well as get to know some colourful characters and interesting creative spirits living in and around this village.

May their inspiring words spark a creative journey within you!

Renate van Nijen

NB: The personal accounts in this book were kindly provided by my interviewees and were current at the time of approval. I sourced other information online or from the following books:

Ŝāt – Jate La Herradura – José Ángel Morales y Carmen Molina Poveda

Un viento inesperado - Tomás Hernández Molina

Naufragio en La Herradura – Juanfran Cabrera

www.ingramcontent.com/pod-product-compliance
Lightning Source LLC
Chambersburg PA
CBHW050159230526
45470CB00001B/162